The Jicarilla Apache Tribe
A History, 1846–1970

The

Jicarilla

Apache Tribe

A History, 1846–1970

Veronica E. Velarde Tiller

University of Nebraska Press

Lincoln & London

Copyright 1983 by the University of Nebraska Press

All rights reserved

Manufactured in the United States of America

The paper in this book meets the guidelines for permanence and durability of the Committee on Production Guidelines for Book Longevity of the Council on Library Resources.

Library of Congress Cataloging in Publication Data

Tiller, Veronica E. Velarde.
The Jicarilla Apache Tribe.

Bibliography: p.
Includes index.
1. Jicarilla Indians – History.   2. Jicarilla Indians –
Government relations.   3. Indians of North America – New
Mexico.   4. Indians of North America – Government relations.
I. Title.
E99.J5T54   323.1'97   82-6973
ISBN 0-8032-4409-6   AACR2

Contents

Maps

Illustrations

Preface

The primary purpose of this study is to describe the nature of the relationship between the United States government and the Jicarilla Apache Tribe of New Mexico from 1846 to 1970. The focus is on how federal Indian policies affected the economic, social, and political history of the Jicarilla Apaches, and what role the Jicarilla Apaches played in determining the outcome of those policies.

Federal-Indian relations have been a recurrent topic for historians during the last two decades. The majority have dealt with federal policies from the period of the Indian wars to the New Deal era, and generally have agreed that the main thrust of the policies has been to Americanize the Indians, rather than to keep them segregated from the mainstream of American society and to treat them as tribal entities.

Despite more objective treatment of Indians in their relations with the federal government, recent studies continue to emphasize how the federal government has rendered the tribes powerless. I have attempted to go beyond this thesis by concentrating on how federal policies, contrary to intent, have tightened the guardian-ward relationship; at the same time, I have considered the capacity of the Jicarilla Apaches to influence the outcome of these policies through their various actions and decisions. The Jicarilla Apaches exercised self-determination before it became a catch-all phrase for recent Indian policy.

I would not go so far as to claim that this book is written from the Indian point of view. There is no composite Indian viewpoint because of the multiplicity and diversity of Indian cultures throughout the United States. More important, the bulk of my sources are government records written and compiled by non-Indians. Furthermore, since I have concentrated on federal-tribal relations, even the background information on culture has been based largely on monographs and articles produced by white scholars.

While I accept the sole responsibility for all errors and mistakes, the organization, contents, interpretations, and evaluations contained in this history, it is my pleasure to acknowledge authors like Morris E. Opler, Dolores Gunnerson, H. Clyde Wilson, Frank Hibben, and Alfred B. Thomas, from whose works I drew heavily.

A special acknowledgment is extended to the Jicarilla Apache Tribal Council for its valuable assistance and support. Its endorsement opened doors to all recent federal and tribal records, and provided access to the historical records compiled by the Stanford Research Institute and to the documents compiled for the Jicarilla Apache Accounting Claims by the Nicklason Research Firm of Washington, D.C., in the possession of the law firm of Nordhaus, Moses, and Dunn of Albuquerque, New Mexico.

Support from the Tribal Council made it possible to obtain the cooperation of tribal members in sharing their oral historical accounts. Particular thanks go to my grandmother, Juana Monarco, who spent countless hours recalling our tribal history, and to Gerald Vicenti, who acted as my interpreter when my Apache failed.

In addition to the Jicarilla Apache Tribe, this volume was made possible by grants from the American Philosophical Society, the University of Utah Research Committee, and the Newberry Library Center for the History of the American Indian.

My gratitude also extends to my college professors Richard N. Ellis and Donald C. Cutter, Richard Crawford of the National Archives, Joel Barker of the Federal Records Center in Denver, Colorado, the staff of the National Records Center in Suitland, Maryland, the Albuquerque BIA Offices, the Jicarilla Agency Staff, the Huntington Library, and the Zimmerman Library of the University of New Mexico.

Special thanks to Betty Dalgleish for her valuable editorial assistance, the secretaries at the University of Utah History Department for the typing, and to all my family for their support—especially to Emily M. Tiller, my daughter, for her understanding and patience.

The Jicarilla Apache Tribe
A History, 1846–1970

Prologue

Jicarilla Apache Origins and
Early White Contact

The Jicarilla Apaches are a vigorous people with a tremendous enthusiasm for life, despite a history of adversity. Their past has reflected this passion for life, the essence of which derives from their conception of a personified universe. This conception includes an optimistic outlook on life, a disposition for patience and understanding, imagination, and an ability to adapt to changing environments. External flexibility and core consistency have been responsible for their survival[1]—since they emerged from their mythical underworld to follow the Sun and Moon.

According to the Jicarilla Apache origin stories, in the beginning Black Sky and Earth Woman bore anthropomorphic Supernaturals who dwelt within the body of their mother, the Earth. Only darkness prevailed in this underworld, where all living things dwelt, and where Black Hac·ct'cin, the first offspring and Supreme Supernatural, created the first ancestral man and woman, animals, and birds out of clay, based on the impression of his own form.

The sole source of light was the eagle plumes that the people used as torches, but these provided inadequate illumination. Consequently, the numerous minor Supernaturals made a miniature Sun and Moon, which were allowed to make one circuit of the heavens. The light cast by these two bodies proved unsatisfactory, so they were brought down and enlarged. The second set was tested and permitted to rise and set four times until it provided sufficient light.

No sooner were the Sun and Moon created than some evil shamans attempted to destroy them. Angered by this, Hac·ct'cin allowed the

Sun and Moon to escape to this earth. The people pondered their misfortune, consulted with each other, sang and prayed, and considered how they could restore their two sources of light. The only alternative, they concluded, was to follow the Sun and Moon. Thus the Jicarillas were united as a people; their emergence from the underworld was necessitated by their attempt to recover the light that they had lost.

The holy people, with the guidance and help of the Hac·ct'cin, the ultimate power, facilitated their own ascent. All the powers that these underworld creatures possessed were used. These powers were given to them by Hac·ct'cin before their world debut, but during the course of the upward journey more ceremonies were given to them. At the start of the journey a ritual was performed. Four mounds of earth that had been piled in a row began to grow into huge mountains, rising toward the hole through which the Sun and Moon had escaped. Then the mountains stopped growing, making it impossible for the people and animals to complete their upward journey. Again it became necessary to use imagination and to perform ceremonies. Several different types of ladders were constructed from feathers, but they proved to be too weak. Failure was not what Hac·ct'cin envisioned; thus, he constructed four ladders of sunbeams and the people and animals were able to continue their ascent. All journeyed up to the opening with the exception of an old man and woman, who were too weak to climb and chose not to leave the land of their youth. They warned that Jicarillas would return to this underworld at death. After their emergence, the people and animals discovered that the earth was covered with water, symbolizing that life on earth was not to be easy. The Wind Deity offered to roll back the waters in the four directions to form the oceans. In his zealousness, he dried up all the waters, leaving nothing for the living creatures to drink. Prayers were offered, and soon rivers, lakes, and streams appeared. The people discovered that the earth was inhabited by monsters, who were eventually slain by one of the culture heroes, Monster Slayer. Finally, with the help of other Supernaturals, all obstacles that made the earth an unsafe place were eliminated.

When the earth was dry and safe, the people and animals traveled in all four directions in clockwise fashion. As they traveled, small groups began to break off and settle down; as they settled, the Supernaturals gave them different names and languages. The Jicarillas, however, continued to circle. The Supreme Deity was getting angry and impatient with their indecisiveness and asked them where they wanted to live. They replied, "Near the center of the earth." The Creator then made four sacred rivers to delineate the boundaries of their country: the Arkansas, Canadian, Rio Grande, and Pecos. This land became the Holy Land for the Jicarillas. They believe that they are the true descendants of the original people who emerged from the underworld, and that they retain the only true language.[2]

After the Jicarillas came to this world, the Supernaturals gave them elaborate laws, customs, traditions, and more ceremonials that were to be observed forever. At this time all the human attributes that the animals possessed were taken from them, though they were allowed to retain the powers they had to facilitate the emergence. For this reason the Jicarillas were warned never to abuse, molest, or otherwise mistreat animals. If an animal were to be hunted for food, the proper prayers and rituals had to be performed. Plants and mineral life were also to be respected since they too retained their supernatural attributes.

The Jicarilla world became a personified universe with which the Indians identified.[3] All natural and living objects, including man, were seen as personifications of Hac·ct'cin. All living creatures and natural phenomena were manifestations of his power. Through ritual, his powers could be used for human purposes. For that reason, the more important sources of his powers—Sun, Moon, Wind, Lightning—are always represented in all the ceremonies. Within this framework, a pantheon of good and evil Supernaturals are recognized. The Jicarillas were made aware that this world consists of both good and evil and that man is not a perfect creature, but one with natural and deep blemishes in his basic character.

The culture heroes and Coyote, the trickster, were responsible for the acquisition of all the cultural and behavioral traits of man, most of which were obtained through theft and cunning rather than physical aggression. All social institutions of the Jicarillas can be traced to the character of the trickster, who points out that man is not infallible and that human foibles can be tolerated with a sense of humor.

The Jicarilla Apaches were so obsessed by their personified universe, absorbed in maintaining their cosmic order through ceremony, ritual, and the observance of their religion, that little else mattered to them. Within this seemingly harmonious and systematic universe, all natural phenomena could be explained or could be attributed to the natural order as they understood it. In spite of the existence of evil in all forms in the world, their faith in their creation seemingly remained unchallenged until the arrival of the white man.

The Jicarilla version of their origin is a symbolic one, yet it shares factual elements with recorded history. The Jicarillas are one of the six southern Athapascan groups, which include the Chiricahuas, Navajos, Western Apaches, Mescaleros, Kiowa Apaches, and Lipans. The Apachean-speaking tribes migrated out of the Canadian Mackenzie Basin, as latecomers to today's American Southwest, some time between A.D. 1300 and 1500, settling eastern Arizona, New Mexico, northern Mexico, southeastern Colorado, the Oklahoma and Texas panhandles, and west, central, and south Texas.

Out of the composite groups of southern Athapascans who relocated in the Southwest, by 1700 an identifiable group known as the Jicarilla Apaches had emerged. As their homeland, they chose the region bordered by the Arkansas River in southeastern Colorado, the northeastern plains region drained by the tributaries of the Canadian River, the flatlands of the Pecos River Valley, and the area northwest to the Rio Grande in the Chama River Valley of New Mexico. This country they deemed to be "near the center of the earth."

The Jicarilla Apaches preserved much of their fundamental Athapascan culture after settling in the Southwest, but over the centuries gradually adopted some cultural traits from their non-Athapascan neighbors. Their material culture was influenced by the Plains Indians, especially by their war and raiding complexes, while their agricultural and ceremonial rituals had definite traces of influence from the Pueblo Indians of the Upper Rio Grande.[4] This cultural borrowing helped the Jicarillas adapt to their environment, which has consisted of two main geographic regions, the mountains and the plains. These geographic distinctions defined the basic social orientations of the Jicarillas into two bands: the Llaneros (plains people) and the Olleros (mountain-valley people).

This dual orientation was not discovered until the late nineteenth century when ethnographic research was conducted—long after the Jicarillas had been placed on a reservation in northern New Mexico. Historical evidence, however, suggests that it had existed for centuries. A description of Jicarilla aboriginal territory provides the key to understanding the dual-band system. Northeastern New Mexico ranges from 2,000 to 14,000 feet above sea level. The highest points are the Sangre de Cristo Mountains, with their component ridges of Culebra, Cimarron, Taos, Santa Fe, Mora, Las Vegas, and Raton. This mountain range parallels the Rio Grande on the east, extending from south of Santa Fe northward in a gentle arc to the Arkansas River in south central Colorado. A considerable part of the region is covered by these mountains, flanked on either side by high plateaus, limited by the Rio Grande on the west to a width of ten to twenty miles. This piedmont is generally level; but on the east it stretches for fifty or sixty miles and drops off in sharp escarpments toward the eastern border of New Mexico.

The semiarid plains receive little rain, usually fewer than twenty inches annually and sometimes not more than ten. The winters are subject to heavy snow and low temperatures, especially in the mountains, while summer days are hot and dry with cool breezes at night.[5] It was in the plains that the Jicarillas began hunting the buffalo and eventually adopting the ways and methods of coping with, and living in, a plains environment.

When the Spaniards arrived in the Southwest in the mid-1500s, they established their first extensive relationships with the Rio Grande Pueblos. It was from the Pueblos that they learned of the Indians east of the Rio Grande, Indians whom the Spaniards later referred to as "Apaches." With this information and high hopes, Francisco Vazquez de Coronado's 1541 expeditionary forces journeyed through the eastern plains of New Mexico in search of the fabled Seven Cities of Cibola. To their disappointment, no cities of gold were located: their chronicles acknowledged, for the written historical record, however, the existence of the eastern branch of the Southern Athapascan Apaches. The Spaniards did not call these Indians "Apaches" until the 1600s; instead they used other names, such as "Querechos" and "Vaqueros."[6]

Until 1700, the Jicarillas were undifferentiated because of the Spanish practice of using only the name "Apache"[7] to refer to all Apache bands (which included the Cuartelejos, Carlanas, Sierra Blancas, Palomas, Achos, and Calchufines). Occasionally the names of chieftains, ecological practices, or physical location were used to distinguish one band from another. The Jicarilla Apaches were not identified by that specific name, however, until 1700, when Governor Pedro Rodríguez Cubero of New Mexico ordered that a condemned criminal's head be stuck on a pole in Taos to warn the "apaches of la Xicarilla" not to harbor Spanish fugitives.[8] This name was applied to the Apaches living in the Taos Valley–Raton Mountains area. The word "Jicarilla" (pronounced hekäre'ya) has since been generally defined as "little basket maker," referring to a small gourd or vessel or basket. The term also designates a hemispherical vessel used to hold food or liquids. By extension, it can also refer to a chocolate cup.[9]

Over time, as a result of continuing contact with the Indians, the

Spaniards noted two cultural orientations among the eastern Apaches. One group comprised semisettled horticultural people living in rancherías, mainly in the Taos, Raton, and Arkansas River region. The other included people following the buffalo on the plains, such as the Vaqueros and Carlanas. This distinguished the two Jicarilla bands.

In the decades before the Pueblo Revolt of 1680, when Pueblo-Spanish relations were becoming strained, a large number of Pueblos from the upper Rio Grande sought refuge among the Apaches. The semisettled life-style of the Apaches was reinforced by the influence of the sedentary Pueblos, and the horticultural tendencies of the Apaches became more pronounced. This was evident in 1692 when Don Diego de Vargas began the reconquest of New Mexico and encountered Apaches living north of Taos in rancherías. Captain Juan de Ulibarri also found a ranchería of Jicarillas in the region between the Rayado and Raton mountains in the Taos Valley (which indicated that the Jicarillas maintained control and occupation of this region from that early time, as they continued to do up to the late nineteenth century).

Throughout the late 1600s and 1700s, two simultaneous events were taking place that helped to establish better the identity of the Jicarillas.[10] The Comanche Indians began migrating out of the Great Basin via the northern plains, down the eastern side of the Rocky Mountains, and south toward the Texas Gulf Coast. As a result, the Cuartelejo, Palomas, and Carlana Apaches were forced out of the plains of southwestern Kansas and east-central Colorado, and they eventually merged with the Jicarillas.

The second event was the beginning of French exploration and settlement along the upper Mississippi River and increased trading activities with the Plains tribes. This commercial tie enabled the Comanches to obtain guns and ammunition, giving them a decided advantage over the Apacheans, who were prohibited from acquiring arms under Spanish Indian policies. The Comanches' superior weapons were only one of the many reasons for Apache vulnerability. By the mid-1700s, the Apacheans were forced to remain closer to the mountains and foothills of northeastern New Mexico and southeastern Colorado.

The French presence contributed to growing Spanish concern over maintaining control of their far northern frontier. To offset French influence, the Spanish government devoted more attention to its relations with the Indians.

The apparent threat from the French and the intensification of hostilities between the Apaches and Comanches were verified in 1706 when the Picuris Pueblo asked Spanish officials in Santa Fe for assistance against the Apaches. Captain Juan de Ulibarrí was sent to help rescue Picuris who had been taken captive. In the course of his mission, he learned that Comanches and Utes were attacking Apache rancherías. Reference to the attacks on the Jicarillas surfaced again in 1714 when the Faraon Apaches from the south central part of New Mexico began rampaging along the Spanish northeastern frontier. They harassed the Spanish and Pueblo settlements, but wreaked havoc on the Jicarillas, who were also suffering from the raids of the Comanches and their allies, the Utes. To stop this onslaught, the Spanish included the Jicarillas among the list of friendly Indians in their campaign against their mutual Apache enemies. This was the start of the Spanish practice of using Jicarillas from time to time as auxiliaries to the Spanish army.[11]

In comparison to the Faraones, the Comanches were even more devastating for the Jicarillas. By 1718–19, the Jicarillas and their close relatives, the Carlanas and Cuartelejos Apaches, were in full retreat. These Apaches asked for military aid from the Spanish government in Santa Fe, but did not receive immediate assistance. Instead the Spaniards took advantage of their situation and began to use them as pawns in their tense relations with France. Viceroy Marqués de Valero commanded Antonio de Valverde Cosio to aid the Jicarillas "with the view of using them as a buffer against the French.[12] Valverde began his campaign against the Comanches and Utes in Apache territory, from Taos up the Canadian River to Colorado along the Arkansas River, where he was joined by the Cuartelejos, Palomas, Carlanas, and Calchufines. Despite formidable preparations, apparently no skirmishes or battles took place.

By late 1719, the Spaniards had become more concerned about the menacing French presence. Within a year, France had declared war on Spain. Governor Juan de la Cruz of Nueva Vizcaya reported that French soldiers were positioned within seventy leagues of Santa Fe and that he had advised the Apaches to take refuge in the Pueblos.[13] Valero instructed Valverde to establish a presidio at El Cuartelejo, "to direct the conversion of the Apaches and induce them to cultivate the land so they might present a barrier to the east."[14] Valverde strongly urged the viceroy to reconsider the location of the presidio; he favored La Jicarilla in Taos Valley because of its strategic location and the friendliness of the Apaches.

In September 1720, a Spanish council of war was won over by Valverde's claim of La Jicarilla as a superior location; but a presidio was never established. The suggestion was repeated from time to time, but policy changes and setbacks always forced reconsideration of the plan. Even after the French threat diminished, efforts to establish a presidio at La Jicarilla continued. Without success, Auditor of War Juan de Olivan Rebolledo pressed for the post for fear of a future invasion by the French or hostile tribes.

The Apaches themselves soon began urging the government in Santa Fe to establish the presidio. In 1723, Apache Chief Carlana and a delegation visited Governor don Juan Domingo de Bustamante to ask for aid against the Comanches. In return, they promised to settle down in pueblos and receive religious instruction from the missionaries. Carlana invited Bustamante to La Jicarilla. Bustamante visited with Apaches at several rancherias and was impressed both by the fertility of their lands and their apparent desire for Christianity. He also saw the immediate need for a presidio, and he recommended its establishment to the viceroy. On May 2, 1724, a second delegation of Jicarillas met with Bustamante, again asking for help against the Comanches.[15]

The Jicarillas even pledged themselves as vassals of the king of Spain, hoping this would induce the Spanish to reconsider the presidio,[16] but they were disappointed again when the Spanish presidial inspector Pedro de Rivera decided it was unnecessary. One of the reasons for this decision was the abatement of the French threat by 1726. Instead of offering aid against the Comanches, the Spanish suggested that the Jicarillas settle closer to the Pueblos for protection from their enemies. Some Jicarilla bands accepted this advice and settled near Taos, where a mission was founded for them in 1733.

Information on the Jicarillas during the 1730s and 1740s is scarce, but there is evidence to suggest that after 1730 the Carlanas, Cuartelejos, and Palomas began to live part of the time in the Sangre de Cristos and that they developed closer ties with the Jicarillas. On a seasonal basis, these Apache bands lived near the Pueblos of Taos and Pecos, but continued to hunt on the plains on a regular basis.

In the 1760s, the Spanish made a greater effort to control the Comanches. In 1768, Governor don Fermín de Mendinueta campaigned against them in the breaks along the Arkansas River, using Jicarillas as guides and auxiliaries. A campaign was carried out by Governor don Juan Bautista de Anza, who had augmented his six-hundred-man force with Jicarillas, Utes, and Pueblos. This effort was followed by more successful attempts. The Comanches were finally forced to sue for peace in 1786.[17] The pressure of the Comanches, however, had forced a merger of the eastern plains Apaches with the mountain-valley Apaches. As a result, the Carlana and Cuartelejo Apaches by 1800 had become the Llanero band of the modern Jicarillas.[18]

The threat of the Comanches and other enemy Plains Indians since the 1700s made the Jicarillas amiably disposed toward the Spanish settlers. They did not seem disturbed by the sparse but growing number of Spanish settlements from Santa Fe north toward Abiquiu and northeast toward Taos. They rather welcomed the opportunity to carry on commerce with the Spaniards, their occasional allies against the Comanches. The Jicarillas continued to maintain their homes in the mountains east of the Rio Grande, where they practiced horticulture and hunted out on the edge of the plains, sometimes venturing beyond the Arkansas to the Llano Estacado.

The Spaniards, preoccupied with the more sedentary Pueblos who offered better hope for Spain to implement its policies of religious conversion, and with the Gila Apaches who were far more threatening to Spanish settlements along the current United States–Mexico border, left the Jicarillas comparatively undisturbed.

By and large, the Spaniards did not radically upset the Jicarilla way of life, though they did leave a definite imprint on Jicarilla society. They introduced Christianity, accepted by only a handful of Jicarillas for short periods of time. The Jicarilla language, however, received Spanish terms to describe and label heretofore unknown objects. A host of foreign material goods and products whetted the appetite for even more material things. The acquisition of the horse was of great importance, since it revolutionized the nature of warfare and transportation. The flexible way in which the Jicarillas viewed their world made them amenable to accepting certain aspects of Hispanic culture.

From 1821 to August 1846, Jicarilla territory was under the loose jurisdiction of the newly formed Mexican government. During this period, there was no lasting peace on the northern frontier. The peace that the Spanish army had established in 1786 was shattered as the Indians again became hostile toward the Mexicans. Indian raids multiplied and upset agricultural, commercial, and mineral activities over hundreds of thousands of square miles.[19]

Although American trappers and fur traders had been traversing New Mexico since 1803 when the United States purchased the Louisiana Territory, Americans now began to trek across the Great Plains toward New Mexico in greater numbers, mainly along the Santa Fe

Trail, to take advantage of Mexico's proclamation of free trade. Mexico soon turned this influx of Americans to its own advantage. Mexico was interested both in establishing peace with the Indians and in developing the northernmost part of its frontier. To accomplish this goal, Mexico offered land grants as incentives to the Americans and to promote peace and economic growth. This paved the way for future assault on the Jicarillas' territory and their way of life.

Between 1821 and 1846, the Mexican government awarded eight private grants and five town grants; included among the latter were the towns of Las Vegas, Anton Chico, and Mora.[20] All were taken from Jicarilla lands without the Indians' knowledge or permission. Under the Mexican Colonization Law of 1828, the provincial governors were authorized to award land grants, but they were to allow the Indians continued use and occupation—full title was not to be issued until the Indians, of their own volition, chose to leave or abandon the land. This law was never fully enforced.[21] In 1841 the largest land grant affecting the Jicarillas, involving approximately 1.7 million acres in northeastern New Mexico, was made to Carlos Beaubien and Guadalupe Miranda.[22] The new owners permitted the Jicarillas continued use and occupation, mainly because, without causing a war, they could not realistically expect the Indians to move out of so vast a region. (Like the Mexican government, these grantees welcomed the Americans.) In 1847 this grant was purchased by Lucien B. Maxwell. He allowed the Jicarillas to remain, maintaining cordial relations, and from them he later profited as the United States government contractor to the Cimarron Indian Agency.

As the white population grew within the Maxwell land grant, there was a greater demand on the ecosystem, increasing the competition for land and resulting in severely strained relations between the whites and the Indians. For the Jicarillas, this meant the beginning of dispossession from their sacred lands, intensification of their raiding activities, the inevitable clash with the American military forces, and ultimate dealings with civilian government officials. The United States took possession of Jicarilla territory when General Stephen Watts Kearny and his army marched into Las Vegas in August to take control of the region following the United States' annexation of Texas in 1846.

By the mid-nineteenth century, then, the Jicarillas already had a long history of cultural adaptation and change. Their ability to adapt to a new environment and accept new cultural traits was an indication of their flexible views and attitudes; still, fundamentally they maintained their original Athapascan culture, even in the face of serious challenges to their way of life. The Comanches had forced the Plains band of the Jicarillas back to the boundaries defined as the sacred lands. A more profound challenge and threat had come during the Spanish and Mexican regimes, with the awarding of land grants. A process of change, affecting the nature and character of Jicarilla native life, and portending future land dispossession, was begun. This process laid the foundation for more profound changes under American suzerainty.

Chapter 1
Jicarilla Apache Culture in 1846

When the Americans arrived in 1846, the Jicarilla Apaches were living in the central and eastern parts of northern New Mexico and adjoining portions of southern Colorado. The latter area also contained enclaves of land belonging to the Eastern Pueblos.[1] The Jicarilla tripartite cultural configuration had altered little since the previous century, notwithstanding the influences of Hispanic culture. The two main bands, the Llaneros and Olleros, persisted as the basic division within the tribe, although the primary economic activities of hunting and gathering were centered in the politically autonomous local groups, which were united only by their common religious beliefs. Culturally, their world "near the center of the earth" remained undisturbed; but this deceptive quiet was not to last long.

The Jicarillas had a matrilocal society: the basic social unit consisted of the extended family, which included the parents, unmarried children, married daughters, and their husbands and children. The next larger unit was the local group, made up of a small cluster of families, who were usually related, and who traveled together and shared common territory.[2] Subsistence patterns necessitated considerable movement from place to place.

The residence groups were highly flexible and mobile. All members were free to come and go as they pleased; however, this physical lack of solidarity was compensated for by a high degree of social cohesiveness through blood or marriage, which bound the individual by obligations or the need for mutual support.

There were favored locations used annually for hunting and gathering purposes where the local groups maintained semipermanent campsites; these were occupied a good portion of the year. The

Ollerites lived primarily along the Upper Rio Grande and its tributaries, in the valleys and along the canyons. In 1850 there were six Ollero extended family units. One family lived west of San Juan Pueblo. Four closely related families lived south of the small Spanish village of Ojo Caliente (on the Ojo Caliente River, a tributary of the Rio Grande) and along the canyons of El Rito. A large subdivision resided along the Chama River north and east of Abiquiu, a Spanish community north of today's Espanola. Northwest from Abiquiu, near Coyote, was another cluster of camps.[3]

In the late spring, small family bands slowly migrated north along the Chama River, toward Canjilón and Tierra Amarilla, to the mountains of southern Colorado. One summer campsite was near the Nutrias drainage southeast of Tierra Amarilla. This migratory pattern was verified by several Jicarilla elders who recalled their own places of birth as well as those of their mothers in testimony given before the Indian Claims Commission in 1953.[4] Juan Monarco related that he was born at Eagles Nest near Taos, but that his mother was born on the headwaters of Antelope Creek in Colorado. Alasco Tiznado recalled that his mother's birthplace was near Saguache, Colorado. Garfield Velarde indicated that his mother was born in Colorado near Los Pinos Creek. He was born near Conejos Creek in the lower San Luis Valley of Colorado.[5]

The Llaneros resided mainly in Mora, San Miguel, and Colfax counties in the northeastern plains of New Mexico and along the foothills of the Sangre de Cristo Mountains. There were approximately eight local groups among the Llaneros in 1850. Cimarron Valley was their beloved stronghold. A sizable branch of Llaneros lived near the village of Cimarron, one north of Mora, and another north of Ocate, toward Agua Fria. Another grouping lived at Ute Park northwest of Cimarron. Several bands made camp along the river tributaries; one on the Little Cimarron River (Red River), one south of the Vermejo River (before it joins the Canadian River), and another along the Ponil River north of Cimarron.[6]

From these headquarter bases, the Llaneros moved easily out into the Plains, raising their hunting camps as far south as Estancia, west of Pedernal Mountain. Many seasonal camps were strung out from Springer toward Taylor Springs and Abbott. Another series of camps dotted the region from Moriarty to Tecolote to Logan, Clayton, and San Jon, on the edge of the Llano Estacado. All sites were chosen for their closeness to traditional hunting and gathering territories in the panhandles of Texas and Oklahoma. Tex Koteen Baldine testified with others in 1953 that his place of birth had been in the panhandle area of Oklahoma.[7]

The Jicarillas shared a common culture, but not an overall formal political organization. The independent and autonomous political units had leaders, influential persons who acquired their positions through skill and wisdom. Each local group had a leader who represented the interests of his followers. It was his responsibility to negotiate disputes with neighboring groups over matters of territory or revenge, and he arbitrated internal conflicts. Having no absolute authority, these leaders governed by persuasion, and their powers were only as great as their abilities to act in the capacity of advocate and to achieve a consensus and promote peaceful coexistence. Leaders gained their positions on the basis of their accomplishments and generosity, but it was not uncommon for incumbents to have received their authority through hereditary succession.

In addition to civil leaders, there were war leaders who commanded a following only in time of war. Both civil and war leaders obtained their positions not only through their skills, but very often by possessing supernatural powers as shamans. For these reasons, the war leader exercised considerable influence in local affairs, either as an individual personality or in his special relationship with the civic leader. The Llaneros' leader up through the mid-1850s was Lobo Blanco (commonly called Lobo), who received considerable notoriety during the Jicarilla Apache War of 1854–55.[8] After he was slain during the war, another leading warrior, José Largo, took the helm.[9] Apparently, he was part Mescalero Apache. In addition to these two figures, who seemed to have gained power through their military skills, there were San Pablo, Chino, Juan Julián, and José Antonio, who were civil leaders. San Pablo, who was sometimes called "Red Coat," led the Apaches in the Cimarron region.[10] By the 1860s, San Pablo, José Largo, and Juan Julián had emerged as the important Llanero leaders, Chino having been killed in 1849, and Antonio evidently having been supplanted by one of the other leaders.

For the Olleros, the leadership consisted of Francisco Chacón, as the main chief, Huero Mundo, and Vicenti.[11] As did Largo, Mundo emerged as war leader during the 1850s and married the daughter of Chacón, which solidified his power. By the 1860s he had succeeded Chacón. Mundo was a half-brother to Ouray, one of the chiefs of the Uncompahgre Utes. Their mother was Jicarilla Apache. It seemed that Mundo was older than Ouray. It is not clear when their mother rejoined the Jicarillas, but Mundo's father was Jicarilla.[12]

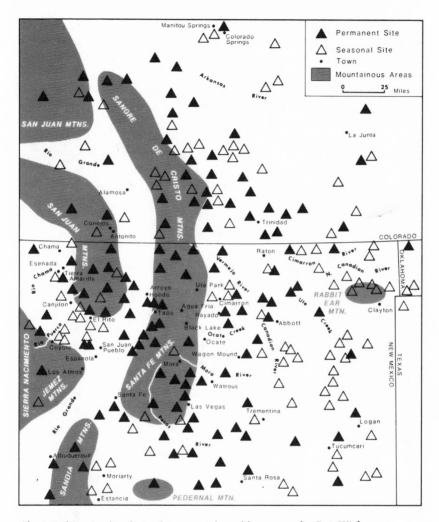

Aboriginal Sites and Early Settlements. Adapted from a map by Greg Wight

Except in warfare, women as well as men achieved leadership roles. Women were important in the practice of medicine, in arbitrating disputes, in advising the male leadership, or simply as advisers to their husbands who were leaders.

Since Jicarilla society was matrilocal, women were not barred from making decisions regarding the welfare of the tribe, though they usually relinquished that role to the men. They preferred their own role as heads of household, a position equal in importance to and as respected as that of hunter, warrior, or chief. Contrary to the popular image of the Apache women, Jicarilla women were highly respected in their society. As one Jicarilla Apache informant put it when discussing that image: "The white *man* made that up....I had two husbands and not one of them was my boss."[13]

As mothers, Jicarilla women held and still hold equal status with the men because children are highly regarded, and the care and rearing of the children are the primary responsibilities of the females. This high regard for children becomes evident in the prenatal stages when women practice a rigid regimen of prescriptions and proscriptions to safeguard the unborn child's health, future luck, mannerisms, and so forth. On the fourth day after a baby is born, a major ceremony is conducted to bind the child to the family and to ensure his life-long association with the Supernaturals. In 1936 anthropologist Morris Opler collected valuable information with regard to Jicarilla childhood and adolescence. He was given accounts of child-rearing practices. One of his informants gave him the following story:

The Gods gave the people this ceremony in the beginning. It was handed down from old times through the tribe. This ceremony was given to the people when they were already on this earth, before Monster Slayer came, however, and before the monsters were killed. It was not needed for life in the underworld before the emergence, for down there, there was no sickness, no death, no need for a "long-life" ceremony like this, but the earth is dangerous and evil; and this takes the children to the puberty ceremony safely.[14]

In the mid-nineteenth century, immediate access to the four sacred rivers was no problem. Here the infants were bathed as part of the ceremonial rituals. During the early adolescent years, a child underwent several more mini-ceremonies such as one on the occasion of receiving his or her first pair of moccasins, or the spring haircut ceremony, both of which were performed to reinforce the initial long-life ceremony.

Still today, many parents and close relatives initiate a process of training which takes on a very serious tone when the child reaches the age of five. The role of disciplinarian is delegated by the parents to the grandparents, who help keep unruly children in line and become the restraining force for difficult youngsters.

The more pleasant side of grandparenting is helping the children learn tribal moral values, sexual attitudes, and familiarizing them with the traditional stories. Storytelling time is important among the Jicarillas. As one of Opler's informants explained,

When the children won't behave or listen, the older people stop talking. They won't allow anyone to make fun of them. When a man has a group of children listening to these stories, he gives them kernels of corn to eat. They eat these while he tells his stories and they never forget them. [15]

Grandparents are protective of their grandchildren, yet stern with them when teaching them their initial skills. Young boys are instructed in the fundamentals of hunting, raiding, and so forth by their grandfathers, while the grandmother provides guidance for the little girls in learning their domestic chores. As part of the socialization process, girls are encouraged to play as if they were sewing and constructing tipis and caring for their dolls. When they have developed sufficient physical strength and better motor coordination, lessons are given in the art of basket making, hide tanning, beadwork, cooking, and other such skills necessary to prepare them for their future roles. In addition to their domestic training, girls are required to learn all the aspects of horsemanship including participation in their capture. Physical fitness is stressed as much for girls as for boys. They are warned, "Perhaps an enemy is near. You must be ready to jump and run. If you make yourself like an old fat lady, when the enemy comes, you will be captured and made a slave. We are not always at peace." [16]

Children are constantly advised of, and cautioned against, the natural and supernatural dangers inherent in their environment. One familiar precaution is not to stand in the path of a whirlwind because the mind could lose its senses and the body might become twisted. Only a shaman with "whirlwind powers" would be able to cure this. Placing a basket over one's head, they are warned, will slow down one's growth. Sickness, ghosts, and harmful things exist and remain in ashes; therefore, playing in them would bring grave consequences. While out in the fields, the children are told to keep a lookout for flying vultures that might cast their shadows on them, resulting in a headache or something worse. Snakes and bears are to be avoided at all costs; not even their tracks should be disturbed. Feathers of night birds such as the owl are not to be handled because they have certain powers that are evil.[17] It is considered necessary for children to learn all the customs and rules in order to maintain a harmonious balance in the personified universe.

The typical Southern Athapascan fear of death is communicated to the children at an early age.[18] The utmost efforts are made to keep children from seeing a dead person or associating with children whose parents or other family members have recently died until the bereaved ones have been through the proper cleansing rituals. Parents do not want their children "marked" by the aura of death.

The seriousness of ceremonialism is also impressed upon the children. Ceremonies are not to be imitated in play, nor are children allowed to witness the performance of certain rituals because their young minds and hearts are not considered strong and it is feared that they may literally be frightened to death. They are introduced to ceremonies gradually, and by the age of six they participate in most of them.

During the adolescent years, the role of women in Jicarilla society is honored when the Adolescence Ceremonial Feast is held for a girl reaching puberty.[19] The purpose of this ceremony is to ask blessings for her long and fruitful life, that she may uphold and honor the fundamental principles and sacred beliefs of Jicarilla society, and that she may bring healthy children into the world. This ceremony is a four-day affair, during which time she and her partner, usually an adolescent male of the same age, listen to the sacred songs about the origins of the Jicarillas. The prayers stress the positive traits that both should strive to imitate in their own lives.

The ceremony is performed in a large tipi that faces east and is presided over by one or several medicine men. During the four days, the two adolescents are expected to eat very moderately, keep themselves busy at some useful chore, observe all the rules and instructions given by the medicine man, heed the admonitions of experienced elders, dance to all the designated songs, and stay up later each night until the last, when they remain awake the entire night.[20]

The feast is a major undertaking for the families of both the girl and the boy. The sponsoring families are obligated to offer three meals per day to all persons attending the ceremony. This task alone requires a massive coordinated effort that calls into play the organizational abilities of the women. The festival gathering serves as a social affair where acquaintances are renewed, gossip exchanged, courtships begun and ended; where old people tell their nostalgic memories, politicos politick, and children play to their hearts' content.

The Adolescence Ceremony focuses on the female, but the role of the adolescent male is also highlighted by the Ceremonial Relay Race, which takes place in the fall.[21] After the Jicarillas were placed on a reservation in 1887, they chose as dates for this Relay Race September 13–15; these are still observed. Although this ceremony emphasizes the participation of the young boys, it is also a harvest festival, staged for the benefit of the entire tribe. Like all Jicarilla ceremonials, it derives its rationale from the story of the Emergence, when there was a race for the Sun and Moon. The Sun and Moon had enlisted the aid of the culture heroes, the deities, and the plants and animals in this race and, as a means of tribute, the Jicarillas were enjoined to carry on the tradition. The deities warned that if the Jicarillas stopped holding this race, they would starve; but honoring the divine as decreed would ensure a balanced and regular food supply. The race was to take place between the Olleros, who represented the Sun and the animals, and the Llaneros, who represented the Moon and the plants. This reflected the duality of the food resources of a people who were primarily hunters and gatherers.[22]

The race track is laid out on an east-west concourse with a circular, kivalike structure, symbolizing the place of emergence, at each end. Two days before the scheduled date, a preliminary race is held to determine the head runners and to make final preparations for the race, including construction of the two symbolic structures, and the making of sacred sand paintings. On the third day, the boys of the two bands run the relay race. Like the Adolescence Ceremony, this event is a gala. Temporary camps are set up by all tribal families to help accommodate guests and visitors from other tribes.

If the Olleros win, animals will be abundant in the coming year; if the Llaneros win, plant foods will be in ample supply. This ceremony is similar to several of the Pueblo races and it has been argued that it was borrowed from them. Opler pointed out, however, that

the Jicarillas already had the social structure to accommodate it [the two bands, and the long-standing respect for Sun and Moon as important Supernaturals], but being primarily hunters and gatherers, they were spurred on by a profound interest in a dual food supply, an even-handed interest that the more agricultural Pueblos could not match. [23]

In Jicarilla society all groups and classes can, and do, participate in religious matters. Any Jicarilla can learn the traditional or long-life ceremonies, which include the Adolescence Rite, the Ceremonial Relay Race, and the Holiness Rite (commonly known as the Bear Dance). For personal shamanistic rites, however, a particular person receives charismatic powers from the celestial bodies, the animals, or some of the other natural phenomena. [24] These powers, which may be good or evil, select their candidate at a very early age and make themselves manifest later in his or her life, whereupon the individual chooses whether or not to accept the role. Sometimes, nonacceptance may have grave consequences for the chosen person, such as poor health, bad luck, and so forth. If the power is accepted, however, a tight bond is established and thereafter the person is completely controlled by the power.

Persons who accept the power are put through a rigid series of tests to determine their courage and sincerity, usually under the guidance of an experienced shaman. Under such tutelage, the individual learns a wide array of prayers, songs, rituals, and a code of behavior; this process can involve several years. After the training, the new shaman becomes a practitioner.

The long-life ceremonies do not require a person to have a direct encounter with the Supernatural Powers. These ceremonies were given to the people at Emergence and have been handed down from generation to generation. The Holiness Rite, [25] or Bear Dance, is the most difficult curing rite to learn and it requires specialization. It obtains its spiritual sanction from the Emergence when two young girls were rescued from an unnamed danger and returned to the people. This rite, which is designed to cure Bear, Snake, and other sicknesses caused by Wind or Fire, is usually performed three days before and during the appearance of the full moon, for a total of four days. It takes place within a large enclosure about eighty feet in diameter, much like a corral, constructed of pine, spruce, or piñon, with an opening to the east. Within this fenced area on the west side is a large tipi with its doorway to the east where the patients are confined while the medicine man prays and sings over them.

The fourth night is the most important: the twelve sacred clowns and twelve T'sa.nati (who represent the Snake) make their appearance four times during the night to cure the patients with their special powers. They pray not only for the sick, but for the health and good grace of the entire tribe. In the intervals between the four appearances, the men and women are allowed to dance within the enclosure. Eight campfires are built within the corral and the women sit on the south side, the men on the north. Outside the corral, camps are set up to serve food to all who attend the Bear Dance. On the fifth morning, all participants may enter the tipi and receive blessings. This marks the end of the ceremony.

Religion always has played a key role in Jicarilla society; everything is in some way related to or explained by religious beliefs, based on the Emergence stories. Economic activities formerly were governed by religious codes and beliefs that helped to maintain certain standards of economic behavior.

Hunting was the foundation of the Jicarilla economy, which depended on extensive landholdings and continual movement. The main large game animals sought were the buffalo, mountain sheep, antelope, deer, and elk. The buffalo were hunted mainly on the plains of the Texas panhandle along the Cimarron, on the Llano Estacado, and south of the Arkansas River.

The Llano Estacado was inhabited by a vast herd of buffalo, which migrated through the area in the spring and fall. These herds grazed through the panhandle of Texas to Palo Duro Canyon, into southeastern Colorado, and continued to the northeast. While in the Colorado region, some of the buffalo went well into the mountain areas. The streams and major tributaries that flowed into the Arkansas River through the deep canyons prevented these animals from crossing and continuing the northward migration.[26] The Jicarillas hunted them during the fall season, from September to November. When the men went out to the plains, some of the women were brought along to assist with the dressing of skins and transporting of the meat to the semipermanent camps.

Some of the highways frequently traveled by the hunters included a trail that led from the Cimarron Valley across the Canadian River, by way of the Point of Rocks, and east to the Big Cimarron on the Great Plains. Another trail led from Mora southeast to Trementina and east to Logan, New Mexico. It was near this trail that the buffalo herds passed on their northward migration. Still another trail went north from the Cimarron Valley to the San Luis Valley, then north to Huerfano toward the Arkansas River.[27]

It was mainly the hunting of the buffalo that brought the Jicarillas to the Great Plains. Articles like the tipi, travois, and parfleche, plus manner of dress, were acquired before 1846. Since the Jicarillas felt more comfortable and secure in their own country, they spent no more time than necessary out on the plains.

The hunting of mountain sheep was as significant as buffalo hunting, and it involved as much time and skill. The regions where the mountain sheep were most likely to be found were north of Blanco Mountain in the northern part of the San Luis Valley; in the Windy Mountains near Culebra Creek, along the Little Cimarron River; and in the San Juan Mountains. A well-traveled trail to the habitat of this animal led from near Taos to Huerfano Butte in Colorado. The Jicarillas believed that the sheep used to live in valleys, but went up into the mountains with the arrival of the Spaniards and their guns. The sheep were a particular challenge to the Jicarillas because they were considered to have excellent vision. Once the sheep were driven into the mountains, bows and arrows no longer sufficed. They could be hunted successfully only with guns.[28]

Elk, deer, and antelope were also major food staples. Elk were hunted in the same general area as the mountain sheep—they roamed along the Arkansas River and into the Spanish Peaks region, though they sometimes could be found in the open valleys. Jicarillas on horseback would drive the elk past waiting hunters. Antelope made their home in the Upper Pecos Basin at the north end of Estancia Valley: one favorite area was at Plaza Largo, along the Tucumcari Hills to the Canadian River. This was a good place to camp for the winter, when the antelope were hunted.

Small animals—the beaver, rabbit, squirrel, porcupine, prairie dog, and chipmunk—supplemented the food obtained from the larger game. Although some parts of their bodies were taken for ceremonial uses, they did supply some meat. In addition to these, some birds (turkey, quail, dove, and grouse) were eaten. Others—eagles, crows, and owls, for example—were taken strictly for their feathers and claws. Hunted for their fur only were wolves, wildcats, weasels, mink, and flying squirrels.[29]

These animals provided all the material goods used by the Jicarillas. The large ones furnished hides for tipi covers, robes, blankets, clothing, rugs, utility bags, rawhide ropes and straps, sinew for thread, and cord for bows and arrows. Certain animal body parts were used for ceremonial paraphernalia: feathers from eagles, claws from bears, teeth from beaver, shells from land turtles, hooves from deer, horns from buffalo, and tails from mountain lions.

Hunting of large animals was the domain of the men of the tribe, and training for this role began in early childhood. According to one of Opler's informants:

When a boy is about four or five years old his older brother, his father or his grandfather gives him a bow and arrow, a little one. They want him to get used to them. Sometimes the older people get the little boys together and show them how to play arrow games. They get them interested in arrows. [30]

The young boys were taught to use the sling, attract birds and animals with whistles, trail the tracks of animals, learn their habits and habitats and the various ways to trap them. The boys were also urged to acquire the necessary habits that would later aid them as hunters.

A boy, even though he is small, is made to get up early in the morning and run. When he is about six or seven years old he is told to run after the horses, to chase them from pasture to a point close to camp so they could be caught by the men. Sometimes the horses go up on the hills during the night, and then the boy is told to go and bring them back before sun-up. [31]

When the young boys became proficient as marksmen and horsemen, they were taken on their first big hunt by the experienced hunters. If the boys made a kill during this hunt, they were ceremoniously initiated into the fraternity of hunters, and were expected to learn the entire array of elaborate rites and the significance of the animals in the origin stories. Such knowledge was necessary before a boy could become a respected member of the hunting order.

Horsemanship was taught to both boys and girls at a very early age. The children were told the story of the horse who did not serve his master at a crucial time because he was badly treated. This story served to emphasize why they must treat the horse with utmost respect at all times. The horse was seen as a special gift to the Jicarillas from the Supernaturals, and as having sacred attributes. Special songs were sung in its praise. Since the gear belonging to the horse was associated with taboos, it had to be handled with great care. One such taboo was that a rope should never be brought inside a dwelling, since it might invite a snake inside.[32]

The important institution of raiding[33] developed as a corollary to the hunting activities. This also involved early training, the observance of certain rites, and learning a code of conduct while on the raid. Its rationale was found in the story of the Coyote, a trickster, who was responsible for acquiring some of the behavioral traits of man through his cunning and "foxy" ways rather than by physical aggression.

With the introduction of the horse to Apache culture, raiding became a highly developed art. The horse, which made buffalo hunting easier, was often hard to come by. The Apaches usually acquired their horses from their Spanish and Indian neighbors to the south, trading buffalo skins and other goods for them. Often they bartered for them with their captives and, infrequently, with their women and children. This animal was also obtained by raiding the Spanish settlements, though it was more challenging to raid their Plains Indian enemies.

Raids occurred whenever a warrior became of age and needed his first mount, when the herd needed replenishing, or when revenge was sought for stolen horses. Permission for raids had to be granted by the chiefs, headmen, or heads of family. After permission was obtained, open invitations were given and a party of about ten males was organized. At least one of them had to be a knowledgeable raid leader who would go through the proper ceremony before the scheduled raid. A dance of final commitment was staged and other preparations were made. The expedition was planned for the four days before the full moon to take advantage of the light it provided. While the men were out on the raid, the women had to maintain a rigid standard of conduct, and observe and perform certain rituals to help ensure the safe return of their men.

As the men approached enemy territory, they began to make more ceremonial preparations, communicate in "raiding language," and adopt a more serious demeanor. After the enemy camps and herds were located, each man roped a horse to ride, at the same time driving off the rest of the herd. Spears were left in the ground nearby to indicate the Jicarillas' contempt for their enemies.

Raiding naturally led to retaliation; when a Jicarilla was killed, this called for revenge, and war parties had to be organized. There were numerous other reasons for war, including trespass, rescue of Jicarilla women and children taken captive, or competition over natural resources. War parties usually consisted of not more than ten men. Again, rituals were performed before the journey began. Unlike the

Plains Indians who counted coup, the Jicarillas preferred to kill their enemies. Individual Jicarilla warriors did not take scalps, but deferred this privilege to the party leader who had made arrangements before the sojourn with the right medicine man. In the event of defeat, no scalps could be taken and any that had been previously taken had to be thrown away.

The war-raiding complex derives its influence from the Plains Indians, but the attitudes "toward the scalp combined the Plains desire for the trophy with the Southern Athapascan dread connected with the dead."[34] Upon returning home, a four day–four night cleansing ceremony and a scalp dance were held so the warriors would not be haunted by enemy ghosts. If any Jicarillas were rescued during the raid, they too had to rid themselves symbolically of their former status in order to reunite with the tribe. The scalp dance was staged for both mourners and victors to help rid them of their frustrations and anguish. When it was over, the warriors were able to keep the scalps without fear.[35] Captives faced a very unpleasant future, being relegated to the lowest level of Jicarilla society: doing the hard and disagreeable labor and being subjected to insults and abuse. Captive children, however, were treated in humane fashion and their adoption by Jicarilla families was not uncommon. When they became adults, they were extended the same social privileges as other members of the tribe.

None of the Plains tribes were friendly toward the Jicarillas, but the Comanches were archenemies. Most fights that the Jicarillas were party to involved the Comanches, who were more numerous and possessed superior arms. While out on the plains in Comanche territory, the Jicarillas took extraordinary measures to ensure their safety. Hunting trips were carefully planned. To facilitate quick maneuverability, camps were small and strategically located near good sources of wood and water in protected and defensible areas. They were close to look-outs such as buttes, mesas, or other points where enemies could be detected over long distances. Two such locations were Dead Man's Mesa, east of Mora at the edge of the Llano Estacado, and Tucumcari Butte, which was also a sacred place. The buffalo flats were visible from the top of this butte for twenty to thirty miles. Seldom did the hunters go beyond the point where the top of this butte could not be seen. Rabbit Ears Mountain near Clayton, New Mexico, also provided necessary protective covering to which hunters could retreat if enemies were met out along the Big Cimarron.[36]

Even the choice of routes required defensive planning. A good trail led down Tequesquite Creek to Ute Creek and on to the Canadian River. This route had wood and water in abundance. East of Ute Creek were three mesas, known as Tres Mesas de la Trinidad, that served as an impenetrable stronghold. Here houses were built for the winter months. The Jicarillas had several skirmishes and battles with the Comanches near Tres Mesas, but they always were able to keep the Comanches from reaching the top of the mesa.[37]

On the prairies the Comanches were devastating, but the Jicarillas were equally so when they had a chance. Nagee, a Jicarilla woman, reported an account of her great-grandmother's involvement in a spring hunting trip to the plains of New Mexico, probably during the late 1850s.[38] Women, children, and young boys remained in camp while the men went out to hunt. One day at mid-morning a boy alerted the camp to approaching Comanches. There was no time to leave and no place to take cover in the barren plains. Nagee's great-grandmother was about seven years old at the time. Given the critical circumstances, her mother dug a small hole in the ground, leaving a tiny air vent, and hid her in it. She was instructed not to come out until she was absolutely certain that the enemies had left. She bid her mother farewell forever and climbed into the hole just in time. Peeping through the vent she witnessed the horror of the Comanches slaughtering all the women and children and burning the camp. She remained for several hours in the dugout. When she got out, she discovered an older boy who had played dead to avoid the disaster and who was the only other survivor. Frightened, they began wandering in the direction of home; she remembered wandering for what seemed like endless days and nights. Once near a settlement they managed to kill a mule, which provided them with food for many days. Fearful of meeting more Comanches, they hid by day and traveled by night. Many weeks passed and in late summer they found themselves in Ute country in Colorado. One afternoon while they were sleeping, a party of Utes came upon them. The men inquired who they were and why they were alone. The children explained their plight, and were taken to the Ute camp. The little girl's hair was a ghastly sight. It took the women several hours to untangle it and wash it. Several days later, the two children were escorted back to their relatives who were camped in the Chama Valley.

Although hunting, raiding, and war constituted the majority of Jicarilla male activity, horticulture was also practiced, and played an important role in Apache life. Its presence was acknowledged from the time of Spanish contact. The origin of horticulture is associated with the wild turkey, who, according to the Emergence stories, brought this practice to the Jicarillas. Although all bands maintained a dual pattern in their subsistence activities, alternating between hunting and farming, the degree to which they relied on horticulture varied. The Ollero band was more involved in farming, although the Llaneros took up this occupation, too, after the arrival of the Americans.

Corn was the main crop, but beans, squash, pumpkins, and other crops were also cultivated. The cultural importance of corn is evidenced in many ways.[39] It became intertwined with many customs, was used as a medicine, and played a leading part in the performance of religious duties. Corn pollen is still the most sacred substance that can be offered to the Supernaturals. Examples of the current ceremonial use of corn include tying it to the top of the flags used during the Ceremonial Relay Race and using the kernels to aid the memory of a person singing sacred songs. During storytelling, children are given ears of corn as they listen to the origin stories so that they will never forget them. Because of its wide usage, the pollen is routinely and faithfully collected from the tassels during the growing season.

The planting and harvesting of crops involved the entire family. After the fields were tilled for planting, a scenario of ritual and prayer signaled the beginning of the growing season. The men made holes with digging sticks. The women and children followed, dropping in the seeds and covering them up. It was believed that the crops would grow faster if the children, who were still growing, put the seeds in the ground. The children had the additional duty of keeping small animals and birds off the fields by scaring or shooting them.

During the growing season, when the new moon was in the sky, the male head of a household engaged in farming puffed smoked ritually on four downy turkey feathers placed at the corners of the fields. In doing this, he was asking that the new moon bring rain. As this suggests, the moon is associated with rainfall and water in Jicarilla symbolism.[40]

After the harvest, the corn and other crops were dried in the sun to preserve them for later use. Some corn was immediately roasted and consumed, but most of it was made into cornmeal, tortillas, and tamales, and stored. If there was a large surplus, some was given to the horses. Grinding the corn was an occasion for the women to get together and test their skills, while some of the old men sang the numerous corn songs. Some men even took a turn at grinding the corn. This was not considered unusual since according to the origin stories, the men had a prominent role in developing agriculture.

Gathering was another important economic function and the responsibility of the women. Like raiding, gathering expeditions involved some praying and singing of songs, but the rituals were less elaborate. The search for wild foods took the people over large areas and great distances and was a year-long endeavor. If the women stayed within the confines of their own territory, they traveled in small parties, but if required to go outside familiar areas, men accompanied them.

Young girls went with their grandmothers, mothers, aunts, and older sisters on these expeditions.[41] The girls were expected to learn to identify the various edible wild fruits, nuts, berries, seedbearing grasses, greens, and tubers. In much the same way, young boys learned the names of the different plants, their seasonal characteristics, and their medicinal uses. The pharmaceutical offerings of nature were numerous and women were expected to know all the major herbs and their proper application. Proper identification was absolutely necessary since many plants were similar and, if confused, could cause harmful, if not fatal, results. The girls were taught how to prepare and store these medicines and administer them to the sick. A class of Jicarilla women healers emerged that developed extensive knowledge and training in the use of herbs. They assisted the medicine men in administering the curing rites, or they practiced as general therapists when called upon. This occupation was handed down to other women and girls worthy of the position. Their knowledge sometimes allowed them to become medicine women, with status equal to that of the men.

While gathering foods and medicinal herbs, the women also collected other vegetal substances used for dyeing their baskets and for coloring and ornamenting their family's clothing. They also gathered wood for carving household objects, and different varieties of soil for cosmetic purposes or for ceremonial use. Times for gathering were happy occasions since they provided an opportunity to get away from the camps and household chores. Often, if the men were not too busy to join them, these endeavors became festive family affairs.

The women were as competitive as the men in fulfilling their economic responsibilities. They were protective, and even secretive, in guarding their natural resources. For example, if the women of a family knew the location of certain kinds of bushes that yielded an abundance of berries, they would make sure no one saw them frequent that particular spot. The tendency to monopolize information concerning resources extended also to essential medicinal herbs and ceremonial materials because it gave a woman extra bargaining power to obtain other items and goods she needed.

This competitiveness was also reflected in the making of baskets, pottery, beadwork, and other craft items. Certain styles, artistic patterns, and sources of materials were jealously guarded and handed down with pride from mother to daughter. The ability to make the best baskets or the most artistically beautiful beadwork, or to tan the softest hide, enhanced a girl's chances of marrying a better warrior and elevated a woman's position among her peers.

This competition was not necessarily for profit, but for social and economic status. It led to greater labor specialization than has generally been recognized. It was highly desirable that a woman have the various skills necessary to make her a productive and useful member of her family. There are women, however, who were especially skilled in making baskets and therefore spent more time at it; others concentrated on tanning hides; still others might spend more time traveling from camp to camp administering herbs or helping with ceremonies. This was possible only because women in extended families cooperated in carrying out the domestic tasks necessary to their everyday existence.

This same competitive spirit also became a source of conflict among the women and their families. Sometimes a dispute would arise over things such as copying someone else's special artistic designs, the actual stealing of materials, or for any number of reasons deriving from the economic activities carried out by the women. Despite this competition, basic social cooperation among the local groups was not undermined.

Perhaps the one single factor that determined the degree of traditionalism for the Jicarilla Apaches in 1846 was geography. Jicarilla native lands were considered the outreaches of the Mexican northern frontier. The lands seemed unattractive to Mexican settlers. This area did not have the reputation of being prime agricultural land, nor did it offer an abundance of mineral wealth. Therefore, it did not invite wholesale invasion by non-Indian people. What resources it contained, and its potential for development, were relatively unknown in 1846. The region's isolation served as a protective shield for the Jicarillas. In this sparsely populated semiarid country, the Jicarillas were thus able to maintain a way of life that was still traditional.

The unsettled region permitted the continuation of the aboriginal economy of hunting and gathering, but there were enough Mexican settlements to provide trading opportunities. The pace of life and amount of Hispanic influence was moderate, allowing Jicarilla native ways to flourish. The pressure for change was not overwhelming, yet the undercurrents of change were there: increased traffic on the Santa Fe Trail, growing Mexican and American populations on the Maxwell Land Grant, and dwindling game. Despite these ominous signs, the Jicarillas maintained their social, political, and religious systems. With the arrival of the Americans, however, all this would change.

Chapter 2
Establishing the Relationship
of Dependency, 1846–55

When General Stephen Watts Kearny occupied New Mexico in 1846, very little was known about the Jicarilla Apaches, a situation that remained unchanged when the Indians were brought under United States jurisdiction two years later. From the close of the Mexican War, until it became a territory in 1850, the area was administered by both military and civilian governments. During this period of ill-defined political jurisdiction, and indeed for many years thereafter, the federal government's Indian policy was vague, vacillating, fraught with ignorance, and subject to the vagaries of political pressures. This led to a very weak guardian-ward relationship between the Jicarillas and the government, whose indifferent and noncommittal attitude toward the Indians, based on a total lack of understanding of their life-style, their needs, and their cultural patterns, delayed the settlement of their affairs for the next several decades, thus beginning a relationship of dependence.

Nor was the New Mexicans' tolerance for their Indian neighbors any better. The predominant attitude of hostility on the part of the settlers in New Mexico was colored by the long history of conflict with the Indians dating from before the arrival of the Americans. This attitude, in turn, affected United States Army policy. When General Kearny arrived in Las Vegas, he promised the settlers security of life and property, specifically from the marauding Navajos and Apaches— a position that was reinforced in the Treaty of Guadalupe Hidalgo, which ended the Mexican War.[1] These promises revealed an implicit prejudice: the military intended to side with the New Mexicans

against the Indians without first examining the causes for the hostilities and without recognizing that Indians had been the victims of an
unfriendly populace equally guilty of offenses.

This ill-reasoned viewpoint put the military in a difficult position.
Many army officers recognized that the hostilities would continue as
long as the federal government postponed the formulation of a plan of
action to administer the affairs of its new wards. Either the United
States had to set aside reservations and supply the Indians with
subsistence until they learned to support themselves under the new
circumstances, or the government had to provide military support for
their extermination. The government, however, was not willing, nor
was it prepared, to take either approach. The political and economic
situations in New Mexico prevented immediate government assistance to the Indians. At the same time, the army's ability to subdue
them was limited by manpower shortages, poorly trained and inade-
quately equipped troops, and a territory too vast to be guarded and
controlled effectively. The stage was set for the resumption of the
conflict between the free-roving Indians and the New Mexican
settlers.

Despite the lack of federal commitment and direction, Kearny tried
to keep the Jicarillas peaceful. In the attempt, he resorted to false
promises. Meeting with a band of Jicarillas on September 23, 1846, at
Abiquiu, he promised them aid and protection if they would settle
down to a life of farming and commit no depredations. The Jicarillas
applauded the idea, though they soon realized that the promise was
not to be fulfilled.[2]

To aid the military and provide a temporary civil government for
the territory, Kearny appointed Charles Bent as governor in 1846. His
duties included overseeing the conduct of Indian affairs. Bent's first
report to Kearny stated that there were about one hundred lodges, or
five hundred Jicarillas, throughout New Mexico. He described them
as an indolent and cowardly people having no permanent residence,
roaming throughout the settlements, living principally by theft, and,
with the exception of a few who bartered a small quantity of pottery,
causing great annoyance to the New Mexicans.[3] The tone of this
report helped to create an image that would adversely affect the
Jicarillas' relationship with the federal government and the military
for years to come. That this image was well implanted in the minds of
military officials by 1850 is shown in a letter written by Colonel
George A. McGill, while he was inspecting the Department of New
Mexico under orders from the secretary of war. He reported that the

Jicarilla Apaches were one of the smallest tribes, but also one of the most troublesome: "This band is considered as incorrigible, and it is believed they will continue to rob and murder our citizens until they are exterminated. I know of no means that could be employed to reclaim them."[4]

In addition to creating this prejudiced picture of the Jicarillas, Bent outlined his recommendations for Indian policy in New Mexico. His suggestions were not original; he merely reiterated what was common practice in the conduct of United States Indian affairs. He felt that it was imperative to demonstrate the power of the United States by sending a delegation of principal men from the various tribes to Washington for a first-hand view of the federal government in action. This display of power, he believed, would serve as a deterrent to warring activities. Bent also advised keeping communication open with the Indians and buttressing that communication with sufficient gifts and agents to control their behavior and regulate their affairs. The governor also supported a policy of stationing troops throughout Indian country and forming independent volunteer companies to help the military.[5] Although Bent's proposals would later be implemented, he did not live to see them carried out. When he was killed in the Taos Rebellion in January 1847, primary control of Indian affairs reverted to the military, where it remained until 1849.

A state of mild hostility among the peoples of New Mexico continued throughout the late 1840s. Indian depredations increased along the Santa Fe Trail. The Jicarillas were willing participants and they were considered especially menacing because of their position on the Cimarron Cutoff. A typical example of their hostile activities occurred on June 12, 1848, when a band of warriors attacked Lucien Maxwell's pack train in the Raton Mountains. Their raids were also felt in the San Luis Valley of southern Colorado and in the Taos Valley, but the army took no decisive measures to control them.

This was the situation that James S. Calhoun faced when he arrived in Santa Fe in July 1849 to become the first Indian agent for New Mexico. Commissioner of Indian Affairs William Medill had informed him that so little was known of the Indians there that he would not be given specific instructions as to his duties, but he was to furnish statistical information regarding Indian conditions in general.[6]

Calhoun's only guidance came from the general Indian policies of the United States; like Bent, he took his cues from those sources.

Establishing proper control of the Indians, he believed, would involve "a strong arm...guided by an enlightened patriotism, and a generous spirit of humanity."[7] He advocated a stern policy of reprimand and reprisal for those who wrought havoc on the settlements, and of generosity toward peaceful Indians.

Calhoun had practically no assistance from the federal government. He had to cope with meager funds, a hostile population, and an uncooperative military establishment. The civilian sector was virtually paralyzed in carrying out any programs to settle the Indians, while the army could not effectively control the marauding bands. His problems were further complicated by the undetermined legal status of New Mexico, which made the application of the Trade and Intercourse Act of 1834 uncertain. This act was designed to define the extent of Indian country, and to regulate trade between the Indians and the whites. The existing trade relations were plagued with fraud, cheating, and the illegal sale of liquor and arms to the Indians, a major cause of conflict between the races that could not be controlled without regulation.

An incident in Las Vegas in August 1849 led to further deterioration of relations. A party of forty peaceful Jicarillas came to town to trade, but ended skirmishing with the troops. Captain Henry M. Judd, who later reported that these Indians had come "with an evident design of committing depredations should a chance be presented,"[8] seemed sure that it was this band that had committed murders and robberies in the vicinity. He felt that his suspicions were confirmed when he learned that they wanted to obtain some gunpowder. Evidently they were unable to buy any, but as they were leaving town, Judd ordered Lieutenant Ambrose Burnside to follow and arrest them. In the ensuing skirmish, six Apaches (five women and one man) were taken prisoner. Three years later, in an interview with Indian Agent John Greiner, Jicarilla Chief Francisco Chacón explained that the Apaches had gone to Las Vegas to trade, but were attacked by the troops. Chacón believed that this incident had occurred because the Apaches had been blamed for the death of two Mexicans and the theft of cattle at Casa Colorado. Chacón believed also that this unprovoked assault had resulted in a later attack on a group of Americans near Wagon Mound, in which the band leader, Chino, was killed.[9]

This type of misunderstanding and distrust led to more conflict. Another incident began on October 28, 1849, when a band of Jicarilla and Ute warriors attacked the White party train near the Point of

Rocks, seventy miles east of Barclay's Fort near the Santa Fe Trail cutoff, and took Mrs. White and her daughter captive. Several days later, they were seen by a party of Pueblo Indians who visited an Apache camp.[10] After discovering the overturned carriage and the male victims, one of the Pueblos hurried to Las Vegas to report to Calhoun, while another went to Barclay's Fort to notify the military. Initially the army seemed reluctant to act without more substantial evidence. Within a week, however, Major William N. Grier and a force of 140 men from the Taos Post went to the Point of Rocks to investigate. On November 3 they picked up the trail, which led them toward the canyons of the Red River. Two weeks later, they found the remains of a fresh camp. The Apaches fled, leaving all their belongings behind, when the soldiers charged in. There they found Mrs. White's body, with an arrow in her head, about 300 yards from the lodges. After pursuing the fleeing Indians briefly, the troops gave up. Although the child was never found, it was believed that she had been killed and thrown into the canyon.[11]

Meanwhile, twenty soldiers from Las Vegas started out with Sergeant Henry Swartwont in pursuit of the Indians. He took along Lobo's daughter, who had previously been captured by Burnside, as a guide and a hostage to be exchanged for Mrs. White. Along the way another incident added more fuel to the fire of hostilities. While encamped for the night, the prisoner asked to go to the top of the knoll. There she began to weep and it was surmised that she had seen some sign of her people and tried, in this way, to warn them. In the morning when several of the teamsters were ordered to put her in the wagon, she seized a butcher knife and tried to stab them. A chase ensued around the camp fire and between the mules and wagon. When she could not catch the teamsters, she stabbed the mules, one of which died shortly thereafter. At that moment, Sergeant Martínez shot her in the head, an act for which her father, Lobo, would later take revenge. The soldiers returned to Las Vegas, where they heard that Major Grier had found Mrs. White's body on the Red River.[12]

The Jicarilla version of the affair, told to Greiner by Chacón in 1852, was that the Utes and Apaches had approached the White party as friends, but were driven away. Then the fight commenced. Mrs. White and her daughter were carried away to the Red River and held until the troops came. Chacón said that she had been given good care and that if the Americans had sent for her, instead of attacking the camp, she would have been returned. He confirmed that her daughter might have been killed, as he had not heard of her since.[13]

The raid on the White party received wide press coverage, which reinforced the Jicarillas' bad reputation and created both a feeling of uneasiness throughout northern New Mexico and a demand for revenge. The people were certain that there was a general conspiracy among the wild tribes to attack them, especially since it appeared that the Indians were well armed and far more familiar with the country than the military, who had been totally unsuccessful in their attempts to bring the Indians to terms.

Throughout the spring of 1850, the Jicarillas continued to raid in the vicinity of the Maxwell Land Grant. On April 5, Maxwell's herders were harassed by a band of Jicarillas, and the following month a more serious attack occurred. A combined Jicarilla-Ute war party killed eleven men on an east-bound mail train near Wagon Mound. Burnside and his men came upon the site about ten days later, and found the mail scattered over a two-mile stretch: it appeared that a running battle had taken place. The remnants of eight bodies were scattered about; all had been eaten by wolves except for the three bodies in the wagon. The soldiers buried the remains and burned the wagon on top of the graves.[14]

Outraged, the army sent an expedition commanded by Major Grier to chastise the Jicarillas. With a force of seventy-eight men, Grier left the Rayado Post on July 23 and moved toward the haunts of the Indians on the Canadian River. Two days later, the soldiers stumbled upon a small party of Apaches, whom they killed and whose horses they confiscated. On this same day, some militiamen surprised another small party, with similar results. The Grier expedition did not encounter any more Apaches for the rest of their 200-mile circuitous trip, and returned to Rayado on July 30.[15]

The citizens would no longer tolerate this type of what they considered an unsuccessful expedition, particularly because the Indians intensified their raids. Consequently, the military began to reevaluate its strategies, and finally concluded that the way to subdue the Indians was to build more forts in the midst of their country. As early as 1849, detachments under Colonel John M. Munroe had arrived in New Mexico and were stationed in the principal towns along the Rio Grande from Taos to El Paso. In 1850 the army sent topographical engineers into the heart of Jicarilla territory to survey the land, assess it natural resources, and determine the feasibility of establishing a military post. Subsequently, Fort Union was built at the junction of the mountain and Cimarron branches of the Santa Fe Trail. It became the headquarters, as well as the largest supply and ordnance depot, for the Ninth Military Department. Later, in the spring of 1852, Cantonment Burgwin was built ten miles south of Taos, and Fort Massachusetts was erected at the foot of Blanca Peak in the San Luis Valley of Colorado.[16]

Evidently this show of power resulted in some positive, but temporary, restraint on the behavior of some of the Indians. During the spring of 1851, reports indicated that Jicarillas were raiding the settlements near Manzano, sixty miles southeast of Albuquerque; but Lieutenant J. P. Holliday, who was dispatched to check out the rumors, found that the raiders were Navajos. Chacón, the Jicarilla advocate of peaceful coexistence, informed Holliday that his band wanted to be at peace with the Americans. Chacón's sincerity was verified by the local people questioned by Holliday.[17]

In light of Chacón's attitude, Governor Calhoun was encouraged. He had heard, however, that a council was going to be held by the Comanches, Utes, and Jicarillas at Bosque Redondo, and while no one seemed certain why it had been called, it was feared that these tribes were plotting war against the Americans. Later Calhoun learned that the Jicarillas, at least Chacón's band, disavowed any plans to participate in such an action.[18]

The governor felt that this was an opportune time to negotiate a formal peace treaty with all the Jicarillas, so he sent runners to gather them in council. On April 2, 1851, a treaty was signed at Santa Fe, with Calhoun and Munroe representing the United States, and Francisco Chacón, Lobo Blanco, Huero Mundo, and Josecito Largo acting for the Jicarillas. The Indians agreed to submit to the United States, to be confined within certain specified territorial limits, to cultivate the soil, to cease their depredations, and to relinquish all captives and stolen property. In return, the United States promised annuities, farm implements, and other gratuities as deemed proper by the government. In effect, the Jicarillas agreed to give up their way of life in return for promised goods. Obviously, the treaty favored the government.

The Jicarillas were expected to comply with the terms of the treaty immediately, yet as far as the New Mexicans were concerned, their part of the bargain would go into effect only after Congress had ratified it. The document stipulated that the Jicarillas were not to roam within fifty miles of any settlement or highway. But since they were now dependent to some extent on trade with the small settlements, which necessitated entering the villages, this unrealistic stipulation led to immediate confusion for all concerned.

About two weeks after the treaty was signed, Lieutenant Orren Chapman reported that a party of Jicarilla and Mescalero Apaches under Quentoz Azules, a Mescalero, was fifteen miles below Las Vegas, but as yet no complaint had been made against them. He added: "None will be made so long as their trade is profitable."[19] Since no Apaches were supposed to be within fifty miles, Chapman was not sure whether or not to treat them as hostiles. His message was relayed to Colonel Munroe, who notified Governor Calhoun. Calhoun dispatched Benjamin Latz to Las Vegas and told the military to ignore the fifty-mile-limit clause for the time being.[20]

On April 21, Chapman gave notice that there were more Apaches in the San Miguel vicinity. A party of seventy Jicarillas near Las Conchas had left for Mora Valley, a band of fifty was near La Cuesta, and twenty-five were near Bernal Springs. A larger group was gathering on the Pecos River to head toward Bosque Redondo to meet with the Comanches for peace talks.[21]

The citizens were disturbed by the presence of the Apaches. Prefect H. Grolman of Las Vegas demanded the assistance of the troops in removing the Indians and forcing them to respect the fifty-mile limit prescribed by the treaty. He was informed that his request could not be honored.[22] On April 25, Chapman was ordered to take twenty-five men to confer with the Indians and explain that they must remain fifty miles beyond the settlements. He was instructed to take prisoners if they did not comply, but was cautioned to exercise extreme discretion. His commanding officer suggested that if any of the principal men desired to come to Santa Fe and confer with the governor, Chapman should furnish escort.

Chapman met Latz in San Miguel on May 1. He remained there for a week, informing the Indians of their violations of the treaty. He also met with Chacón and inquired as to his future intentions. Chacón was more concerned with his present needs. He explained: "I and my family are starving to death, we have made peace, we do not want to do harm as you see from our bringing women, and children with us, we want to go to the clay bank at San Jose and make vessels to sell so as to procure an honest living, we can't steal and must do something to earn a living."[23] Chapman told Chacón that he could remain in San Miguel until instructions were received from the governor, but he did not feel that Chacón's overtures should be taken very seriously. He attributed this stance to Chacón's dire economic situation, but remained suspicious because he noted that the camp where most of the

Indians were located commanded a strategic position overlooking the valley of Pecos, the Tecolote, the Bernal, and Las Gallinas.

On May 7, Chacón met with Colonel Munroe and Governor Calhoun at Santa Fe. He agreed that the Indians under his control would comply with the government's wishes and move on through Anton Chico by the following week. He was warned that this agreement would be binding on all Apaches in the area and that two military companies would be sent to Las Vegas and San Miguel to ensure compliance. Latz was to inform the other bands of this directive. As an added incentive, the Apaches were promised fifty bushels of corn. Chacón and his band were to receive twelve to fifteen bushels. Munroe and Calhoun were to meet Chacón at Anton Chico on May 14 to make sure that Chacón moved two days' travel beyond that point, but evidently Chacón did not understand that he was supposed to meet them again, for he did not appear on that day.[24]

Later, Captain Ewell informed Munroe that he had met Chacón at Mora on May 24. At this time it came clear that there had been a breakdown in communication between Chacón and the United States authorities. Chacón stated that he had not been aware that he was to meet Calhoun and Munroe two weeks earlier. Also, he did not totally understand the fifty-mile-limit clause of the treaty. He protested that the limit did not make sense now that they were at peace. Ewell permitted Chacón to remain in Mora on his pass from the governor, and Chacón stated that in eight days he would like to confer with the governor again.

The governor was evidently aware of the absurdity of the fifty-mile stipulation. He knew that the Jicarillas must steal or starve unless some plan were devised to feed them. It would be folly to suppose that they could be subjected to proper restraint without subsistence. He informed military authorities that all that could be done at that point was to watch their movements and leave them unmolested so long as they were peaceful. The military, in the absence of instructions from Washington, followed his advice and took precautionary measures, but it did not antagonize the Jicarillas.[25]

Despite Calhoun's hopes, no policy statements were issued by the Indian Department. This prompted him to write Commissioner Luke Lea, asking: "Where are they to be located, and what shall be the extent of the limits to which they are to be restricted, and from which are they not to depart except under rules and regulations to be adopted?"[26] Calhoun felt it was only fair to the Indians that the government answer these questions. He was particularly mindful of the Jicarillas' efforts to comply with the treaty and regarded their behavior as meritorious, deserving of some token of commendation.

After Calhoun and Munroe had established guidelines regarding the fifty-mile stipulation, some of the Jicarillas made sincere efforts to remain at peace. In late May, military authorities became aware of another council to be held by the Comanches, Utes, and Jicarillas at the Bosque Redondo,[27] and again assumed that some clandestine plans were in the making. The Jicarillas disavowed any intention of participating since they were determined to live up to their part of the treaty, believing that it was being seriously considered by Congress. Throughout the balance of 1851, they were generally peaceful, having only minor squabbles with some of the local townspeople, all involving the sale of liquor.

Calhoun also made a real effort to live up to the spirit of the compact by extending piecemeal aid, but no support was forthcoming from Washington. In March 1851, John Greiner, the Indian agent assigned to the Taos Agency, assumed the duties of superintendent of Indian affairs for the ailing governor, and established a good rapport with the Jicarillas. He realized that, because of their location and intimate knowledge of the country, they were a potential threat to communications between New Mexico and the United States, and felt that their daily contact with the settlements was good reason to keep them at peace.

By this time the Jicarillas were aware that their neighbors, the Navajos and Utes, had received much more favorable consideration from the government. The only gratuities they themselves had received were the few distributed at Anton Chico and Taos. This treatment seemed unfair. They had also heard malicious rumors that the government believed that they were not deserving of any presents. In an attempt to placate them, Greiner sent messengers to ask all Jicarillas to meet with him at Pecos on March 20. Approximately one hundred warriors with Chacón, Lobo, San Pablo, and San Antonio came to this meeting. Good feelings prevailed. The Jicarillas informed Greiner that Arapahoes had killed some of their people and stolen their horses. They also complained that the alcalde at Anton Chico had unjustly imprisoned some of their people. After gifts were distributed, Greiner promised them that Calhoun would present their case to the president in Washington. Thus reassured, the Jicarillas returned home.[28]

Unfortunately, Calhoun never reached Washington; he died on June 22, 1852. This ended any hope of establishing a decent relationship between the Jicarillas and the government. Greiner, however, as acting governor, was quite successful in maintaining relative quiet in the territory until September, when the new appointee, William Carr Lane, arrived.

Without specific support from Washington, but basing his actions on a bold interpretation of the territorial governor's powers over Indian affairs, Lane launched a program to settle Indians on lands of their own choice. Greiner stayed on to help implement the plan until the new agent, Dr. Michael Steck, took office in late 1852. This straightforward, reformist approach, however, did not conform to the policies that officialdom considered proper and it was doomed to failure from the start.

Lane decided to move all the Jicarillas west of the Rio Grande, an act that further alienated the majority of the Llaneros because the area east of the river was their heartland. Steck had suggested this move after a council with the Utes, Mescalero Apaches, and the Jicarilla bands under Lobo and San Pablo in December. He presented the plan to them only to learn that the Jicarilla leaders had no interest in the proposition. One headman, Sanchua, a political orator of sorts, retorted that they were under the protection of the American flag and that they had the right to choose any mode of life, so long as they did not violate the 1851 treaty. Presumably this meant that they did not want to become farmers. In spite of this information, Steck concluded that it was in the best interest of New Mexico to move these Indians out of the wave of settlement in the eastern part of the Territory.[29]

On this trip Steck also obtained information about the Jicarillas. He reported that there were approximately 400 of them, divided among four chiefs (Chacón, José Largo, Lobo, and José Chavis) and four headmen (San Pablo, Huero, Sanchua, and Chino). He described them stereotypically as fond of spirits and unreliable in their word. Still, he did sympathize with their predicament.

On February 24, 1853, Governor Lane ordered Steck to move the Jicarillas to suitable agricultural locations and to establish communities with self-governing bodies to maintain peace and order. In this setting, the Jicarillas were to adopt a "civilized" way of life. Only Chacón's bands supported Lane's plans, and in a cooperative spirit they selected some land along the Rio Puerco, twenty miles west of Abiquiu, near a small stream that emptied into the Chama River. This location was well watered, surrounded by beautiful mountains from which timber could be obtained, and abundant in game. The valley was excellent for grazing and provided good winter camping grounds. It was also the only place west of the Rio Grande and still within Jicarilla territory that had not been claimed. By March, Chacón and his people had begun to clear over one hundred acres and to plant corn, wheat, squash, pumpkins, and melons.

The willingness of the Jicarillas to participate in Lane's program led Steck to believe that the situation was changing for the better. To ensure the success of the enterprise, Steck promised further technical assistance and provisions until the crops matured. He requested that Congress grant these lands to the Jicarillas to secure their rights and to keep the settlers off.

Despite the apparent success of Lane's efforts, Commissioner George W. Manypenny remained skeptical. In April, he began undermining Lane's program, which he described as visionary and extraordinary. He wrote Lane on April 9, 1853, that "if the new locations should prove to be insufficient for the support of the Indians placed upon them or unsuited to their tastes and habits, there is little room to doubt that they would soon abandon them [and] return to their old places, and resume . . . their predatory and vicious practices."[30] He ordered Lane to suspend all operations until further notice.

Lane attempted to save his program. He explained that, because the military had failed to protect the country, he had decided to keep the Indians at peace by feeding them and settling them down to cultivate the soil. Besides, he said, "I considered that I was fully authorized to take the steps which I did take; I was simply carrying out the long established and benevolent policy of the United States in relation to the Indians."[31] Lane had even received the endorsement of the press in Santa Fe, which reflected opinion throughout New Mexico. It seemed that the white people preferred his policy to unsuccessful military chastisement. Lane's defense, however, did not succeed. Manypenny insisted that Lane's proposals were unintelligible: had they been clearly outlined from the beginning, he might not have suspended the operations. In essence, the commissioner admitted that he agreed with Lane, but funds were not available for the program. Furthermore, Lane had already spent all the funds appropriated for the Indians of New Mexico for that fiscal year on this plan.[32]

When Lane resigned to run as territorial delegate for Congress in May 1852, David Meriwether became governor. Manypenny informed

Meriwether that the continuation of Lane's program would involve a sum of money beyond the appropriations for New Mexico for Indian affairs, and cautioned him to keep this in mind when advancing the policy of the government, a policy that was still no more than a set of vague guidelines. With this crippling financial situation, disaster was inevitable. Meriwether had to cope with the reality of his predecessor's overzealous use of funds and the federal government's unrelenting hold on the purse-strings for the conduct of Indian affairs. Nor was there any attempt made to communicate with the Jicarillas and explain this difficult situation. Without an explanation, they were left with the impression that the government had not acted in good faith.

The absence of rainfall was a further complication. Edmund A. Graves, the agent appointed to the newly created Abiquiu Agency, reported that the Jicarillas had "commenced the cultivation of a farm which has been very well worked, when it is considered that it has been mainly done by the wild and roving Jicarilla Apaches."[33] One hundred and twenty acres had been placed under cultivation when the Rio Puerco dried up, making irrigation impossible. There was no harvest, but the Jicarillas pledged that they would remain on good terms with the government despite the failure of the farming effort. They hoped that the government would see them through until the next growing season. Graves, however, placed little reliance on their promises, recalling the White party incident. He discredited all their good-faith efforts. Without government aid, the Jicarillas could not make a decent living, even if they returned to their old lands; the only viable alternative, which they had wholeheartedly supported, had failed. Meriwether was convinced that they would not remain peaceful even if he were to extend assistance. Graves realized, however, that if they were not fed, the plundering would begin again.

The spark that ignited open hostilities occurred in February 1854 when Samuel Watrous, the beef contractor for Fort Union, reported the theft of several cattle. On February 20, troops under Lieutenant David Bell were ordered to recover the stolen cattle, which were thought to be seventy miles east of Cañón Largo on the Canadian River. It was believed that a band of Jicarillas and Utes, led by the Ute Chico Velásquez, were responsible for the theft.[34]

On March 2, Bell, accompanied by Brevet Captain George Sykes, Lieutenant George Maxwell, and thirty-five men of Company H, Second Dragoons, made a scouting expedition down the Canadian River. Within three days, one of the guides discovered a fresh trail that led them about a mile. Then they spotted several mounted Apaches on the other side of a rocky ravine. One of the Indians saw them and immediately fled, but was cut off from his party and taken prisoner.

Meanwhile, another group of warriors was seen about three-quarters of a mile away. Bell took after them, but before he could gain much ground, the war party charged the dragoons at full speed. Within a short distance of the soldiers they halted, and gave an invitation to battle. When Bell approached, he noticed that Lobo Blanco was leading them. Bell informed them that the soldiers had not come to fight, but to talk and be friends. Although several of Lobo's warriors came up and shook hands with Bell, most remained at a safe distance, holding strung bows and arrows. One of the Apaches asked why they had disarmed one of his companions if they wanted to be friends. Bell replied that the soldiers had intended to obtain a guide to the camp. After the captured Indian was released and his weapons were returned, tentative talks began.

Bell inquired as to the whereabouts of Velásquez, about whom the Indians claimed complete ignorance. The officer told them that three weeks previously cattle had been stolen from Samuel Watrous by Indians who had headed toward Cañón Largo. He explained that he had trailed them to the nearby river and had also found evidence at the campsite north of Cañón Largo. The Apaches denied the implicit accusations and assured Bell that they had not been west of the river. They said that it was the Utes who had committed the depredations, but Bell was not dissuaded by their denials. He demanded that the thieves be delivered. Another spokesman replied that, without a council of the different chiefs, they could not be given up. He offered to go down into the Canyon of the Red River where he would unite his people and come up with a plan of action.

Bell absolutely refused such a plan. He announced that Lobo would be held prisoner until the thieves were surrendered and that their ponies would be taken to satisfy Watrous's claims for damages. The spokesman objected to the confiscation of the ponies but, according to the report, did not seem to care if Lobo were taken. When the Apache returned to inform his awaiting party, the warriors responded with the war cry and a messenger was dispatched to warn their families in the woods about three miles away. One by one, some of the warriors rode toward the rear of the dragoons; only twenty remained to face the soldiers. Then Bell ordered Lobo's arrest. He resisted, and the other Jicarilla warriors formed a semicircle, outflanking the dragoons on both sides. The soldiers were ordered to charge and a skirmish ensued. When closely pressed, some of the Indians threw themselves under the necks of their horses, discharging arrows at the soldiers and dexterously avoiding being trampled. The fight lasted but a few minutes. Then the Indians scattered. The soldiers did not follow, fearing an ambush. Lobo was killed in the skirmish; his slayer remains unknown. Bell reported that the Apaches lost five men; he lost two; and the soldiers returned to Fort Union with four wounded.[35]

The following day some Jicarillas and Utes raided a herd of two hundred cattle near Fort Union, killing two herdsmen. Velásquez, who was believed to have joined the Jicarillas, saved the remaining herdsmen from the raiders and thus proved his innocence. Again troops were sent to scour both sides of the Canadian River in an attempt to punish the Apaches, who had apparently headed toward Anton Chico and Pecos.[36]

Although neither military nor civilian authorities took this outbreak very seriously, both attempted to prevent further violence. Moreover, not all of the Jicarillas were in favor of outright war. Some were not engaged in the fighting at the beginning of 1854. Acting Governor William S. Messervy appointed Lafayette Head as special agent to keep open communications with Chacón, who wanted to remain neutral and had not supported Lobo's band in the outbreak. Head was told to settle them near Abiquiu and provide assistance for any farming efforts if convinced of Chacón's sincerity; otherwise, this band was also to be considered hostile.[37]

After the battle on the Red River, forty-five lodges of Apaches who desired peace moved toward Mora. When word of this reached Fort Union, forty-five to fifty mounted troops from Cantonment Burgwin were ordered to keep watch over them and enforce neutrality. If any Apaches were caught leaving the camping grounds three miles out of Mora, they were to be attacked. Otherwise, the band was to be assured that they would not be held responsible for the actions of the hostiles.[38]

Unfortunately, they did not remain near Mora. It seems that a man of Mexican descent told them that the troops planned to attack them. Not knowing what to believe, they left. Some went toward the Rio Grande, while others headed toward Taos to meet another peaceful band camped near Picurís Pueblo. Kit Carson, the recently appointed Indian agent at the Taos Agency, was instructed to determine the intentions of the Jicarillas in that area. He held council at Taos on March 25 with six Jicarilla warriors and two chiefs (presumably including Chacón). These Jicarillas disavowed participation in any depredations or in the fight with Lieutenant Bell. They professed friendship and asked for government protection against hostiles, soldiers, and citizens. Carson urged Messervy to appoint a special agent who would live among these friendly Indians and supply them with provisions to prevent raids.[39]

At this crucial point, Governor Meriwether was unfortunately granted a four-month leave of absence by the State Department. That saddled Messervy with all the difficult decisions concerning Indian affairs in the Territory. The disposition of the Jicarillas posed a particularly difficult problem. Approximately one-third of the tribe was belligerent; the remaining two-thirds sought the protection of the superintendency. Had the Jicarillas been united in hostility, the government would have been relieved of its responsibilities; the War Department would have had sole authority in dealing with the Indians. Messervy, however, was faced with the dilemma of either recognizing the band at Picuris as peaceful or considering the entire tribe at war and abandoning this group of Jicarillas. Messervy knew that if he chose to recognize the peaceful band, they would have to be fed. If they were to leave the Pueblo to hunt, they would be in danger of attack from soldiers who could not distinguish them from unfriendly Indians. Underlying his dilemma was the reality of insufficient funds, the prohibition against incurring more expenses, and the fact that he lacked the necessary administrative manpower to carry out any sort of plan.

Messervy finally decided to keep the Indians as quiet as possible until Washington officials defined a policy or Congress provided the means to improvise. He appealed to the commissioner for funds, and instructed Carson to feed the peace faction if he were convinced of their sincerity.

Carson had obtained prior assurances from the friendly Jicarillas that they would remain near Picuris until he returned from Santa Fe, but the band fled. They encountered Major Phillip R. Thompson's detachment of dragoons en route from Fort Union to Taos. Major Thompson demanded that four of them accompany him to Cantonment Burgwin and remain there as hostages to ensure the good conduct of the whole band. They consented and proceeded to Taos; but the following morning they all fled, including the prisoners.[40] This action meant that another band of the Jicarillas had become openly hostile.

On March 30, while following them, Lieutenant John W. Davidson was attacked by a combined force of 100 Jicarillas and Utes on

Embudo Mountain near Cienequilla, twenty-five miles south of Taos. In this three-hour battle, twenty-two dragoons were killed and thirty-six were wounded; all of their arms and ammunition and twenty-two horses fell into the possession of the Indians.[41] This engagement convinced the military, the territorial government, and the New Mexico citizenry that the Jicarillas and Utes were both a serious and a threatening problem.

One of Davidson's men immediately sent a message to Cantonment Burgwin asking for assistance. A detachment of dragoons under First Lieutenant Samuel D. Sturgis and the troops of Company D, Second Artillery, under Sykes were sent to aid the defeated company. All forces within the northern territory were alerted and, under orders from General John Garland, began serious preparations for campaigns against the Jicarillas and Utes.

While traveling back to Picuris, Carson was informed of the Embudo Mountain fight. He immediately decided, without further investigation, that his peace mission had ended.[42] When Messervy heard the news, his dilemma was solved. He concluded that he would listen to no more proposals from the Apaches "until they have received that chastisement which they have so long perpetrated upon our citizens."[43] Messervy advocated total punishment of the Jicarillas that they might serve as an example to other tribes. Peace, he argued, should not be concluded until the Jicarillas had been made to feel the strength of the government and had suffered the full penalty. Although he believed that "the best interests of this territory and the highest dictates of humanity demanded their extinction,"[44] he also considered settling them near the Pueblos. On April 10, however, he issued a declaration of war against the entire Jicarilla Apache Tribe.

For the next four months, a vigorous campaign was conducted by Lieutenant Colonel Philip St. George Cooke and his two hundred men. They had the assistance of a thirty-two-man Spy Company under James H. Quinn, who was employed to track the Apaches through the broken and unknown wilderness where they sought refuge.

Although Carson volunteered to accompany Cooke, he remained somewhat sympathetic toward the Apaches. He later wrote that they were driven to war by the actions of the troops; when they were vigorously pursued, thinking there would be no mercy shown them, they resorted to desperate means to escape. If they had been sent for and a fair and just treaty had been made with them, he was quite certain that they would have surrendered all the government property they took in the Davidson incident. There might have been some chance of this, especially since Chacón, the chief who commanded the largest number of lodges, had previously made overtures of peace. On the other hand, Chacón had no control over the Llaneros, who wanted a showdown. Moreover, New Mexicans were eager for an all-out war.

On April 4, Cooke began to march south and west of Taos from Arroyo Hondo, crossing exceedingly precipitous country west of the Rio Grande. His pursuit of the Jicarillas was hampered by a violent wind and snow storm. The Apaches led their pursuers over the most rugged terrain in which they had ever campaigned. The mountain ranges, which often rose to 7,000 feet, were covered with three feet of snow.

On April 8, after a long, hard march and the loss of some stragglers, the soldiers discovered an Apache camp in the rocky and steep ravine of the Rio Caliente, a tributary of the Chama River, which was almost impassable. The Apaches spotted the soldiers and hurried their women and children onto horses as they were fired upon from above. The dragoons attacked the warriors, drove them from the river, and put them to rout. Cooke surmised that this force of over 150 Apaches was commanded by Chacón. Although there was no conclusive evidence that Chacón had even been present at the Embudo Mountain battle, the soldiers pursued this band to avenge Davidson's men. The soldiers later returned and destroyed the deserted camps.[45] It seems that the dragoons were concentrating their efforts on the wrong band, while the real hostiles escaped to the Mescalero country.[46]

Some Utes later told Kit Carson that four or five Jicarillas had been killed and five or six wounded. Seventeen Apache women and children were also missing and were assumed to be prisoners; in fact they had perished in the deep snow and freezing temperature. During the fight, one woman drowned in the stream while trying to escape, but her baby was rescued by one of the soldiers, who gave the infant to a family in Taos.

Cooke continued his search for the Jicarillas in the mountains overlooking the Chama Valley. The snow was so deep that the pack mules bogged down and had to be unloaded; horses that lost the path floundered helplessly in the crusted snow and drastically slowed the pursuit. The Apaches had taken a southwest course toward the valley of the Canjilón. The soldiers were briefly encouraged when the Spy Company discovered a fresh trail in the forest. Cooke's men wearily continued their fruitless search. On April 12, although more tracks and trails were discovered, further efforts were halted and the troops headed back toward the settlements at Abiquiu and along the Chama River.[47]

Meanwhile, Major Brooks and his force trailed Chacón and Huero, with their fourteen lodges, north to the Conejos and the Rio Culebra, east of the Rio Grande. The Jicarillas, however, managed to evade these troops, who were also forced to return to Taos.[48]

Shortly thereafter, Cooke learned from shepherds that some Apaches had camped west of Cebolla Stream. It was believed that they were headed east toward the Sangre de Cristo Mountains, fifteen miles below Fort Massachusetts. Cooke dispatched James H. Carleton from Taos on May 23 to intercept them. With his force of one hundred men, including Quinn's Spy Company, Carson, Major Brooks and eighty infantry, and Sykes' Riflemen, Carleton traveled north. Carleton and Carson agreed on a strategy that included searching both sides of the Sierra Blanca for the Apaches believed to be concealed there. Quinn's Spy Company marched thirty miles west of the mountain and through Mosca Pass to await the main force on the middle branch of the Huerfano River, while Carleton and Carson proceeded along the eastern base of Sierra Blanca to Sangre de Cristo Creek and up the Vallecito. Having discovered only some old Apache trails and camps, the entire force met near the base of the mountain on the Greenhorn road of the Huerfano.

The following day Carleton's column went south across the valley of the Cucharas River, a tributary of the Huerfano, where they found the remnants of an Apache camp. They were convinced that they were indeed trailing the hostiles. The soldiers continued reconnoitering across the west side of the Spanish Peaks, just below timberline, where they encountered another three-day-old campsite. One June 1, they descended south to the Arishapa, a tributary of the Arkansas. The following morning their strenuous journey took them south to the Purgatoire and on to Dragoon Park, about twenty-five miles west of Bent's Fort Road. Signs indicated that the distance between them and the Indians was decreasing. Then, on June 4, some spies discovered fresh footprints leading toward Raton Pass.

When the soldiers reached the north end of Raton Pass, they took the utmost precautions to prevent discovery. Protected by dense timber, the column cautiously climbed the steep and rugged Fischer's Peak. After much toil, which wore out many of the horses, the Spy

Company reached the summit by the only gateway to the area. There lay level land, protected in a deep amphitheater surrounded by thick, impenetrable woods with a stream flowing through the center. Quinn's spies caught the twenty lodges in this Apache refuge unawares. As soldiers descended upon the panic-stricken people, three Apaches attempted to save the horses. They succeeded in salvaging only one horse and a mule from a herd of almost forty. The rest of the Apaches fled into the deep woods. The troops attempted to cut them off by covering all escape routes and searching the woods thoroughly, but the Indians had concealed themselves so effectively that none could be found. Carleton later was uncertain how many Apache casualties had occurred, but believed several had been killed or wounded.[49]

Shortly thereafter, the troops returned to the abandoned camp, where they probably found the food cooking on the fires rather palatable. They destroyed the camps and apportioned the thirty-eight captured horses among the Quinn's men, most of whom were on foot. This capture, however, was not considered a military advantage because it made trailing much more difficult. Carleton's consolation was that the Apaches, with all their cunning, could be pursued and found even in their own strongholds.

The main column retraced its steps across Raton Pass while Lieutenants Johnson and Moore and Quinn's Pueblo spies remained in the amphitheater to kill any Apaches who might return. When a party of warriors did return, one of the Pueblo guides took the scalp of an Apache believed to be the son of Huero.

The column moved south toward the Canadian River in search of the band under Flecho Rayado, another Apache war leader. On June 9, after searching the valley of the Vermijo, the soldiers became convinced that Rayado's band was not there. The tired troops agreed to keep moving on to the Cimarron and back to Taos.[50]

While the army combed the mountains for the evasive Jicarillas, militia forces were chasing other destitute bands who appeared among the villages stealing livestock. On June 30, Companies D and H, Second Dragoons, under Sykes and Second Lieutenant Joseph E. Maxwell, Third Infantry, followed a band of ten to fifteen Indians along the Mora River into the mountains. Maxwell and four of his men pursued them as they escaped up the side of the canyon. When the soldiers reached the top, they were met by a volley of arrows and Maxwell was killed instantly. The Jicarillas escaped, and the men returned to the fort with the body of the fallen officer.[51]

For the most part, hostilities subsided after these incidents, although scattered clashes occurred between the Jicarillas and the soldiers and citizens. By the end of June, General Garland was convinced that the war had come to an end. He reported to army headquarters that "the Jicarilla Apaches have been most thoroughly humbled, and beg for peace."[52] This reflected wishful thinking more than reality. In late August, however, Chacón did send three Ute Indians bearing a message of peace to Governor Messervy. The Utes informed him that Chacón's band of sixty lodges had gone to the San Juan River area in northwestern New Mexico to avoid the soldiers and hoped to return after a peace was made. Messervy responded willingly to this overture, but he wanted Chacón to know that his safety would be guaranteed only if he was prepared to live up to the agreement.[53]

Thereupon plans for peace negotiations were set in motion. As a result of this unfortunate war, Congress had appropriated $30,000 in July 1854 for negotiating treaties with the Navajos, Apaches, and Utes, and $25,000 for the Indian budget of New Mexico. Messervy recommended that "the Jicarillas should relinquish their present claim to lands and be removed to the country of the Gila Apaches, and that an annuity of $5,000 be paid them for the first three years and $3,000 each year thereafter." In addition they were to be furnished one farmer and one blacksmith for ten years.[54] The superintendent made tentative plans to hold peace talks and distribute provisions to the Utes and Apaches after July 1855. The negotiations would depend partially on presents for the Indians, which were not to be delivered from the states until after July. Messervy thought it was highly desirable that invitations for the coming negotiations be sent out during the winter. In this way, the Indians could be notified by February and the peace council could meet in the spring. Half of the provisions could be purchased in the territory in time for the negotiations; the other half could be purchased at a later date.

On September 6, 1854, Chacón visited Meriwether with the intention of suing for peace. Chacón was tired of the war that had caused so much suffering and poverty among his people. Meriwether reminded him that blame for the war lay entirely with the Jicarillas, who had committed thefts and failed to surrender stolen property. Chacón claimed that the difficulties had arisen because of the actions of one band of nine lodges headed by José Largo, who had escaped south to Mescalero and left Chacón's band to face the army. Chacón offered to apprehend Largo if he were given a month to do so, and if his women and children were provided with food and provisions. Meriwether agreed and corn was distributed to Chacón's followers, who were camped near Abiquiu. Meriwether, however, was not very optimistic, feeling that hostilities would not end "until the Indians were given one or two good thrashings."[55]

Although Chacón favored peace, he was reported to have taken part in all the battles. The evidence suggests that he participated as fully as the notorious Geronimo of the Chiricahua Apaches, who was seen in every battle that took place in Arizona. By 1854, Chacón had probably reached his late sixties, and his leadership was being challenged. In his conversation with Meriwether, he admitted that he lacked the necessary authority to control his warriors. Since some Jicarillas were allied with the Utes, he could not have controlled their actions. Chacón's visit to the acting governor indicated that the Jicarillas were not united and had no single chief. They were scattered over a wide territory; there was probably little, if any, real communication among them. While Chacón sought peace, Jicarillas and Utes continued to fight, but neither the army nor the Jicarillas made any apparent progress during the fall of 1854.

On September 18, 1854, Colonel Thomas T. Fauntleroy replaced Lieutenant Colonel Cooke as the new commandant of Fort Union. As winter set in, supplies were replenished and preparations for a spring campaign began. Governor Meriwether issued a proclamation in English and Spanish calling for the enlistment of mounted volunteer companies, who would provide substitutes for the diminished troops in the New Mexico military department and increase manpower. General John Garland, the departmental commander, planned to use a combined force of regulars and volunteers to defeat the Indians in the spring campaign. Citizens responded immediately, forming six companies of mounted volunteers headquartered at Taos under the command of Lieutenant Colonel Ceran St. Vrain. Colonel Fauntleroy had command of the overall military operations and all three military posts (Fort Union, Fort Massachusetts, and Cantonment Burgwin).

Meanwhile the Indians had regained their strength and were making more daring attacks on the settlements. Indian depredations that took place near Ocate Creek, the Red River, and Las Vegas forced the soldiers to step up their preparations. In the lower San Luis Valley, 150 Utes and Jicarillas drove off nearly 4,500 head of settlers' livestock. By March, Fauntleroy was nearly ready to carry out his duties. He gathered his entire force at Fort Massachusetts: two dragoon companies, four companies of mounted volunteers, and thirty guides and spies under Captain Lucien Stewart. The Indians, in the meantime, successfully drove off another 1,000 head of livestock from the San Luis Valley, the Red River region, and the Las Vegas area.

Fauntleroy began his campaign on March 14, 1855, when his 500-man force left Fort Massachusetts for the San Luis Valley and the headwaters of the Arkansas. When the Apaches realized that they were being followed, they split away from the Utes and divided into several parties. The troops picked up the trail of Chacón and his warriors, the largest of the groups. On the headwaters of the Arkansas, the soldiers came upon a camp of Jicarillas; their horses were captured, but the Indians disappeared into the countryside. The pursuers' supplies were running low and their horses were exhausted, so Fauntleroy ordered a return to Fort Massachusetts.

Fauntleroy regrouped his forces and headed back toward the San Luis to finish off the Utes. St. Vrain was assigned to press the Jicarillas between the Sangre de Cristo Pass and the headwaters of the Huerfano River. He succeeded in finding one camp of Indians on the Rio del Oso, or Bear Creek. For two days the troops fought the Indians, killing or wounding thirteen of them. The remainder fled toward the Purgatoire River. St. Vrain encountered this group or some other on the Purgatoire near Long's Canyon. When they saw the approaching troops, most of the Apaches fled toward the Raton Mountains, but a few engaged in a skirmish with the soldiers. A company was ordered to overtake them; some prisoners were apprehended and taken to Fort Union.[56]

In May, the volunteers continued their search for Chacón and his band in the Red River area, again with little success. Also again, the forces had to rest and resupply; they returned to Fort Union. In June, the military reconnoitered the intermountain region of southeastern Colorado once again. Invariably the Indians escaped even after the soldiers spotted them. At times the chase must have seemed a futile game of hide-and-seek to the soldiers. At the end of four months, the frustrated volunteers found relief when the enlistment period ended and General Garland issued orders for them to disband. "The record of the New Mexico Mounted Volunteers was good, but they never inflicted a defeat on the Jicarilla of sufficient certitude to end their depredations."[57]

By that time, however, the Utes and Jicarillas were weary of being constantly pursued; they had suffered from the harsh weather and the casualties inflicted by the military and volunteers. In August 1855 a delegation of Muache Utes and Jicarilla Apaches opened negotiations with Governor Meriwether. A peace treaty was signed on September 10 at Abiquiu.

In the eleven years of America's tutelage over the Jicarilla Apaches, a relationship characterized by misunderstanding on both sides developed. The Americans arrived with a set of preconceived notions about the Indians, a rigid set of practices for dealing with them, and an indifference toward their predicament. The superficial concern exhibited by the Americans was governed by the needs of the white population, whose overriding desire was to push the Indians out of the path of settlement and then keep them out at minimum expense.

On the other hand, the Jicarilla Apaches did not seem to discriminate among the settlers whom they raided, with the possible exception of long-proven white friends. The Jicarillas had their own way of "sharing the wealth" as prescribed by their cultural deities and their notions of what was theirs by right since it came from the land assigned to them by the Supernaturals. This point of view ensured that the newcomers would not understand them. Moreover, their experience with the Spanish and Mexicans led them to believe that they would be able to carry on their way of life without much interference from the Americans. Here they made a gross misjudgment. When they recognized this error, it was much too late to deal with it effectively.

Many complex issues and deep-rooted problems prevented the establishment of a mutually beneficial relationship, but the burden of finding solutions rested primarily with the United States, which had the means to enforce its will. It was the duty of the federal government to deal directly with the Indian tribes as authorized by its own laws. While the political status of the Territory of New Mexico was suspended, hanging on the Compromise of 1850, a muddled policy was applied to the Indians that no other governing body or institution could change. As a result, the territorial government was practically paralyzed and the army bungled along, both looking to Uncle Sam for guidance and direction, since no form of action was legitimate until sanctioned by the federal government. Governor Lane found this to be true when he implemented a farming program for the Jicarillas; he was reprimanded by the commissioner of Indian affairs. Likewise, Congress refused to ratify the Treaty of 1851. To its credit, the New Mexico territorial government attempted to deal with the "Indian problems," but the federal government extended no support and constantly undermined these efforts.

While the Jicarillas did not have direct influence in determining their future, a sizable number of them, especially the band under Chacón, proved that they were willing and flexible enough to adopt the more congenial and permanent life-style of farmers. Their attitude, however, was interpreted to be of questionable sincerity. Had the officials taken the time to acquaint themselves with the Jicarillas, perhaps they would have realized that agriculture was neither a recent nor an unfamiliar occupation for them, especially for the Olleros. Perhaps then they would have recognized that the Jicarillas were sincere in their attempts to find a partial solution to the economic problem of limited land and resources, which was the overriding cause of the political conflicts; but the officials refused to admit that this was in fact the answer they had searched for.

With this solution to the Jicarilla dilemma undermined, raiding resumed. The military had solved its problems and was ready for a fight, and so the unnecessary conflict of 1854–55 began. The Jicarillas entered this war very reluctantly; the majority risked their lives in coming to the authorities to seek protection and to express their desire to remain neutral. Once again, however, misunderstanding and lack of communication forced all Jicarillas to take up arms. They entered the war at a severe disadvantage. Despite their apparent weakness, however, they managed to alarm the whole territory and inflict some military defeats. Although the entire military force in the northern New Mexico area was on their trail, they managed to evade the soldiers time and again. This hide-and-seek version of war discredited the army, but it also eventually wore the Jicarillas down.

The worst mistake made by the military was the pursuit of the Jicarilla band most inclined toward peace. The Olleros realized that their survival depended on settling down to agriculture. The Llaneros, on the other hand, had more cause to start a war; as hunters, their game was threatened and their life-style more in jeopardy. A good portion of them escaped the pursuit of the army.

It was also unfortunate that the federal government was quick to use force against the Jicarillas but very reluctant to carry out its trusteeship responsibility, which would have been less costly in the final analysis. The events of these eleven years reduced the Jicarillas to a life of poverty and hardship as they roamed through the communities of northern New Mexico. Although they continually pressed the government to establish a reservation for them, their request was not granted until 1887.

1 Whero Mundo
2 Pabtelon
} Apaches.

3 Wm E Arny
4 Capt Jhs. M Davis.

5 Piquitigon. {Utah Indian
6. Vicento.
   Jicarilla Apache Lawyer.
   and Orator.

7 Martine Ute Capote Band

W.F. M. Arny.
Indians "Talta"

Jicarillas and Utes taking part in the 1868 treaty council. The Jicarilla delegation included Huero Mundo (back row, left),

Vicenti (back row, fourth from left), and Panteleon (front row, left). Courtesy of the Edward Ayer Collection, Newberry Library.

Jicarilla delegation sent to Washington in 1880 for negotiations about the reservation. Left to right: Santiago Largo, Augustin

Vigil, Huerito Mundo, San Pablo, and Juan Julian. Smithsonian Institution, National Anthropological Archives.

Chief James Garfield Velarde, wearing a Garfield peace medal.
Smithsonian Institution, National Anthropological Archives.

A trilogy of Jicarilla leadership, 1896. Left to right: Edward Ladd Vicenti, interpreter; Emmitt Wirt, post trader; James Garfield Velarde, chief of the Olleros. Smithsonian Institution, National Anthropological Archives.

Augustine Velarde, ca. 1900. He was an important Ollero headman in the 1890–1930 period. The Thomas Gilcrease Institute of American History and Art, Tulsa, Oklahoma.

Laval Largo, ca. 1925. He succeeded his father, Santiago Largo, as headman of the Llaneros. Smithsonian Institution, National Anthropological Archives.

This photograph taken at the 1904 St. Louis World's Fair shows Darcia Tafoya weaving a traditional Jicarilla basket. Smithsonian Institution, National Anthropological Archives.

Emmett Wirt's store. National Archives.

Chapter 3
The Ration System: 1855–72

The Jicarilla Apache Treaty of 1855 was not ratified by Congress, so none of the problems that had led to the war were resolved. The Jicarillas continued their precarious, but traditional, life-style on their denuded homelands, which were rapidly being settled by whites. The competition for the limited natural resources made the Jicarillas increasingly dependent on the food rations issued from the Abiquiu, Taos, and Cimarron Indian agencies. The ration system was to have been a temporary arrangement until the government established a reservation on which the Jicarillas could become self-supporting.

Under the treaty, the Jicarillas agreed to remain at peace and to surrender claim to their northeastern New Mexico lands. In return, the government was to set aside a reservation approximately forty miles long and ten miles wide in Rio Arriba County, northeast of Abiquiu. The Jicarillas were also offered bimonthly rations and yearly annuities consisting of small farming implements, clothing, blankets, shoes, and household items. The rations were to be obtained from the Abiquiu and Taos Indian agents, who were also issuing rations to the Muache, Capote, and Weeminuche bands of the Southern Utes.

The Jicarillas spent 1855 quietly recovering from their wartime losses. There was a constant flow of families to the areas around both agencies. Lorenzo Labadie, the Abiquiu agent, observed that they were so demoralized that they exhibited no particular aims for their future and constantly reminded him of their misery.[1] Carson also echoed this theme: that both the Jicarillas and the Utes were destitute and the steadily dwindling wild game was not helping matters.

Especially disturbing to Carson was the situation of those Indians who lived miles from the agency and who were forced to travel long distances—wearing out their horses, and having to steal food along the way. It was ironic that pillage was necessary to obtain the meager rations that were to prevent this very thing.

Although the majority of the Jicarillas pledged peace, a number of small disaffected bands continued to commit depredations near Mora and on Maxwell's Ranch at Rayado. Carson attributed these raiding activities to the alienated warriors. When they were likely to ask for peace, Carson did not speculate, but explained that these parties vowed they would take revenge for the killing of their families by the whites.[2]

Improvement in the psychological attitude of the Jicarillas was noticeable in the spring of 1856, although their economic situation remained static. The more industrious families began planting crops on land "loaned" to them by their Spanish friends around Abiquiu and El Rito. Labadie was optimistic. He felt that if the government would only assist with implements, seeds, and other provisions, the Jicarillas would soon be self-supporting.[3] The Jicarillas squatting near Carson's agency were also trying to provide for themselves by selling earthenware and willow baskets, and some even earned wages by working for the people of Taos. Others hunted in the mountains of Colorado and when they managed to get a surplus of meat, they sold it.

Another cause for good spirits was the reunion of José Largo's band with tribal kin. Largo's small band returned from its self-imposed exile in Mescalero country in the latter part of March. Soon after the outbreak of hostilities in 1854, this band had sought refuge first among the Comanches and later with the Mescaleros. Largo told Acting Governor William Davis that he had nothing to do with the recent war.[4] His claim seems doubtful. According to Chacón, Largo was one of the instigators of the depredations that led to the war. Also, Largo succeeded Chief Lobo as the leader of the Llaneros; had he not supported Lobo all along, it is highly improbable that he would have been Lobo's successor. The acting governor instructed Largo to join the Jicarillas west of the Rio Grande, but Largo found Cimarron more to his liking. Largo would not have been welcomed at Abiquiu among the surviving relatives of Chacón (who appears to have died after the treaty was signed). Concurrent with Largo's homecoming, another band—probably one of the estranged bands—under a leader named Negro, was reconciled to and rejoined the Apaches at Abiquiu.[5]

The few efforts made toward self-support and the general optimism did not prevent sporadic raids nor did they eliminate economic destitution. In June 1856, seven New Mexicans were killed near Mora. The Jicarillas were accused of the crime. Meriwether ordered Labadie to investigate the charges. Labadie denied that the accused were responsible, but four Apache men were absent during a count he took. He speculated that perhaps a war party of Cheyennes and Arapahoes who had been seen in the area might have been the perpetrators.[6] There was no sure way of determining the assailants. Carson's agency was also flooded with reports of Indian depredations, but he had similar difficulty in properly identifying the guilty parties. This reinforced the conviction held by the white population that all plundering and killings were committed by the Indians. It was hoped that the approval of the 1855 treaty would end the depredations and put the Jicarillas on the road to self-support.

Congress did not consider the treaty until the first session of 1856 and by that time the New Mexicans had organized to defeat its ratification. Judge Charles Beaubien, president of the Convention of Citizens of Taos, had petitioned the president of the United States to veto the treaty, and he had more than a hundred signatures to support his petition. The members of this organization believed that it would be dangerous to their safety to have the Indians so close to their settlements.[7]

The odds were working against the ratification of the treaty. A last-minute claim to a parcel of land within the proposed Jicarilla Reservation was an added complication. In July 1856 a citizen from Abiquiu claimed that he had inherited a small land grant located within the boundaries. The surveyor general of New Mexico accepted his claim and notified the commissioner of Indian affairs on July 28, 1856, that the grant appeared to be valid, asserting that the claimant had prior rights to the land and to deprive him of it would be unjust. Furthermore, he felt it would be impolitic to "donate" lands to marauding Indians adjacent to or in the vicinity of lands owned by individual citizens.[8]

After filing with the Land Office, the claimant and his group of fifteen men visited the proposed reservation apparently for the very first time. Labadie tried to stop them, but was overwhelmed by their forceful insistence that the surveyor general had given them the go-ahead to take possession. Having no choice but to acquiesce, Labadie quickly sent word to the governor, informing him of the situation.

When Meriwether received the information, he was more than irate. He promptly wrote the commissioner, defending the selection of the reservation site and refuting the existence of any prior claims. Meriwether recalled that during the treaty negotiations the large assemblage of informed and public-minded citizens from throughout the area were asked whether anyone owned land within the proposed reservation. No one came forth. Furthermore, at some point during the discussions Meriwether had suggested another location, but this brought immediate objections. This led him to believe that the people present at the peace conference were reasonably knowledgeable about the local ownership of land.[9]

Meriwether's defense proved useless, for on July 6 he learned that the treaty had been defeated. To add to his despair, he also found out that the claimant had presented only a petition for a grant and not a title as had been implied by the surveyor general. The governor commented disgustedly that "since the failure to ratify the Indian treaties, I presume that it is of little importance whether this reservation is covered by a grant or not."[10] Congress, however, did approve $35,000 to locate all New Mexico Indians on unclaimed and unoccupied lands, a provision with no direct bearing on the Jicarillas. The rejected treaty prevented the Jicarillas from obtaining a permanent reservation, though the rations were continued. Then the problem was submerged as the nation turned its attention to the events leading to the Civil War.

One of the greatest consequences of the Civil War for the Southwest was the increase in Indian raids. With the army's concentration on the fighting in the East, the Indians took advantage of the small regular and volunteer forces remaining in the West. The Navajos and Mescalero Apaches were two New Mexico tribes that became more daring and caused havoc throughout the territory. By comparison, the Jicarillas and the Utes remained relatively peaceful. They probably engaged in the raiding activities that plagued Mora and San Miguel Counties, but the presumption of innocence was on their side since it was public knowledge that the Mescaleros were openly hostile. The New Mexico superintendent was afraid to accuse the Jicarillas without substantiated evidence for fear that it might drive them into open hostilities.

The superintendent's cautious approach did not deter the Jicarillas and Utes, however, who began to escalate their raiding activities in the Taos area. Consequently, the whites began to agitate for the removal of the Taos Agency to the less populated region near Cimarron.[11] It was not only the depredations that annoyed the Taos people; the free trafficking in liquor on ration day bothered them. As a result of pressure, the Taos Agency was relocated near Cimarron in 1861.[12] Carson resigned as agent and was succeeded by William F. N. Arny.

Tensions mounted as Confederate troops marched through Albuquerque and occupied Santa Fe. By March 1862, Union troops under Colonel John P. Slough and Major John M. Chivington had captured their supply lines and forced a Confederate retreat to Texas.[13] The threat of a Confederate take-over subsided, but the "Indian problems" remained.

Arny returned to Cimarron to resume his "civilization program," in spite of the Cimarronians' displeasure with the proximity of the agency, which brought the Indians closer to their homes. Lucien Maxwell, however, welcomed the presence of the Indians. He leased a 1,280-acre tract to the government for the agency site (and ensured himself lucrative government contracts in the coming years). An allocation of $2,000 was made for an adobe building that contained an office, a council room, a kitchen and dining room, sleeping quarters, and a storeroom. Corrals were also built near the agency. To encourage industrious habits, Arny plowed twenty acres, to be assigned in small plots to the Indians,[14] for cultivation of wheat, corn, and vegetables. Eventually he hoped this would become a model agricultural community, but his plan had to be abandoned when he was appointed secretary for the Territory of New Mexico in late 1862. Levi Keithly, the new Cimarron agent, was less interested in "civilizing" the Indians. He was satisfied with the mundane job of doling out rations at Maxwell's flour mill. The boredom characteristic of an Indian agency led him to reside in the village of Cimarron rather than at the agency. Gradually, the building constructed by Arny fell into disrepair and the Indians came to the mill site to pick up their rations, thus negating Arny's justification for the existence of an agency.

As secretary, Arny continued his campaign to establish reservations for the Indians as a way of ensuring their survival and assimilation.[15] The secretary believed that as long as the Indians were allowed to roam, as long as a generous government afforded them a means of subsistence, and as long as they were permitted to beg and steal, they would sink deeper into degradation. The Abiquiu agent disagreed with Arny's implication that the Jicarillas were freeloaders.[16] In his opinion, the Jicarillas were unwilling to settle down and start farming because they feared dispossession. The agent was disappointed because the few Jicarillas who had engaged in agriculture were not encouraged by the government. This agent agreed with Arny, however, that serious agricultural efforts would not become a reality until a permanent land base was secured from the government. The agent at Cimarron offered an altogether different version; he did not feel that the Jicarillas or the Utes were interested in settling down and farming, but were occasionally friendly only because of their peculiar dependence on the government.[17]

About all that the government was able to do at this time was listen to arguments and recommendations. It frowned on any suggestions for establishing separate reservations throughout New Mexico for the different tribes. It hoped to consolidate them on as few reservations as possible. In line with this informal policy, Arny suggested that the Jicarillas be located on the Warm Springs Reservation at Santa Lucia in southwestern New Mexico.[18] This suggestion was not carried out because the Civil War was drawing to a close, and General James H. Carleton's military campaign, which began in 1863, against the Navajos and Mescaleros was proving successful. By 1864, these tribes were driven to the Bosque Redondo Reservation in southeastern New Mexico near Fort Sumner. Since this consolidation was temporarily working out, officials began to contemplate the possibility of also placing the Jicarillas there, instead of at Warm Springs, as suggested by Arny.

In January 1864, New Mexico Superintendent Michael Steck instructed Keithly to use his influence to relocate the Jicarillas at Fort Sumner. The Cimarron agent announced that no rations would be issued except at the Bosque, hoping that this would lure them there. Keithly succeeded only in persuading José Largo and his band to visit the Bosque to check it out for themselves.[19] The other bands would not even consider visiting the reservation. After looking it over, Largo concluded that the Bosque was an undesirable place; other bands accepted his assessment. The plan to put the Jicarillas at Fort Sumner fell through when it became clear that the whole operation was quickly turning into a fiasco. Subsequently, the Navajos and Mescaleros were allowed to return to their homelands.

There were other factors besides the failure of the Bosque Redondo experiment that contributed to the delay in establishing a Jicarilla reservation. In 1866 the New Mexico superintendent offered one interesting insight into the advantages of not finding a solution to the territory's "Indian problem." In his opinion, the commercial and agricultural enterprises in New Mexico were supported by the government's disbursements to the military. The presence of the troops stimulated the economy: the agricultural sector found a market for its products, and the mercantile community handled the flow of goods for the military. Without the purchase of military supplies, the economy of New Mexico would suffer. To carry on the intermittent warfare against the Indians, the military was augmented by volunteer forces. The practice of encouraging whites to volunteer for expeditions and campaigns against the Indians was sanctioned by territorial law. Volunteers were rewarded with plunder, and any captives taken were to be reported to the territorial offices; instead, according to the superintendent, they were sold for prices ranging from $75 to $400, or kept as slaves. He estimated that between 1846 and 1866 the Indian wars had caused a reduction in the Indian population from 36,880 to approximately 19, 857.[20]

The superintendent also believed that many unscrupulous private individuals and parties stood to gain by seizing every opportunity to claim damages from the government by making unfounded charges against the Indians for depredations. This was common practice. On numerous occasions when the agent investigated the charges, he failed to find any real evidence. The difficulty in identifying the guilty party, whether Indian or white, was an argument used by the superintendent to support his plea for the establishment of definite reservations.

At the end of the Civil War, some semblance of normalcy returned to the conduct of Indian affairs, and the westward movement, which determined their nature, resumed. In the immediate post–Civil War period, when the line of settlement was in the Great Plains area, the government concentrated its efforts on the pacification and consolidation of the Plains tribes on reservations; consequently, those tribes that posed no direct threat to westward expansion received relatively little attention.

Based largely on the experience with the Plains tribes, Indian policies began to take shape, and they were eventually formulated as Grant's Peace Policy of 1869. The consensus for the Peace Policy had been reached before the end of the Civil War, but the policy was not legally recognized until 1869. The salient feature of Indian policy was the concentration of all Indians on reservations, there to be educated, Christianized, and helped toward agricultural self-support. This was what Arny had advocated, and basically it was no great departure from standard policies. Specific additions under the Peace Policy were the nomination of agents and superintendents by the various religious denominations, the creation of a Board of Indian Commissioners, composed of philanthropists, to oversee the disbursement of Indian appropriations, and an end to the treaty system, which had dealt with Indian tribes as though they were sovereign nations.

The desire to place all Indians on reservations had always been a concern of New Mexico territorial officials, but they had never been sufficiently empowered by the Washington office to carry it out. Now that an agreement was reached as to what federal Indian policy was, the New Mexico superintendency felt more at ease, only to discover that the Jicarilla Apache were not high on the federal government's list of priorities. Nonetheless, they offered many suggestions. A plausible recommendation was made by the superintendent in 1866: to purchase the Rayado Tract where the Cimarron Agency was located for the Jicarillas and Utes.

There were several supporters of this idea, mainly former Indian agents. In 1863 one agent, rather optimistic about the Indians' farming operations, wrote, "The Jicarillas, or at least a part of them, understand and appreciate to a good extent, the benefits of industrial pursuits, and avow their willingness to work, if they could be made sure of obtaining adequate returns for the labor; . . . They have planted small patches of land, loaned them by the Mexicans."[21] Manuel S. Salazar, agent for a short period at Cimarron, endorsed the superintendent's recommendation, since he had a favorable opinion about the Jicarillas' interest in agriculture and manual labor, noting that the women made earthen vessels, which they sold to supplement their rations. Salazar reasoned that it would present no problems if the two tribes were put together on one reservation since they were intermarried and friendly.[22] E. B. Dennison, a later agent, also expressed similar sentiments. To his recollection, the Jicarillas were never disloyal to the government, lawless toward their neighbors, or unkind to him; they were trustworthy, although "deprived of knowledge, moral teaching, and kind treatment." For his times, Dennison paid the Jicarillas a rare compliment by stating that they exhibited such traits of character as devotion to truth, attention to their young, kindness to their sick, and charity to their aged ones. He felt that they should be commended and given greater opportunities because of their willingness and abilities.[23]

The opinions expressed by the agents were based on the actions and behavior of the Indians residing near the agency. Those Apaches who did not live near the agency or near the settlements were as industrious as those described by the agents. A rare account is provided by Juan Dedios, who served as an informant for Dr. Frank Hibben, an anthropologist from the University of New Mexico, in 1933.[24] Dedios's insights into Jicarilla life not only are interesting, but they differ from governmental officials' viewpoints. Dedios portrays the Jicarillas as a group of people trying to sustain themselves by hunting and trading, making the best possible use of their land and its diminishing resources, and deemphasizing reliance on rations.

Dedios was born in the late 1840s, a Navajo by birth. As a very young child he was captured by a party of Spanish and Ute slavers who invaded his homelands in the San Juan River area. He was traded to the Gonzáles family in Abiquiu, and later adopted the name of Juan Dedios. In the service of his family, Dedios was a livestock herder and occasional farmer. He had no opportunity to learn the Navajo language, but soon became fluent in Spanish, Apache, and Ute. A memorable event occurred in Dedios's otherwise routine existence sometime in his late teens. The privilege of accompanying a trading expedition to Mexico City was offered to him; this trip took approximately one year, traveling by ox cart from Abiquiu via Santa Fe, El Paso, and Chihuahua. In Mexico City, the expedition traded for items such as porcelain, guns, powder, knives, metal, cloth, and gold. On this trip he obtained a gun (which later gave him an advantage when he went hunting with his Indian friends). After his return from Mexico City, he married a Spanish girl from a family named Chávez and had two daughters, both of whom married. It is not clear how long this marriage lasted. Apparently after the death of his wife, Dedios hunted with his Jicarilla and Ute friends out of Fort Bent on the Santa Fe Trail, and sold dried meat to the wagon trains headed toward Santa Fe and to the people of Taos and Picurís. These hunting activities brought him into close association with the Jicarillas. He began to travel widely over their territory and eventually came to know them quite well.

Buffalo were becoming scarce, but Dedios and his companions continued to hunt them east of the Canadian River and northeast of Mora on the Cimarron River. In Dedios's opinion, the Jicarillas were better buffalo hunters than the Utes and some of the Pueblos from Taos and Picurís. When he went hunting with the Jicarillas, they lived in tipis made of buffalo skins. While he used his gun, his Indian friends used bows and arrows, the arrowheads being made from iron obtained from the rims of wagon wheels.

While moving from place to place, Dedios invariably came upon other Jicarilla bands. He recalled meeting them at their hunting camps in the Jemez Mountains, along Huerfano Creek in Colorado, in the Estancia Valley, and even on the Llano Estacado in Texas. He became acquainted with the major trails and campsites used by Jicarilla hunters and travelers.

The seminomadic Jicarillas moved from place to place, following game, but there were favored places where they always camped while on hunting expeditions. Dedios showed many of these sites to Dr. Hibben, most of them being near hunting areas. In the upper end of the Estancia Valley were three camping spots that accommodated Jicarilla hunters when they were out after deer and antelope. For buffalo hunts, Dedios identified one near the small town of San Jon at the edge of the Llano Estacado, another east of Logan on the Canadian River, and one at Trinchera Pass east of Raton.

Dedios and the other Hibben informants located many sacred places within Jicarilla territory: for example, Rabbit Ears Mountain and Tucumcari Butte. These were meeting places where hunters gathered and prayed before leaving for the Plains. Dedios recalled that once he and some other Jicarillas discovered a herd of buffalo east of Tucumcari Butte in a river bottom. They killed the whole herd, but could not butcher them all and so they left some behind. Killing more buffalo than were needed was rare. The next year, he lamented, they experienced little luck with their hunting.

One fall Dedios went hunting in the Arkansas River region with Julián and his entire band of thirty-six lodges. Several of these Jicarillas had good buffalo horses. Their trip began at Vermejo on the Little Cimarron, headed north, and wound up on the Plains. While on this trip, they met another Jicarilla leader, San Pablo, who was camped near Cienega, one day's travel east of Rabbit Ears Mountain. Cienega was a camp where the men left the old men and boys while they hunted buffalo.

Dedios described the trading among the Jicarillas, Utes, and white travelers who came through the Raton Mountains. The Indians traded beaver skins, hides, and medicinal plants for meat. Trade camps were also set up, two of which he attended, at Cimarron and Mora. Here all kinds of goods were exchanged.

The government rations issued at the Abiquiu and Cimarron agencies did not escape Dedios's attention. Everyone received rations; some hung around the agencies just for the rations, which they sold and ended up without food. Others had their rations stolen by the soldiers. These Indians retaliated by stealing from settlers. He recalled one incident when some Apaches raided the ranches near Tierra Azul and soldiers were called out who shot the Indians.

Inadequate rations and scarcity of game led to the raiding, but also forced some Jicarillas to cultivate crops. Dedios remembered the corn fields along the Little Cimarron that were planted by the Llaneros.

Despite all the favorable views about the Jicarillas attempting to prove their worthiness and efforts toward self-reliance, there was little chance that the people of Cimarron would consent to the purchase of the Rayado Tract or any area of land for a permanent reservation. Inextricably tied to the inevitable rejection of the Jicarillas was the 1866 discovery of gold on Willow Creek, and prospectors overflowed into the nearby gullies on the western slopes of Baldy Mountain.[25] A second group of miners also found that the flats of Moreno Valley contained gold. Confident of the enduring prosperity of the mining district, a movement was afoot for the permanent development of the area. The first of the new settlements was Elizabethtown, which was swarming with merchants there to take advantage of the boom atmosphere. Maxwell was not to be left out, leasing plots of his land at low prices as an incentive to help develop the region. He was even involved in a scheme to build another town in Moreno Valley. This fell through, but he prospered and gained substantial income from his other business ventures, including supplying the miners and leasing two placer mines.

The invasion of miners and businessmen transformed the tranquil farming region into a bustling community. For the Jicarillas it meant an assault on their sanctuary. As one agent put it,

they had so long held this section as their home, as a resting place, retreating to it as a point of safety if punished in war with their enemies, the Indians of the plains, most of them were born here, their ancestors for years past have been buried there, they entertain heathenish superstitions, they hold these valleys sacred, there they make medicine, hold their feasts, and perform their ceremonial of lamentations for their dead.[26]

The newcomers intensified the strain on already limited resources. As a result they demanded the removal of the Indians. This, in turn, increased the Jicarillas' reliance on rations. While their dependency increased, the amount and quality of the rations decreased: they arrived in Cimarron at irregular intervals and produced only problems for the Indians. To add to these logistical headaches, the agents at

Cimarron were not the least interested in the welfare of their charges. At the height of the gold rush, agent Captain Alexander S. B. Keyes was so preoccupied with his personal affairs that he neglected to distribute the rations when they were available and failed to follow up when they did not arrive. Obviously, he did not have total control of the appropriations that bought the rations, but his lack of concern compounded the problems.

The dire economic situation facing the Indians did not help. In the early summer of 1866, the small herd of buffalo on the plains and the deer in the mountains were unusually scarce, while back at the agency, Maxwell was running a deficit from feeding the Indians and refused to extend any more credit. Out of desperation, they resorted to their only alternative: requisitioning the livestock of the people around them.

Superintendent A. B. Norton calmed the settler's nerves when he authorized the payment of $500 in July to Maxwell to provide meat and flour for the Indians. Norton was immediately reprimanded by Commissioner D. N. Cooley, who made it clear that Indian policy was not a question of humanity but of law. He pointed out that so long as Indians were fed at public expense, they were not going to make an effort to support themselves, especially Indians whose habits were nomadic and whose hunting grounds were unlimited.[27] It was crystal clear that Cooley was completely ignorant of the conditions under which the Jicarillas and Utes lived.

Norton was astonished by Cooley's disapproval. Norton knew that peace hung on the subsistence of the Jicarillas and the Utes. He was rendered helpless and let Cooley know that if war broke out, he would wash his hands of any blame. Driven again to desperation, the Indians began scouting for livestock. An incident involving a skirmish over some sheep ended with the slaying of a Ute. The assailant took refuge at Fort Union, but the Utes followed him there and demanded that he be surrendered to them. Carleton, the commanding officer, refused and wired Arny to have the matter investigated. Acting Governor Arny's first reaction was to call for volunteers in case of conflict.[28]

Carleton dispatched soldiers to Cimarron, but began an investigation of his own. His probe led him to believe that the Indians were not to blame. He wrote: "We have taken possession of their country. Their game is all gone, and now to kill them for committing depredations solely to save life cannot be justified."[29] He was convinced that this "was not only a true story but the whole story."[30] Moved by the

Indians' predicament and concerned about the safety of the community, he ordered Lieutenant George J. Campbell to buy some provisions from Maxwell with army moneys and disburse them to the Indians, but he was to make it understood that this was only a temporary measure and that if the Indians committed any infractions they would be without food. This goodwill gesture ameliorated the immediate suffering, but guaranteed no future goodwill.

The recurrence of depredations and counterbribes of food was monotonous. The welfare of the white and Indian communities called for a more sensible approach. Looting was getting so bad that Maxwell warned the government that there would be an uprising, and he appealed for the stationing of troops on his ranch. On December 16, 1867, one hundred soldiers were sent from Fort Union to comply with his request. The government again sent goods to ward off the impending rebellion, but finally decided to take other measures to deal with this chronic and cyclical problem.

Concomitantly, the Jicarilla problem was given some attention in 1868, when it was treated as an appendage to the resolution on the removal of the Utes from New Mexico. A year before the Peace Policy became the Indian policy, on November 6, 1868, the leaders of the Southern Ute bands and the Tabeguache, Yampa, Grand River and Uintah bands of the Northern Utes entered into one of the last treaties with the United States, in which they agreed to a cession of Ute lands. The intent behind the Peace Policy was written into this treaty, which called for the establishment of two agencies, one at White River in the northern part of the new reservation and the other at Los Pinos, about 165 miles northwest of Fort Garland in southern Colorado.[31]

All the Southern Utes were to be removed from New Mexico and relocated on the Colorado reservation. The government lacked the manpower to carry out this scheme, so the Cimarron Agency was ordered not to hand out rations or annuities to the Indians, irrespective of tribal grouping. As a result of this ill-conceived strategy, rations were withheld from the Jicarillas, yet no provision was made to include them in the rations at Los Pinos or to continue disbursements at the Cimarron Agency.

During the treaty negotiations, the Indian Office representatives hinted at the idea of settling the Jicarillas on the newly created Ute Reservation. Arny, who was reappointed Indian agent at Abiquiu in March 1867, had been aware of the Ute situation all along and saw this as an opportunity to begin the civilization program for the Indians. At Abiquiu he had attempted to renew the program he had started several years before at Cimarron, but he soon realized that the relationship between the government and the Indians was centered in the ration system; and that no progress had been made to develop agriculture or to help the Indians become self-supporting. He could see that he had no control over the Indians, who inhabited a vast country and who refused to be assimilated. To overcome this, he had a special agent appointed to a small subagency at Tierra Amarilla, a village located about twenty-five miles north of Abiquiu on the Chama River. A few troops were also stationed at nearby Camp Plummer (this camp was later renamed Fort Lowell). This subagency provided more contact with the Indians, who came in mainly to receive their rations.[32] Arny could see that something more had to be done, so when the suggestion came up to locate the Jicarillas and Utes on a reservation, Arny supported the idea.

At first Arny was preoccupied with the Utes and their relocation, but he soon turned his attention to the Jicarillas, who were just as absorbed in the disposition of their own affairs. The agent at Abiquiu knew of their desire to remain in that area, but he also was aware of the government's plan to consolidate the administration of Jicarilla affairs in the defunct Cimarron Agency. Initially, when the Ollero chiefs and headmen urged that a permanent reservation be established in the vicinity of Abiquiu, Arny had insisted that they should go to the agency at Cimarron to settle their affairs, but he could not resist the concept in principle.

On his return to the Abiquiu Agency in August 1868, he encountered the Apache leaders Huero Mundo, Vicenti, Pantaleón, and a large party of their followers, assembled and waiting to hear the outcome of the Ute meeting Arny had just attended. Arny heard them out at a council where they expounded on their desire to remain west of the Rio Grande, a right, they contended, that had been granted to them several years back by Colonel Munroe. They proposed entering into a treaty with the United States whereby the government would purchase all their lands with the exception of an area to be designated as their reservation. In the event the government went along with this proposal, the Jicarilla leaders urged that their annuities be protected from theft and fraud by having the government disburse them outside of the towns and settlements. In this way, unscrupulous whites would not steal them, nor would the Indians forfeit them to whiskey peddlers. Furthermore, this Jicarilla council reaffirmed their commitment to peace and self-support and hoped that the government would make diligent efforts to establish a reservation for them.[33]

Arny could not dispute the rationale behind this proposal. He was inclined to believe this band since they furnished about half of their own subsistence by raising corn, wheat, and vegetables, and by manufacturing and selling pottery and willow baskets. Arny recalled from his experience that this band had demonstrated their willingness to work and that they had the potential to become good farmers with proper encouragement and advice. Some doubt lingered in Arny's mind because the band had engaged in some raiding, but, as the Jicarillas explained to him, they considered this perfectly legitimate as "payment" from the settlers for the use of their lands.[34]

Arny's enthusiasm can only be surmised; but by November he had managed to get himself appointed agent for the Jicarillas west of the Rio Grande. Part of his duties included obtaining their consent to merge with the Utes in Colorado. When he approached them with this possibility, he already knew that they would be unwilling to move out of New Mexico. As they put it, "if the Great Father desired them to go to Colorado or Utah, he would have to kill them and take their dead bodies."[35] Their former proposal was the only acceptable way to deal with the issue. Arny concurred, and he later recommended the establishment of a separate Jicarilla Reservation in northwestern New Mexico, adjacent to the Ute Reservation. This recommendation was also endorsed by John Ayers, the new Abiquiu agent, who also was familiar with Jicarilla wishes. The territorial governor of Colorado, A. Cameron Hunt, informed Commissioner Nathaniel G. Taylor that the Utes likewise did not approve of consolidation with the Jicarillas, but gave wholehearted support to an adjacent Jicarilla Reservation.[36] This ended the government's efforts to locate these Jicarillas in Colorado, although when the Utes were again approached in 1872 and 1873 to negotiate with the United States, the Ollero Jicarillas took that opportunity to renew their appeal for a reservation.

Unfortunately, the plans to consolidate the Jicarillas with the Utes seem to have excluded the Jicarillas at Cimarron. This was indicative of the lack of unification among their leaders. Each band had its own ideas as to where its permanent reservation should be located. Naturally the Llaneros wanted to have a reserve in Cimarron, but realities soon dissipated this dream. The flow of white people into their country was not subsiding any more than was the pressure they were putting on the government to rid the country of the Indians. What actually gave the Llanero dream its death warrant, however, was the sale of the Maxwell Land Grant.

In 1869 a group representing Colorado mining interests inquired about the purchase of the Maxwell Grant. Excited by the possibility, Maxwell employed several experts, including lawyers and land surveyors, to oversee the probable sale, which was soon consummated. The Colorado businessmen began promoting their new real estate holdings for development and reaped immediate benefits when on January 28, 1870, a British company negotiated a six-month option to buy the grant for $1,350,000. The option was quickly transferred to the newly created Maxwell Land Grant and Railway Company, which then assumed the responsibility for making final arrangements for the purchase.[37]

When the Jicarillas and Utes learned of the sale, their reactions were mixed. Some were dismayed; others were extremely restive and outright hostile, insisting that the land commonly known as the grant was still in their possession, and that they had permitted Maxwell to live on it because he had been their friend. Grave doubts were expressed about Maxwell's professed friendship since he failed to consult them about the sale or to share the proceeds with them. Not realizing that their legal right to the land had long ago been negotiated right out from under them by the Mexican government, they persisted. Maxwell probably anticipated this type of reaction, but the law was on his side and he knew it. Occasionally Maxwell was summoned from his new home at Fort Sumner to help explain the situation to the discontented Indians.

Less tolerant of the Indians than Maxwell had been, the British landlords renewed the effort to get them off company land. Happy to act as a disguised intermediary rather than as an adversary, the government took this opportunity to remind the Indians that the time had come for their removal. The government pretended it had nothing to do with the removal, but threatened to withhold rations if the Llaneros did not cooperate.

In the fall of 1870, the Indians returned from their fruitless summer hunts in a rather rambunctious mood, ready to make trouble if their rations were not waiting for them. Forewarned about the probable trouble, the agent was ready with rations and annuities on August 30 and had called in Arny, who was on a mission as a special agent for the Indians of New Mexico, to act as mediator. An atmosphere of tension prevailed on ration day, when Arny met with the Llanero leaders. José Largo, who was the main spokesman at this council, possibly realizing the futility of his plea, nonetheless made a last ditch effort to have a reservation established in the Cimarron region, with hunting privileges in Colorado. As a concession, he offered the white settlers the consideration of recognizing their land claims though he would not allow further settlement.

On the subject of rations, Largo adamantly complained that the supply allotted could not feed an average family for ten days. Arny was left with the impression that if these people were not furnished with adequate rations, blankets, and clothing, Cimarron country would be fighting a war during the coming winter. Largo assured Arny, however, that this would occur only as a last resort. Arny recommended to the Superintendency that the Jicarillas be given an increase in rations, especially since they had not received their annuities the previous years. While the special agent was holding council with the Indians, a company of soldiers from Fort Union under Colonel John J. Gregg made their presence known by camping across from the site of the mill where rations were being disbursed.[38]

September was a potentially explosive month. A series of events occurred that nearly led to violence. The officials and new owners of the grant began arriving, and Keyes was transferred to Fort Sill, Indian Territory, at this inopportune time. In this crucial and transitional period, the Cimarron Agency was again without an administrator. Fortunately the government soon appointed Captain W. P. Wilson to that post. Wilson's appointment did not help matters. Preferring to associate with his fellow soldiers at Fort Union, he was not around to perform his duties. He went to the agency mill only to hand out rations *when* they were available.

While Wilson was agent, an incident took place that almost ignited an "Indian war." It involved three youngsters, an Anglo boy, a Spanish boy, and an Indian boy, who started quarreling when one was kicked by a cow.[39] This battered youth ran to the village yelling that the Indians had beaten him and driven off the herd, creating such a commotion that a dozen armed men stormed off to the field where the alleged beating had taken place. To their embarrassment, they found only a peaceful herd of grazing cows. Had any Indians been nearby, they probably would have been shot on sight. The Cimarron newspaper later reported the incident as if it had been a serious matter. The villagers' unthinking response to this childish prank illustrates just how strained the relationship was between the Indians and whites concerning the pending removal.

Wilson's lack of interest in his job soon led him to hand in his resignation. The position was filled by a former agent, E. B. Dennison.

His appointment was challenged by the land company officials, who found his character unsavory and his actions detrimental to the welfare of both Indians and whites. He was in office for less than three months, but during that time he managed to gain the confidence of the Indians and learned the reasons for their discontent. Shortly after he took office on October 26, 1870, he made a report to Nathaniel Pope, New Mexico superintendent, explaining the marked change in the disposition of the Jicarillas and Utes over the past two years—from a relatively cheerful to a very despondent people. He attributed the dissatisfaction to the possession of Indian lands by the miners and to the actions of the government resulting from the Ute Treaty of 1868. The camaraderie that had existed between the two tribes was under severe stress, largely because the Jicarillas blamed the Utes for their main problem, lack of rations.[40]

By mid-December 1870, Dennison was replaced by Charles F. Roedel as farmer-in-charge, a new designation for agents who were in charge of helping the Indians raise crops. This was a misnomer. During December, Roedel was asked by Pope to make an estimate of the agricultural implements and seeds necessary for issue in the spring, but he did not do so. Roedel felt that the Indians would not be able to use them since the grant lands were being rapidly sold to settlers and other interested parties. Roedel did request that other provisions, especially clothing, be forwarded to the agency for distribution as the cold weather was taking a severe toll on the Jicarillas.[41]

The spring of 1871 found the Indians no better off, although rations were parceled out on a more regular basis; however, they were still insufficient. Perhaps driven by desperation, an Apache by the name of San Francisco tried to break into the Maxwell Company store, and was shot by the clerk. A party of Apaches demanded that the clerk surrender and open the store, but Roedel was able to quiet them when he agreed to meet with some of the leaders of the tribe. A compromise was reached when the company agreed to pay damages.[42] Some relatives of the slain Apache did not feel that money and ponies were enough. The following month, Roedel was shot at by two Apaches, one of them a brother of San Francisco. The agent's troubles did not end here. A pistol was also drawn on his interpreter and the Indians refused to take the wheat meal rations, which contained bran. Evidently they disliked the bran, which they sifted out of the meal. This left very little wheat. The company store agreed to exchange the wheat meal for second-grade flour called shorts, a commodity the

Indians found more palatable. The company seemed willing to improve its relations with the Indians, but it did warn that it would not make a practice of paying for "dead Indians." Roedel was told in no uncertain terms to warn the Indians that any found drunk on the streets and any others not out of town by sundown would be jailed and that the company men would not hestitate to enforce this policy.[43]

The absence of the Indians produced an unusual quiet around the Cimarron Agency during the late spring, but it was not due to the company threat. This suspicious tranquility caused some apprehension among the residents. Roedel was not disturbed because at the April ration issue San Pablo told him that the people were going to Colorado to hunt and would return in July. Largo's band was headed for the Red River. Only Chino and his lodges came in during May to pick up their goods.

The hunt proved very successful, so late in June the Indians drifted back to Cimarron to get their rations, which were not forthcoming. For the next six months, rations continued to be irregular. The Indians resumed raiding. The government attempted to placate the raiders in December by distributing the annuities and doubling the rations.

By comparison, the year 1872 was uneventful for the Apaches of Cimarron. The rations came in on a more regular basis, and Elizabethtown was slowly depopulated. The entire Baldy Mountain District was being deserted because of a decrease in mining activities. The Jicarillas hoped that they would cease entirely. This apparent return of peace, however, was only temporary.

The Jicarillas were still clinging to their traditional ways in 1872, and the government had not yet begun its reservation program for them. The best portion of their territory had been usurped by agrarians and miners. The Jicarillas were becoming strangers in their own lands. Little effort was actually spent on finding them a reservation. The Olleros had shown a willingness to compromise their life-style in order to support themselves, and the Llaneros also recognized its ultimate necessity. All chances for compromise, however, were lost due to lack of government action. A feeling of insecurity was permeating all aspects of their lives. Their total existence was geared to poverty: the rations were by no means adequate and wild game was no longer abundant.

The constant variable in this unpleasant history was America's belief in its manifest destiny and the prevailing mood of Social Darwinism in this Gilded Age. Americans were indifferent to the plight of the Indians, and considered the government's meager rations adequate compensation for their losses. This bargain ration system did not make for good relations between the Indians and the whites. Neither was it an investment in the Jicarillas' future. The Jicarillas no more wanted this degrading form of payment than was the government willing to subsidize it.

The ration system, which was to have been a provisional and tentative arrangement, became the government's way out of facing up to its responsibilities to its Indian wards. The classic trilogy of Indian dispossession—the encroachment of white settlers, dwindling wildlife, and the uncaring government—left the Jicarillas no alternative but dependency on the ration system.

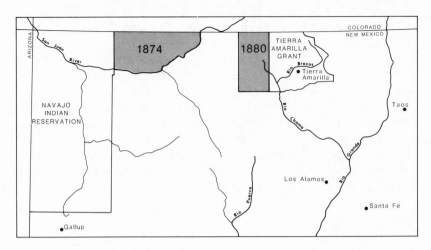

Executive Order Reservations of 1874 and 1880

Chapter 4
Removal: 1873–86

The final dispossession of the Jicarilla Apaches from their traditional homeland occurred in 1883 when they were removed to the Mescalero Apache Reservation in southern New Mexico. This feat was accomplished only after two Jicarilla Apache Reservations had been created by Executive Order, one in 1874 and the other in 1880. Each was subsequently abrogated. The Mescalero consolidation was to have been the final solution to the Jicarilla problem, but the Indians found it totally unacceptable. In 1886 they engineered their own solution.

The deceptive peace and quiet experienced by the Apaches at Cimarron in 1872 was completely eroded by the rapid series of events that took place within the next decade. The tumultuous pace of events threw the Jicarilla life-style into greater turmoil and disarray than ever before. Sam A. Russell, the special agent in Tierra Amarilla, best explains the Jicarilla situation in the decade after 1873. In 1876 he wrote, "The Jicarilla Apache Indian has no home. As a people, they have no country that they can call their own. No incentive to improvement has even been placed before them; they are left to roam over a section of mountainous country of uncertain ownership; or it may be included in a Mexican land grant."[1]

In 1878 he made a similar report: "They have been left by a paternal government without a home, and compelled to become wanderers, by being driven from place to place when they have attempted to locate and cultivate the soil. They have, through me, been for almost four years begging for a home; a place where they could farm and have schools for their children. It has thus far been denied them."[2] But amid the adversity, the Jicarillas met the serious challenges confronting them.

After the 1868 Jicarilla-Ute conference, William F. N. Arny had recommended a separate Jicarilla Reservation to be located in northwestern New Mexico. This plan was reactivated in 1872 because by then federal Indian policies required that all Indian tribes be placed on reservations and the program outlined by the Peace Policy of 1868 be carried out.

On April 23, 1872, Congress passed an act that authorized further negotiations with the Ute Indians of Colorado for the cession of the middle portion of their reservation, which had been set aside in the Treaty of 1868. United States commissioners met the Ute representatives in August. It was during this meeting that Huero Mundo was given the opportunity to inform the government of the Jicarilla preference for a reservation in northwestern New Mexico rather than for consolidation with the Mescaleros.[3] He had been invited by his half-brother Ouray to attend the negotiations to make his position known to the government. The officials listened to Mundo, but took no action. Since the commissioners were not able to secure the Ute land cession that they desired, another meeting was scheduled for the following year.

Meanwhile, the government stepped up its efforts to move the Jicarillas south. In June 1873, New Mexico Superintendent L. Edwin Dudley held a council with San Pablo, José Largo, and their 376 followers, informing them that the lands they were living on now belonged to a company over which the government had no control and that the country was rapidly being settled by people whose actions could not be predicted. The superintendent explained that the government could not guarantee protection against unfriendly settlers. If they would transfer to Mescalero, land would be assigned to them and their rations would be doubled.[4] The Apaches were impressed, but reluctant to make a commitment without first conferring with the rest of the Jicarillas at Tierra Amarilla. This was one indication that there was a movement toward greater cooperation among the leadership over a common concern that affected the entire tribe.

In September 1873, Felix Brunot and Nathan Bishop of the Board of Indian Commissioners again attempted to persuade the Utes to cede the San Juan portion of their reservation. They met with the Ute people at Los Pinos Agency in Colorado and again Mundo attended. This time he secured a promise from Brunot that all information would be presented to the proper officials in Washington. Mundo made it clear that the Jicarillas were opposed to locating with the

Mescaleros, but that a reservation near Abiquiu where the land was suitable for farming was highly desirable.[5] Again no action was taken on the Jicarilla position, but the commissioners were successful in securing title to the San Juan cession (this became known as the Brunot Agreement of 1873).

A Ute delegation, headed by Ouray, went to Washington in November to witness congressional approval of the Brunot Agreement. Huerito Mundo, son of Huero Mundo, was allowed to accompany the Utes to present the Jicarillas' case. As a result of his efforts, definite plans were made to establish a reservation on the headwaters of the San Juan River in northwest New Mexico. Special Agent Thomas A. Dolan was instructed by Commissioner Edwin P. Smith to call a meeting of the Jicarillas to obtain their consent to give up the lands they occupied in favor of the anticipated reservation.[6]

In mid-winter Dolan sent messengers inviting the various bands to meet with him at Tierra Amarilla. The tribesmen gathered there on December 10, 1873. This was the first tribal meeting attended by both Jicarilla bands where they jointly considered their permanent location. Dolan presented the predrafted Articles of Convention: these defined the boundaries of the proposed reservation as commencing at the headwaters of the San Juan River, following along its course south, until it intersected with the eastern boundary of the Navajo Reservation, and then east along the Colorado boundary to the place of beginning. The Jicarillas were to relinquish their rights to all other lands, and, in return, the United States promised $10,000 over a five-year period and $3,000 for educational purposes over the next ten years. The terms also included the usual promise of protection under United States law. The Jicarillas were to allot their lands, send their children to school, have their affairs administered by the Southern Ute Agency, and grant the United States the necessary right-of-way through their lands.[7] This document, known as the Agreement of December 10, 1873, resulted in the Executive Order of March 25, 1874, setting aside the reservation outlined in the agreement. This was the beginning of a barrage of inchoate executive orders setting aside several Indian reservations in various locations for the Jicarillas.

While awaiting the next move of the Indian Office, the Jicarillas remained close to Abiquiu and Cimarron. Second thoughts about the unfamiliar San Juan location surfaced in disagreements over the impending relocation. The government, too, was becoming apprehensive about the executive order, which did not come to the Jicarilla agent's attention until November 1874. Even after the agent learned about the transaction, he did not bother to carry out the intent of the executive order. He did not favor moving the Indians, because the San Juan and Uncompahgre Mountains were proving to be rich in ores, assuring migration to the region.[8] As it turned out, this was the very reason the government was procrastinating.

Throughout 1875, the Indian Office made almost no efforts to move the Jicarillas to their newly created reservation, and the Indians were not anxious to leave their country. The Apache leaders at Cimarron insisted that the recent agreement was made entirely by the Abiquiu faction and that it did not apply to them.[9] These stirrings of factionalism delayed the actual occupation of the reservation—a move that might have validated their claim to it. While the Indians squabbled among themselves, the Indian Office revived its plans for the Jicarilla-Mescalero merger.

On September 14, 1875, W. D. Crothers at the Mescalero Agency reported to Commissioner Smith that he had conferred with the Mescaleros and secured their permission for joint tenancy with the Jicarillas.[10] The secretary, however, felt that it would be best to wait until spring to carry out the consolidation. In the meantime an incident at the Cimarron Agency prompted the Indian Office to speed up plans for removal. A dispute arose between two Indians over an allegedly unfair distribution of rations. This resulted in an exchange of gunfire, and the wounding of the agent and two Indians. The incident later led to the arrest of three tribal members and the stationing of troops at the Cimarron Agency. By December the agency was placed under the complete control of the army, which began preparing estimates for the cost of removing the Apaches from Cimarron and Abiquiu.[11]

The new year ushered in more protests against the implementation of the intent of the Executive Order of 1874. On January 25, 1876, Agent Sam A. Russell of the Abiquiu Agency wrote the commissioner that a gentleman from Santa Fe had informed him that efforts were being made to rescind the executive order. Russell wanted to know if this were true. He understood that the effort was being made because greater benefits would be derived from the San Juan area if whites occupied it, and that there was, after all, an absence of game to sustain the Indians. He naïvely wondered why, if the country was so immensely valuable for agricultural purposes, it was not suitable for the Indians.[12]

Russell's inquiries were answered when he learned that citizens from the San Juan area had petitioned the president, the secretary of the interior, and the commissioner to annul the order and move the Jicarillas to Mescalero.[13] They argued, as the gentleman from Santa Fe had implied, that the Jicarillas' presence would keep settlers from some of the country's best agricultural lands.

The government used this request to reinforce its previous decision. Edward C. Kemble was appointed as the inspector to look into the removal, which was now rescheduled for May. He and Russell met with the chiefs and headmen of both bands at Tierra Amarilla to discuss their impending transfer. The Jicarillas promptly objected and argued that only two winters ago the government had wanted them to go to the San Juan area and that they had gladly agreed to do so. Huerito Mundo stated that when he went to Washington in 1873, the president had told him that the San Juan would always be their home. But, he added, if the president could not keep this promise, there was no reason to believe that he would ever keep any other promise. The Jicarillas were aware that the quality of the lands at Mescalero was not as good as had been represented, and they also knew that the water was too alkaline to permit successful agriculture. Furthermore, Mundo indicated that if the government prevented them from claiming their reservation, they felt capable of finding their own homes without this kind of government help. Kemble could not convince them that the Mescalero Reservation offered any advantages; but despite their objections, he recommended that the Abiquiu and Cimarron agencies be abolished and that the Jicarillas be removed to Mescalero. As a result, the Indian Office abolished the Cimarron Agency in July 1876.[14] President Ulysses S. Grant also abrogated the Executive Order of 1874 and returned the San Juan lands to the public domain.[15]

Just as the move to San Juan had been thwarted by the refusal of the Jicarillas to leave their homes, in similar manner the government encountered resistance to the transfer to Mescalero. The Jicarillas were scattered over such a large area that the agents could not get them together to start the trip. A year later, the authorities were still trying to arrange for the removal. Agent Benjamin H. Thomas of the Pueblo Agency wrote the commissioner on December 20, 1877, that it was no more possible to move the Jicarillas "than a flock of wild turkeys."[16] The Jicarillas successfully continued their delaying tactics. The following March, Commissioner E. A. Hayt issued orders to the military commander of the district to effect the removal and Russell was instructed to provide the Indians with supplies for their journey south; in July, preparations were still under way. Another inspector,

E. C. Watkins, was sent to meet with all the Jicarilla leaders, but he succeeded in finding only San Pablo, who voluntarily promised to escort his band to Mescalero. When the agency was closed in July, San Pablo and his followers began their journey. Apache runners were dispatched to make contact with the other bands in the mountains, who were to join the column en route. Wagons loaded with supplies pulled out; cattle were driven by the men and boys. From all outward appearances it seemed that the government was going to accomplish its objective. All hope was dashed, however, when San Pablo's people began to slip away and head back toward Abiquiu to be with their other kinsmen. On October 1, 1878, F. C. Godfrey, Indian agent at Mescalero, reported that only San Pablo and thirty-two of his people had arrived. San Pablo explained that for some unknown reason his people had deserted him on the road. He graciously asked that he be allowed to go and look for them, but was refused permission.[17] Later, he returned north to rejoin his tribe.

Removal from Abiquiu was not attempted until August 1878, when Inspector Watkins returned from Los Pinos Agency in Colorado after relocating the Utes (who had previously lived in northern New Mexico). On August 18, Watkins called a council with the Jicarillas, who assembled immediately. Watkins reiterated his plea, but it fell on deaf ears. This time the Jicarillas used the excuse of the Lincoln County War for not wanting to go there.[18] They had heard that while San Pablo was down in Mescalero he had lost his horses to some outlaws and had not recovered them. Watkins was in a quandary since he was aware of the conflict and the consequences of placing the Jicarillas in the midst of it. He did recommend that they be removed to Indian Territory (present Oklahoma), but nothing came of this suggestion.[19] Thus ended the government's abortive efforts to move the Jicarillas to Mescalero in the 1870s.

Since the Jicarillas were all at the temporary Abiquiu Agency in Tierra Amarilla, Agent James H. Roberts was ordered to keep them from returning to the Cimarron country and to give them rations in order to obtain their cooperation. The Cimarron Jicarillas disregarded the orders, ignored the bribe, and began returning to their own country. When the agent tried to enforce the orders, minor conflict seemed inevitable, so he decided to ask for aid from the troops at Abiquiu.[20] No troops were sent, but on November 7, 1878, he received authorization to organize an agency police force. The police were to see to it that all the Indians stayed in the vicinity of Abiquiu. The force consisted of other sympathetic Jicarillas, who were no more effective than the agent. On May 16, 1879, the entire force resigned, refusing to compel their relatives from Cimarron to remain in Abiquiu.[21] The agent was now helpless and the Cimarronians spent the entire summer of 1879 back in their own territory.

In Abiquiu the other Jicarillas remained peaceful, but not idle. Mundo and his son Huerito went to visit Ouray on the Ute Reservation to seek advice about the pending removal to Mescalero. Ouray supposedly advised his half-brother that the Jicarilla leaders should request a visit to Washington to see if they could obtain a permanent reservation in northern New Mexico. When Mundo returned home, he sought the opinion of the other elders, who agreed that there was time enough to bid for a conference with the president. They went with their decision to Thomas, who on November 20, 1879, wrote to the Washington office requesting permission and support for four or five men to meet with the president in Washington. Thomas received a wire on December 13, 1879, granting the request. Three months later, San Pablo, Juan Julián, Santiago Largo, Huerito Mundo, and Augustín Vigil began their trip. They met with Acting Commissioner E. J. Brooks to discuss the location of a reservation. The outcome was a victory for the Jicarillas. Brooks appointed E. B. Townsend to select land for the tribe.[22]

For the second time it seemed that the government was acting in good faith. The Jicarillas were proud of their efforts and happy that they had not gone to the Mescalero Apache Reservation. By August 13, 1880, Townsend had examined some land the Jicarillas wanted west of Tierra Amarilla in northern New Mexico. He described this place as one of the best that could be found in the territory. He reported that "along the Navajo River, in both Colorado and New Mexico are considerable areas of land finely adapted to agriculture, thus far almost entirely neglected by ranchmen in choosing their locations."[23] Townsend evidently found only four or five settlers on this land. They had erected some buildings that Townsend thought potential agency headquarters. He proposed to pay the settlers for their claims. In his opinion, the president should be requested to set these lands aside for a Jicarilla reservation.

The Indians anxiously awaited word from the agent about the new reservation and the go-ahead for relocation. Having learned a valuable lesson from the previous experience, they decided against employing any delaying tactics. Looking ahead to planting their fields in the spring, they hoped a favorable decision would be reached soon. Their hopes and expectations were fulfilled when on September 21, 1880, by

Executive Order, President Rutherford B. Hayes set aside the reservation Townsend had recommended. It appeared that the Jicarillas had finally been given a permanent home; but before they could be resettled, special-interest groups again began pressuring the Interior Department to consolidate the Jicarillas with the Mescaleros.

After the president created the reservation, the agents were instructed to relocate the tribe near Amargo, a town that was to become the temporary agency headquarters. Preparations did not get under way until almost a year later because of administrative lag and the slow communications between the agency and Washington. In October 1881, after the bureaucratic clearances were obtained, Thomas received only $1500 from Commissioner Price for the removal expenses. On October 20, Thomas urged Frank N. Roedel, farmer-in-charge at Tierra Amarilla, to gather the Apaches in the most expeditious manner and have them en route to the new agency by the first of November.

Roedel faced no small task. The Jicarillas were scattered from Tierra Amarilla to Cimarron. Nevertheless, by the end of October he managed to notify all members, who hastily returned to Tierra Amarilla. By December, the supplies had been transported to Amargo, and by January the last of the stragglers arrived. Subagent Holt's monthly report for February 1882 indicated that there was an atmosphere of general satisfaction with the new reservation.

The apparent feeling of content was soon clouded by intratribal feuding. The conflict was essentially political in nature and it primarily involved the factions headed by Mundo and the two bands under Largo and San Pablo. The last two groups suspected that Mundo had something to do with abolishing the Cimarron agency, which had given the Llaneros no choice but to move to Amargo. Mundo's followers were accused of wanting to be "domesticated" farmers. Mundo and his band in turn accused their critics of being unrealistic in trying to remain in Cimarron, especially since all the buffalo had long since been killed. The verbal feud got so intense that the Olleros set up camp as far away from the Llaneros as possible.[24]

Conflict between these two bands never reached the point of armed hostility, but it was a contributory factor to San Pablo's and Largo's unauthorized return to Cimarron. Compounding their displeasure was the lack of sufficient rations. It was their feeling that they could provide for themselves in a more adequate fashion by hunting buffalo and other game back in the old country.[25] For their trip Largo's men began stockpiling ammunition and refused to disclose the amount in their possession to the agent, insisting that they had no ulterior motive except to go hunting. Reed suspected that they intended to leave the reservation, a suspicion that was soon confirmed.

In May, a resident of Taos reported that a few Apaches had been seen in the vicinity.[26] This alarmed Thomas, who ordered Reed to make sure that San Pablo (who by now had been joined by an additional 150 Jicarillas) returned to the reservation. Reed asked for Jicarilla volunteers to go after San Pablo, but not a single person responded.[27] Thus he and Steward, an agency employee and perhaps an interpreter, started the search for the stubborn chief on June 4. By June 9 the two had reached Taos, where they learned that San Pablo was camped in the mountains west of Mora. When Reed finally found the Apache campsites, he asked for an explanation for the exodus. San Pablo calmly explained that his chances for making a living outside the reservation were far better than on it, and he had no plans to return. Reed informed him that he had no choice in the matter. He was to return within two weeks or troops would be called out. Hesitantly, San Pablo then promised to go home, but he gave Reed no definite date of departure or arrival.[28] A month went by, and San Pablo and his people were still absent, which caused some apprehension among citizens of the area. They appealed to the military to get the Indians out of the Wagon Mound vicinity. On July 10, 1882, Brigadier General Ranald S. Mackenzie telegraphed Thomas about the complaints he had received. Thomas requested that the general send an officer to help him impress upon the Indians the necessity of returning to their reservation.[29]

Shortly thereafter, Thomas and an army officer went to Wagon Mound to meet with San Pablo. Thomas uncomfortably noticed that the camps were well supplied with meat and flour and that the condition of the Indians was very good. This was quite a contrast to the situation at the agency, where supplies were scarce. He was reminded of the letter he had recently written stating his position of sympathy for these absentee Jicarillas, considering that back on the reservation there was little food and that all other supplies were exhausted.[30] San Pablo, forgetting or ignoring his previous promise, told Thomas that he intended to move farther east during the next four months. When he was reminded of his earlier promise, San Pablo could not understand why he was not able to hunt without everyone making such a fuss. Thomas did not hazard an explanation, but neither did he press the issue.[31] He returned to Amargo without San Pablo.

The agent's patience was wearing thin by August, when he decided it was high time to compel San Pablo to obey orders. Accompanied by troops, Thomas searched for the renegades for nine days. Thirty-nine of the band were apprehended and taken to Fort Union, after their weapons were confiscated, but the hunt for San Pablo continued.[32] On August 18 Reed heard that the chief and some of his followers were on their way to Amargo, evidently convinced that Thomas was serious. Within a few days all the Jicarillas were back on the reservation.

During the period from July 1881 to October 1882, while the agents were trying to locate the Jicarillas at Amargo and chasing after San Pablo, attempts were under way to prevent the Apaches from permanently occupying the land that had been assigned to them. When certain interested parties heard of the newly established reservation, an avalanche of complaints flooded the Indian Office. In the forefront of the onslaught was M. B. Ritch, acting governor of New Mexico Territory, who had been petitioned by the people of that area. On July 19, 1881, Ritch wrote the secretary of the interior requesting that the "Jicarilla Apache Reservation be opened to settlement and that the Jicarillas be removed from the section they now occupy to one that will not be detrimental to the public interest."[33] He felt that the Jicarillas' removal to Indian Territory would have no negative consequences, especially when compared to the positive benefits to be derived from settlers who had property interests as well as prior rights to the land. Ritch also argued that the Jicarillas would be demoralized inadvertently if they lived near the communities due to the liquor traffic.

Thomas objected to moving the Jicarillas again. Somewhat prophetically he stated, "The proposition to continue to carry the Apaches further back away from the demoralizing influences of society is absurd, because the time for hiding away the Indians from civilization . . . has passed, and they must stand or fall in the very midst of civilization."[34] The Indian Office was not the least bit interested in such exhortations: it was attuned only to political pressure. Still, it appeared to be walking the tightrope on this issue. On the one hand, it was not outright in favor of abolishing the Jicarilla Reservation, but on the other, it was also being pressured by the citizens of southern New Mexico to rid that country of the Mescaleros. At the risk of alienating the northern New Mexicans back in August 1881, Commissioner Price had instructed Townsend to reexamine the conditions on the Jicarilla Reservation to make sure that no unnecessary complications would be encountered when the Jicarillas arrived.

Pagosa Lumber Company sawmill at the Jicarilla Agency, early 1900s. The site is now part of a residential area. National Archives.

Gathering of Jicarilla men at the agency to sign an authorization for the expenditure of timber moneys, November 1918. National Archives.

A new Jicarilla cabin, abandoned because of a death in the family, 1917. Note the lack of windows and the vent above the door. National Archives.

A Jicarilla camp in La Jara Canyon in the northern portion of the Jicarilla Reservation, 1920s. Branch of Land Operations, Jicarilla Apache Agency, Dulce, New Mexico.

Jicarilla men shearing the tribal herd at Stone Lake, 1932. Branch of Forestry, Jicarilla Apache Agency, Dulce, New Mexico

Sheep dipping at La Jara Canyon, 1939. National Archives.

Jicarilla men vaccinating cattle, 1939. National Archives.

Evidently Townsend was then to go south to persuade the Mescaleros to move to the Jicarilla Reservation. Townsend was also to get the consent of the Jicarillas to share their home with the Mescaleros. It appeared that Price was trying to appease the southern constituency by agreeing to consolidate the two tribes on the northern reservation and ignoring the northerners' pleas. He even abandoned the idea of moving the Jicarillas to Indian Territory.[35]

After inspecting the Jicarilla Reservation in 1881, Townsend compared the existing conditions to those of his first visit a year earlier. The Southwestern and Rio Grande Railroad was under construction across the northern portion of the reservation, and a temporary railroad town had sprung up at Amargo. He also found a coal mine operating near the town, but the number of settlers within the boundaries of the reservation had remained constant. Townsend recommended that the original intent of the Executive Order of September 21, 1880, remain, but that compensation be given the settlers for their lands and improvements. He also recommended that the operation of the coal mine be halted and that some kind of restitution for this privilege (which had been unlawfully obtained) be paid. Townsend urged that Thomas not delay the removal of the Jicarillas to this reservation any longer. His last recommendation was that the Mescaleros be consolidated with the Jicarillas.[36]

Townsend met with Mescalero chief Naitzellia concerning removal to the Jicarilla Reservation, but the chief was unwavering in his refusal to relocate. The Jicarillas expressed a similar attitude when told that the Mescaleros might join them. Huerito Mundo made it clear that they were not friendly with the Mescaleros and did not wish to have anything to do with them.

Unable to get their cooperation, Townsend complained to the commissioner that when the reservation had been set aside, it had not been expected that other Indians would be moved there. Townsend, however, advised that the reservation be enlarged by thirty miles on the west side, should such an eventuality occur.[37] Fortunately for both tribes, the plan to consolidate them at the Amargo Agency was abandoned. Thereupon, landed interest groups intensified their efforts to get rid of the Jicarillas by reviving the old plan to remove them to the Mescalero Apache Reservation. This time the groups had the support of Henry M. Teller, the secretary of the interior, who may have had land interests in southern Colorado. With his assistance they succeeded in convincing Congress of the feasibility of their plans. William Llewellyn, the Mescalero agent, was given the unpleasant job of gathering evidence to present to the commissioner—evidence that would overwhelm the commissioner, who would then have to order the consolidation. Llewellyn's compensation was appointment as agent for the Jicarillas as well as the Mescaleros.[38] In October 1882, Llewellyn diligently began his duties and on the twenty-sixth filed a report with the commissioner concerning his trip to Amargo (where he was to have ascertained whether the Jicarillas could ever become self-supporting). He had observed that "except for a strip of land near the Navajo River, the reservation was barren and sterile, and could not be made to sustain either man or beast."[39] Llewellyn also discredited the location with his reference to the demoralizing effect that the unscrupulous railroad employees and Mexicans, who freely trafficked in liquor, had on the Jicarillas. These observations later proved to be partially true, but at the time Llewellyn made them they were specious. He did not have the welfare of the tribe in mind: he was collaborating with the interest groups. Furthermore, he knew that conditions at the Mescalero Agency were no better than at Amargo. Only a couple of months before his trip, military officials at Fort Stanton had expressed grave concern about starvation among the Mescaleros.[40] Llewellyn was aware of this, but he nevertheless maintained that moving the Jicarillas was for their own good.

If conditions were not favorable at Amargo, it was not because the Jicarillas were unwilling to try; neither was it a situation that could not be corrected if proper attention were devoted to it. Reed reported that during the previous year the Indians had repeatedly expressed the desire to go to work and raise a small crop, but that it was impossible for them to do this without the necessary equipment and supplies.[41] Reed agreed with Llewellyn, however, that harsh winters made the climate unconducive to farming. Although it appeared that there was ample rationale for Secretary Teller to give the go-ahead for the removal, in reality it was not the undesirability of the lands, but political pressure, that provided the leverage he needed.

To allay any future criticisms and to go through the motions required by policy, Teller instructed C. H. Howard, Indian inspector, to hold a council with both the tribes concerning the removal. On February 13, 1883, Howard found the Mescaleros willing to accept the Jicarillas as co-occupants of their reservation, but suggested that a delegation of Jicarillas be brought to Mescalero to decide for themselves.[42] In June, he met with the Jicarillas. About half of the tribal members were willing to give the idea a chance, but specified that they must be assigned a portion of the reservation where they could live apart from the Mescaleros. The others would not even give a final answer until they had an opportunity to examine the Mescalero Reservation. Howard was inclined to agree to this latter condition; however, as it turned out, there were no funds available for this purpose. On this trip Howard reiterated Llewellyn's previous contention that the Jicarillas could not become self-sustaining in the high country.

On June 20, 1883, Llewellyn made another trip to Amargo. This time he reported to the commissioner that he found it was impossible to raise corn, that there was no grass for grazing, and that the water was not fit for human consumption. This exaggerated report was so effective that within a month, on July 13, the commissioner authorized the expenditure of $5,000 to move the Jicarillas to Mescalero.[43]

Active opposition to removal began with Llewellyn's second trip to Amargo. Mundo's followers, especially, resisted; they were tired of looking for a permanent home. Since their reservation was a recognized legal entity, they were not willing to give it up easily. The loss of their "holy lands" still rankled. Mundo's band insisted that they be allowed to remain where they were. Llewellyn's callous response was that his orders were final and that the Amargo agency's supplies had already been rechanneled to Mescalero. He made it clear that those who were willing to go with him would be treated kindly, fed well, and given land, but that those who were not cooperative would be placed in the hands of the military.[44] Given this type of intimidation, many Jicarillas were forced into compliance. The bands under San Pablo, for example, were not only willing, but eager, to go. Llewellyn, in his ignorance, explained to the commissioner that one of the reasons for the opposition of the Olleros under Mundo was that they did not speak exactly like the Llaneros since they were a detached band from either the Navajos or the Utes. It is true that Mundo was a nephew of Ouray of the Utes and that the Olleros were intermarried with the Utes, but this was also true of the Llaneros. Llewellyn did not want to acknowledge that there were Jicarillas brave enough to stand up for their rights.

On August 15, the Jicarillas, Llewellyn, and General David S. Stanley held a council to discuss the removal to Mescalero. For the record, General Stanley certified that Mundo had finally consented, but only under protest, and that he was strongly inclined to yield only to force. Mundo believed that the removal was not legal and was not willing to give credence to the statements of this group of men. He wanted Congress to investigate. (At his conference, the Jicarillas strongly contemplated a surprise attack on the conferees, and fights nearly broke out among the factions, but they finally decided that the consequences would ruin all chances for ever getting back their reservation.[45] Mundo demanded that his protest be recorded in writing and presented to Congress. This protest was to document the Jicarillas' claim to the reservation. Mundo requested that the reservation not be opened to settlement pending congressional consideration or until the Indians were amply compensated for their losses.[46] Llewellyn recommended that San Pablo and his people be included in the claim, that the reservation be sold, and that the proceeds be used for the purchase of farming implements.

Five more days were granted to make final preparations—days in which the Jicarillas held prayer meetings, asking the Great Spirit for divine guidance and assistance in returning home in the near future. On August 20, the Jicarillas began their "Trail of Tears" or "Long Walk" to Mescalero. The Amargo Agency was closed, and notices of the reservation's status as government land was posted. It remained closed to settlement and it was not made available for sale,[47] as Mundo had requested.

The Jicarillas, escorted by soldiers, traveled by horse and wagon. The route was determined by the availability of water for the animals, for the Jicarillas owned two thousand horses. They stopped off in Santa Fe on September 2. They crossed over the Río Pecos at San José, where smallpox broke out, resulting in six deaths. They had intended to continue to Roswell across the plains to the Rio Hondo, up the Rio Ruidoso, and on to Mescalero. Instead, alarmed by the smallpox, they cut across the country to El Capitán and Fort Stanton, then went on to the Mescalero Reservation. The total journey was about 350 miles. Rations were issued once, at Carrizo River.

The majority of the Jicarillas made the best of their situation while at Mescalero, carrying out their promises to cultivate the land, construct irrigation dams, send their children to school, support the police force with manpower, and generally to work toward making Mescalero their home. Robert S. Gardner, United States Indian inspector, selected land especially suited for grazing. He optimistically hoped that these lands could be irrigated and farmed without much expense to the government. The inspector intimated, however, that the land was better suited for grazing than for agriculture.[48]

Since San Pablo and his people, numbering 234, had not opposed removal, the best agricultural lands near Three Rivers were assigned to them. They proved to be good farmers. By the following year, 500 acres were under cultivation. San Pablo personally farmed 45 acres. In recognition of San Pablo's support, Llewellyn in 1883 purchased a house for him near the agency with government funds.[49] In comparison, Mundo's people did not fare so well. They held fast to their objective of returning to their reservation at Amargo, and for the next three years consistently worked toward that end.

On October 22, 1883, Gardner met with the Jicarillas to reassess their attitudes. San Pablo was pleased, but Mundo and his principal men, Augustín Vigil (son-in-law of Mundo) and Augustine Velarde (brother to Mundo, despite his different surname) were still dissatisfied. Gardner told them that they should forget about returning to Amargo; that the government had acted in their best interests. The Jicarillas were aggressive enough, however, that Llewellyn and Gardner requested the Indian Bureau to allow a delegation of both Jicarillas and Mescaleros to go to Washington to talk to the authorities.[50] Evidently only Llewellyn made the trip, as he wrote in his letter to the commissioner on April 25, 1884: "Shortly after my return from Washington last January, I had a talk with all the leading Jicarilla men in council. Most of them were well pleased with the outcome of the visit to Washington, except Huerito and Augustine, who, however, finally submitted to the sentiment of the others."[51]

Llewellyn tried to offer some concessions to the disaffected Jicarillas by offering them what he thought was the best land near Carrizo Creek, but in fact it was not the best. Mundo and Augustine Velarde continued to be uncooperative. They obstructed the planting of crops and the construction of dams. Llewellyn tried to cope with this behavior by allowing their wives to cook noon meals on the ground where the men were at work. This was an attempt to keep them working the rest of the day since they usually did not return after their mid-day meal. Mundo's band also refused to support the police with manpower and tried to discourage other Jicarillas from cooperating in important matters. Llewellyn threatened to take their horses away if they did not stop obstructing his plans. He also used the tactic of playing this band against the other Jicarillas, which exacerbated the already bad relations between them.

The Indian Office had been aware of the problems of inadequate acreage for farm lands long before removal; even Llewellyn admitted that this situation existed. In November 1884, he informed the secretary of interior that there was a great need for more land. "There is but little land susceptible of cultivation in the vicinity of the agency not already occupied by the Mescaleros," he wrote, adding: "The Jicarillas are laboring at a great disadvantage from insufficiency of good lands and difficulty of irrigation."[52] The absence of good arable land formed the basis for Mundo's and Vigil's resistance. It provided them with further ammunition in their battle to leave Mescalero and regain their old reservation.

On November 15, 1885, Fletcher J. Cowart replaced Llewellyn as agent at the Mescalero Agency, and developed a friendlier relationship with Mundo's band. In February 1886, he allowed Augustine Velarde and Vicenti to visit their children at the Santa Fe Indian School.[53] Velarde became leading headman of Mundo's band. He, with Vicenti, Augustine Vigil, and José Martínez, confronted Cowart with the idea of severing their tribal relations and homesteading on the public domain in northern New Mexico.[54] They said that all their people, 107 households, wished to take this step. Cowart explained the effect of severing their tribal relations, but they replied that they totally understood the step they were taking. They wanted land where they could live close together as one people. Cowart knew they were serious and at first supported their efforts. He wrote the surveyor general in Santa Fe regarding the matter, informing the commissioner that originally he did not think that any of the band wished to leave unless the whole band could do so, but that the departure of this group, which was always complaining, would be beneficial to the other Jicarillas. He did not think any harm would come of the experiment. Velarde, Vigil, Vicenti, and others then applied to Governor Edmund G. Ross of New Mexico for permission to leave the reservation and to homestead on the public domain.[55]

In the summer of 1886, the commissioner informed Cowart that only the four headmen would be allowed to take up homesteads.[56] The four Jicarilla leaders were angered because it had been their understanding from the governor that this would not be the case. Handicapped by not knowing English, they believed that there was a conspiracy between the agent and the interpreter to keep them on the Mescalero Reservation. Since they did not trust government bureaucrats, they insisted on going to Santa Fe to find out the truth. Cowart told them that their affairs were managed, not in Santa Fe, but in Washington. Disregarding this fact, the four Apaches left for Santa Fe without Cowart's permission. Cowart notified the commanding officer at Fort Stanton and told him to arrest them.

On their return from Santa Fe, however, this was not done. They again confronted Cowart with their homestead plan, and then offered a compromise. They proposed that Velarde, Vigil, Vicenti, José Antonio, José Martínez, Vicentito, and Pedro Sánchez take their immediate families and homestead in Rio Arriba County, where they were well acquainted with the settlers. If they could set an example by successfully farming and living in peace, in a year or two the government would allow the rest of their people to join them.[57] The degree of give and take in their efforts gave evidence of these Jicarillas' sincerity.

Cowart wrote the commissioner that "it has been the wish of the government to civilize them and now when they want to homestead, they are restrained."[58] He added that if the Mexicans could do it, why not these Indians? Cowart even offered to go with them to protect their interests while they were getting settled, but the Washington office seemed unable or unwilling to respond promptly. The Jicarillas failed to understand why so many letters and so much time were required by Washington when a simple yes or no would have sufficed.[59]

Although there were no immediate results from the plan for acquiring homesteads, it did serve, for the Jicarillas, as a stepping stone toward returning to their rightful reservation. When they realized that the homestead project would not prove fruitful, they developed another plan. They appealed directly to Governor Ross for assistance in getting back their reservation, whereupon Ross ordered an investigation. Before applying to the governor for help, however, about 200 Jicarillas began their own return or escape back to northern New Mexico. Along the way they took temporary refuge with their friends at the San Juan and San Ildefonso Pueblos near Española. The governor assured them that they could remain at the Pueblos without interference. He informed them that Indians were entitled to claim homesteads within the territory and offered to assist them in this regard.[60]

Ross took an active interest in the return of the Jicarillas to their old reservation and supported their efforts against the special groups that were interested in the lands around Amargo. The Jicarillas were also fortunate in enlisting the support of General Nelson A. Miles, who placed Colonel Benjamin H. Grierson in charge of looking into their case.[61] Grierson eventually secured the cooperation of Commissioner of Indian Affairs J. D. C. Atkins, who in turn appointed Special Indian Agent Henry S. Welton to assist in finding them suitable lands for a reservation in northern New Mexico.[62] With the backing of these able men, the Jicarillas finally achieved their objective.

The actual move to their designated lands in northern New Mexico was not easy, and demanded still more perseverance and negotiation. When the Jicarillas left the Mescalero Reservation in October 1886, Cowart informed the military about the "runaways" in an attempt to force their return. Fortunately, General Miles had gained accurate knowledge of both their condition and their peaceable disposition. Miles took extraordinary measures to meet with the Jicarilla headmen on November 13, 1886, near Santa Fe.[63] He completed a full investigation and authorized the Jicarillas to remain in the vicinity of the Pueblos north of Santa Fe.

At this meeting the Jicarillas explained their reasons for leaving Mescalero, the most important being that they had never willingly given up their old reservation. Furthermore, the Jicarilla leaders explained that they had been given to understand that they could return in a few years if Mescalero proved unsatisfactory. Miles learned, in addition, that all the arable agricultural lands had been assigned to the Mescaleros, while the lands unfit for farming were assigned to the Jicarillas. Moreover, they had been ill provided with food and clothing. Consequently, the principal men told the general that they wished to take advantage of the act of Congress allowing them to sever their tribal relations and take up homesteads as individuals or separate families.[64]

Miles promised the Jicarillas that he would bring their grievances before the proper authorities. In turn, the Indians promised him that no depredations would be committed. Miles recommended to the adjutant general of the army that these Apaches temporarily be attached to the Pueblo Agency and that their portion of the Mescalero supplies be sent there. He also sent a detachment of soldiers to examine the availability of land. When Miles left for Washington to carry out his promise, he turned the Jicarilla case over to Colonel Grierson, commander of the 10th Cavalry, who diligently carried out his orders.

In November 1886, a second group of Jicarillas, numbering about a hundred, left the Mescalero Reservation. Fearing that the tribesmen who remained behind would be imprisoned, Velarde and Vigil attempted a rescue. Many parents were unwilling to leave without their children, because they feared the possibility that the children might be unduly punished for their parents' actions. Thus, during a violent snowstorm, just after dark, they stole their children from the agency school. Evidently the attempt was well planned and executed because they were not discovered by the school personnel. The Mescalero Apache students must have been sympathetic enough to give their passive support by not alerting the school officials. After the Jicarilla pupils were sneaked away, the telegraph lines connecting the agency with Fort Stanton were cut as a precautionary measure.[65]

The escapees were well on their way when Colonel Grierson was informed about the second exodus. An interpreter was sent to interrupt the Jicarillas and to try to persuade them to go back to the Mescalero Agency. They refused absolutely, saying they would rather die than return. Grierson allowed them to join the other Jicarillas who were already near Santa Fe, charging Lieutenant John J. Crittenden of the 22nd Infantry with ensuring their safe journey to the Pueblos. Subsequently, the commanding officer at Fort Stanton was ordered to prevent any more Jicarillas from leaving Mescalero.

As Miles had promised, he brought the Jicarillas' story of their grievances to the attention of the proper authorities in Washington. On December 24, 1886, the commissioner sent Special Agent Henry S. Welton to Santa Fe to set in motion the selection of a reservation. Welton proved to be the right man in the right job. He was efficient and determined to deal fairly with all parties involved. For example, he asked the Jicarilla headmen to assist him in the selection of land. Their first choice was near Ojo Caliente on the Chama River near Bear Creek. Welton looked into the matter, but was convinced that the old reservation was more suitable and politically easier to obtain. Lieutenant Crittenden was sent by Grierson to assist Welton in determining the number of settlers in the old reservation. He found that some Mexicans were occupying land there, and that they had built pens and shanties to give a false appearance of homesteads. Welton informed the settlers that their claims were illegal and would not be recognized.[66] In fact, these settlers were trespassing, since the old reservation had not been opened up to settlement.

Welton encountered considerable opposition from both the Mexicans and the stockmen of the area. He wrote the commissioner telling him that he feared an uprising by the settlers. Thereupon Major David Perry was sent to Amargo with troops to prevent any possible conflict. Welton also recommended that Perry forbid any further settlements.

On January 26, 1887, Welton recommended to the Indian Office that lands as defined by the Executive Order of September 21, 1880, again be set aside, with the exception of the towns of Amargo and Monero, which were within the mining area. As compensation for these exceptions, additional lands on the west side of the reservation would be included in the boundaries.[67] Welton strongly urged that prompt action be taken to obtain presidential approval because opposition to the Jicarillas' reoccupation was mounting. The lobbyist "pets" of Henry Teller, who was now a United States senator, were desperately trying to get rid of Agent Welton, and unfavorable stories about both him and Commissioner Atkins appeared in Denver newspapers.[68] Finally, on February 11, 1887, by Executive Order, President Grover Cleveland set aside a reservation for the Jicarillas, the boundaries being those recommended by Welton.

The opposition, led by Teller, continued to lobby, quite confident that they could still prevent the reoccupation, which they tried to do by deleting from the Indian appropriation bill a $1500 allocation for moving the Jicarillas to their old reservation.[69] The Jicarillas were so determined to return, however, that the lack of funds did not stop them. The military, too, cooperated. Governor Ross wrote to the commissioner stating that "the failure of this appropriation need in no way interfere with the removal of these Indians. . . . The Indians can easily remove themselves, and Grierson will be able to help them . . . in the matter of transporting their goods and substance."[70] Ross stated that his office might also be able to expend some funds for construction of temporary office buildings for the agency.

Welton was given complete control of the removal. On April 11, 1887, while he was in Washington, the acting commissioner advised him to delay moving the Jicarillas until July. Welton at first agreed. Two weeks later he decided not to delay any longer since this might give the opposition still another chance to prevent the reoccupation. He left for the new reservation with 500 Jicarillas and approximately 2,000 head of livestock on April 25.[71] On the way they were joined by their fellow tribesmen who had been waiting at San Juan and San Ildefonso Pueblos.

The journey was slow. Welton rode on ahead to double check the situation on the reservation. He found that more settlers had poured in as soon as it was known that the lands had been withdrawn from the public domain for Indian purposes. The land was nearly stripped of vegetation from excessive grazing. In addition, more improvements had been made, more land broken, more fruit trees planted, and more irrigation ditches dug.[72] All the arable lands and all water places had been claimed. The settlers' manifest intentions were to defeat the removal of the Indians, or, failing that, to establish fictitious claims for damages. Welton recommended to the commissioner that these settlers be dealt with firmly and investigated to determine which held bona fide claims. The settlers were neither investigated nor dealt with firmly; they would remain a burden to the Jicarillas in the following decades. Yet the Jicarillas were home at last.

The signing of the Executive Order of February 11, 1887, marked the end of an era in Jicarilla Apache history. The Indians had finally found a permanent home where the government could reasonably assure them of noninterference from the whites. They had struggled to keep part of their once vast domain, but succeeded in maintaining only a small portion just outside their traditional homelands. The experience associated with their displacement had given them a sense of insecurity and a distrust of the government. It had also sharpened the division between the two bands; but both had learned some valuable lessons in dealing with the government.

The government's indecisive posture toward the Jicarillas had prevented the Indians from obtaining a reservation in their traditional homelands, the Abiquiu–Tierra Amarilla region for the Olleros and the Cimarron Valley area for the Llaneros. The flood of settlers into these regions had led to the dispossession of the Jicarillas, forcing them to wander among the settlements, being constantly pushed about as the white population increased. They acquired a reputation as undesirables, yet they clung to the conviction that, like other tribes, they were entitled to a reservation in their own country, on land that was rightfully theirs. They were pragmatic enough to realize that they could not stem the tide of settlement or turn back the pages of history. In a way, they acknowledged this reality by appealing to the government for a reservation, but the government was seemingly helpless in the face of the political pressures from different interest groups. At one point the Jicarillas even offered to solve the problem by requesting that they be allowed to find their own homes.

As a consequence of the government's vacillation, the Jicarillas found themselves relegated for a time to unfamiliar lands on other reservations. They obstructed removal plans, but delaying tactics backfired in 1876 and 1881 when their reservation was returned to the public domain. Thus they defeated their own objectives. Their uncooperativeness, however, stemmed from their own intratribal conflict, and, consequently, part of the responsibility was theirs. At the same time, a consciousness was developing toward tribal unity, reflected by the consensus on the need for a permanent reservation. The specifics concerning this issue continued in dispute, and while there was union in common purpose, the band system did not diminish in importance.

During this period several other significant changes occurred. Their first extensive interactions and negotiations with the government were beginning to teach the Jicarillas just how it operated. They saw that there was no "Great Father'" who directed all the action, but a bureaucracy that wielded powerful influence. In their initial dealings, the Jicarillas seem to have put all their faith in the federal government to protect their interests, but when they lost their reservation in 1883, they were disillusioned. Within the next few years, however, they successfully gambled by playing off one group against another. With the aid of the territorial governor and the military officials, the Jicarillas offset the interest groups' influence with Congress and the Department of the Interior. Thus they were able to get back their reservation. They also found out that the agent was really the low man on the totem pole, and within the coming years they often appealed to higher authority, sometimes with good results. Credit must be given to the Jicarilla tribal leaders, especially those of the Olleros, for their persistence in pursuing their desire for a permanent reservation. Without their initiative, tenacity, and determination, chances are that the tribe would still be in Mescalero today.

In 1887 they were victorious. Their victory soon appeared to be hollow, however, because in the next half-century they witnessed some of the worst suffering they had ever known. Once again, their prime antagonist was their "guardian." At times it seemed that the government was punishing them for their victory. Eventually they overcame the hardships and succeeded in developing a decent way of life, although the process was long and slow.

Chapter 5

The Jicarilla Apache Economy:

1887–1934

When the Jicarillas returned to their reservation in northern New Mexico in 1886, it was understood that they would take their lands in severalty. The following year the Dawes Act was passed, authorizing the allotment of land on Indian reservations. For the Jicarillas, this policy created economic hardship and retarded social progress, instead of helping to make them capable, self-sustaining American citizens, as was intended.

On February 8, 1887, three days before the Jicarilla Apache Reservation was set aside by executive order, the Dawes Act formally became law. Its essential purpose was to accommodate and implement the assimilation of the Indian into the body politic of the nation. The Indians were no longer to be treated as half-wards or half-citizens—at least in theory. They were to gain self-respect and independence by substituting white Anglo-Saxon culture for their tribal customs.

The main provision of the act granted the head of each family 160 acres. Every single person over the age of eighteen, including orphans, received 40 acres of land. Patents in fee were issued and held in trust by the government for the next twenty-five years. If a substantial amount of excess land remained after allotment, it was to be returned to the public domain or sold for the benefit of the tribe. This arrangement proved extremely unprofitable for the Indians, since literally millions of acres of Indian land were transferred to white ownership as a result.[1]

The allotment of lands was carried out on the Jicarilla Reservation by a small supervisory agency staff. As a preliminary step in this process, a survey of the entire reservation was required. The reservation, consisting of approximately 416,000 acres, was located in northwest New Mexico in Rio Arriba County, with its northern boundary on the Colorado–New Mexico border. The Continental Divide crossed the eastern part. The drainage pattern included four major lakes on the eastern slope; the Navajo River was the only waterway that drained west, becoming part of the San Juan River system.

The terrain was mountainous, cut by deep, narrow canyons and covered with forests. Since the altitude ranged from 6,000 to 9,000 feet, the winters were rigorous and the growing season short. Average rainfall measured between nine and fourteen inches in the good years.

On these unproductive lands, the government began ineptly to implement its ill-reasoned policies with the survey of the out-boundaries and the allotting of the land. In July 1887, the secretary of the interior received a presidential order to survey only that portion of the reservation with water resources and arable land.[2] The undisclosed motive behind this was apparently to save government funds by surveying only lands that were to be allotted.

Surveys for the eastern out-boundaries and the allotments were well under way in 1888, but because of insufficient funds, the work was discontinued until late 1889. Evidently, numerous errors were discovered in the internal surveys. Out of the twenty-one townships, only nine had been sectioned; the western boundary was not marked; and the sections that had been surveyed were not properly marked for clear identification. In 1889 the Jicarilla subagent complained that the landmarks for the allotments had been obliterated and urged an accurate survey immediately.[3]

The commissioner must have had to offer a convincing argument before the secretary could request a cancellation of the 1887 presidential order. Special Allotting Agent John K. Rankin was appointed to oversee the survey.[4] After some difficulty in contracting a new surveyor, Rankin was finally able to resume the work in December.

Three months later, the Indian Office had to discard Rankin's allotment work, which he had completed during the winter of 1890–91, because Congress had amended the Dawes Act on February 28, 1891, to provide for the allotment of one-eighth section of agricultural land or one-fourth section of grazing land to each member of the tribe.[5]

Rankin began again and finished his job in November 1891. Eight hundred and forty-five Jicarillas received land assignments, which were still subject to the Indian Office's approval. The total area of allotted lands was 129,313.35 acres, leaving about 286,686 surplus acres. Southern Ute and Jicarilla Agent Charles Bartholomew proposed the remaining lands be sold for the benefit of the Jicarillas rather than returned to the public domain as the government had intended.[6] Fortunately, as matters developed, the lands were neither sold nor reclaimed by the federal government.

For the next five years, the confirmation of the Jicarilla allotments was of little concern to the government. In June 1896, the commissioner finally recommended to the secretary that the allotments be approved,[7] but the patents were not forwarded to the Jicarilla agent for issue until 1898. The delay was due in part to the need for minor corrections in the surveys.[8]

When the agent was ready to distribute the patents, another problem surfaced. It seemed that no one could match and identify the names on the patents with the rightful owners. Evidently, Rankin had not concerned himself with full legal and proper names of the Jicarillas to whom he made assignments. Also, over the years some had changed their names, while in other cases, badly translated Apache names could not be recognized even by the Jicarillas themselves.

Another problem contributing to the growing chaos involved actual boundaries for allotted lands. Many corner landmarks had been obliterated or destroyed over the nine-year period since the surveying had begun, making identification of the allotments difficult or impossible. Often, the agent thought he was able to locate a certain tract from the description on the patent; but the allottee would dispute the assignment and claim a different tract.[9] By 1899, only 154 Jicarillas had received their patents. Six hundred and ninety-one remained unidentified.[10] The exasperated agent had to admit that another survey was necessary in order to reestablish boundaries by township, section, and quarter-section lines. All patents were withheld until the embarrassed Indian Office could take the necessary action to correct the situation. The allotment process on the Jicarilla Reservation continued in this manner until 1909, when the reservation was once more resurveyed and reallotted.

The allotting of lands on the reservation was not an isolated process; rather, it was complicated by the claims of settlers who had homesteads within the reservation. These people presented a most difficult and lasting problem for both the government and the Jicarillas. A number of them had legitimate homestead claims, protected by the Executive Order of February 11, 1887, though the claims of squatters who had settled on the reservation after the Executive

Order was issued were not recognized. Both groups, nevertheless, proved to be irritants to the Jicarillas.

These settlers occupied and controlled the majority of the arable land with water resources. This prevented the Jicarillas, who were expected to engage in agriculture, from benefiting from those lands. The question of the settlers was the sole responsibility of the Interior Department: only it could settle this potentially inflammatory matter. The Department was aware of the negative impact that the presence of settlers had on implementing the Dawes Act. Beginning in 1880, when the reservation was first set aside, agents had recommended the removal of the settlers in order to give the Jicarillas the full advantage of their lands, and "in order to place all questions between the Indians and non-Indians beyond dispute."[11] Adequate compensation to the settlers was advised. In 1882, the commissioner of Indian Affairs issued an opinion that non-Indian squatters on the Jicarilla Apache Reservation possessed no legal claim either to the land they occupied or to their improvements.[12] He felt, however, that they had equitable rights and, to be fair, he drew up a proposal for the secretary of the interior, requesting an appropriation from Congress to compensate the settlers upon removal.[13]

The Interior Department did nothing because plans for the transfer of the Jicarillas to the Mescalero Apache Reservation had begun. In 1883 when the government had succeeded in implementing its removal plans, notices were posted announcing that the Jicarilla Reservation was not open for settlement. In 1884 the lands were returned to the public domain, but remained closed to homesteading.

During the three years that the Jicarillas were on the Mescalero Reservation, tracts on their old reservation were claimed by many squatters, but, apparently, many did not file with the Land Office since the lands were not yet surveyed. The real flood of squatters, however, began in 1886 when it was rumored that the Jicarillas would return.

In January 1887, when Henry S. Welton reexamined the area, he found an abundance of water and arable land. At that time he felt that there was sufficient land to accommodate the Jicarillas, but estimated that there were fifteen to twenty settlers who together had a total investment value of $3,000.[14] Welton discovered coal mines and stone quarries on the land, but recommended that they be left out of the proposed reservation. He also excluded the area most heavily populated by settlers.

On this trip Welton sensed potential trouble in the near future between settlers and Jicarillas. He noted that a ring of wealthy Mexican ranchmen controlled most of the land; and it was they who led the opposition to the Jicarilla reoccupation. Cowboys employed by the ranchmen were evidently instructed to build log shanties to fix claims on the government in the event that they were not successful in discouraging the return of the Jicarillas. Because Welton had anticipated conflict, he had recommended that troops be stationed there to prevent further settlement.

In contrast to what he found in January, by June Welton learned that squatters had swarmed onto the reservation with their livestock. Convinced that all the arable land was claimed, he reversed his initial findings and reported that the Indians could not take lands in severalty on this reservation should the squatters' claims be recognized.[15] Welton was now convinced that the presence of the settlers would have negative impact on the Jicarillas.

From February to October, Welton recorded 10,000 head of livestock on the reservation, which overgrazed the ranges, indeed denuded them. Settlers were daily encroaching upon the lands of the Indians, cutting their hay and taking possession of their stock if it happened to stray upon the settlers' unfenced pastures. Some settlers claimed the stock belonging to the Indians by cutting off the animals' ears, while others impounded them and demanded payment for their release. Several Jicarillas were assaulted when they attempted to retrieve their animals. An incident occurred when a Jicarilla woman asked a settler for her burro and was nearly struck down. Indian police arrested the assailant and Welton ordered that he be turned over to the nearest civilian authorities three miles down the road from the agency. Welton requested that the soldiers escort the man off the reservation, but they refused.[16] This lack of cooperation pleased the settlers, who continued their abuses.

A cavalry unit had been ordered to the reservation to assist Welton and to facilitate the removal of settlers who were there illegally, to prevent further settlement by squatters, and to protect the rights of the Indians. Since the military was partially instrumental in aiding the Jicarillas in returning to northern New Mexico, Colonel Benjamin Grierson, commander of the district, acquiesced when the Indian Office requested a detachment of troops and endorsed the plan.[17]

The troops were not entirely sympathetic to Jicarilla problems. They refused to enforce the trespassing laws on the reservation because of uncertainty about the exact boundaries. Field agents and military personnel continuously urged the Indian Office to finish its survey, but the Indian Office was unable to overcome its own inertia.[18] Not until 1890 were the boundaries completely marked. By that time, however, the troops had been withdrawn, and the settlers' abusive behavior went unchecked.

The government not only left the Jicarillas practically defenseless against the settlers, but also chose to bargain away their rights to a decent livelihood, which was possible only through the use of all lands within the reserve. In December 1888, the Indian Office recognized the rights of twenty-five bona fide settlers, who occupied four thousand acres of the best agricultural lands. The Indian Office was in no position to alienate a group of citizens who, compared to the Indians, had political "pull." The Indian Office reasoned that it would be unjust to eject forcibly any settler who in good faith had made actual settlement before the Executive Order of 1887, unless the lands were absolutely required for the Indians. The Executive Order clearly stated that "it did not intend to deprive any settler of any valid rights acquired under laws providing for the domain."[19] The commissioner felt that although the squatters possessed no valid rights, it might be unjust to dislodge them. He was not inclined to recommend the use of force to remove them from the reservation.

While it would have been unjust to dislodge the bona fide settlers out of hand, it was certainly within the power of the government to appropriate ample funds to compensate such settlers for their improvements, some of which were makeshift. It was well known that most of the reservation could not be cultivated and that the acquisition of the settlers' lands was absolutely mandatory if the Dawes policies were to be implemented successfully. For several decades following Welton's recommendation in 1886, government field agents and inspectors constantly reminded the Indian Office of the need to remove the settlers. In 1888, Special Agent Thomas McCunniff reported that the Jicarillas would never succeed in agriculture unless they had good land and water for irrigation. He recommended that all lands claimed by settlers be purchased for the Jicarillas or that the patterns of land ownership be clarified and the rights of the Indians strictly enforced.[20] The following year Agent Bartholomew echoed the same sentiment. United States Indian Inspectors Arthur Tinker, Robert Gardner, and James Cisney all urged the government to take similar measures in 1890, 1891, and 1892.[21] Even Allotting Agent

Rankin had an opinion supporting this viewpoint. He wrote that although the United States government proclaimed a policy of fair treatment of the Indians, "it hardly appears to be treating the Indians with fairness [by telling them to] wait and accept the little that is left of the water and arable lands."[22]

The Indian Office did not feel it just to remove the settlers to benefit the Jicarillas, yet when government interests were involved, it did not hesitate to eject them. When Welton decided that settler Gabriel Lucero's claim was necessary for the agency site, the commissioner declared: "It is true that no person has acquired any valid rights in the tract wanted for the agency because no plats of survey for the townships have been filed with the local land office; hence settlement on the lands in question would not constitute a valid right against the United States."[23] The commissioner made it clear that if the site was all that Welton claimed, he would favor an $800 appropriation for its purchase.[24] Implicitly this should have been applied to all reservation land.

In December 1887, the Indian Office announced that no one living upon unsurveyed lands could acquire title unless the government chose to allow it.[25] The commissioner ruled that once the land passed from the government to the Jicarillas, the government could then make an ex post facto law allowing the squatters to remain on the land even though it no longer belonged in the public domain.[26] It was of secondary concern to the Indians' trustee that the Jicarillas were experiencing economic hardship by being deprived of the best lands.

It was obvious to the agents that the Jicarillas could never become self-supporting agriculturalists since the settlers occupied the most valuable sections. Under the circumstances, the Jicarillas could hardly be expected to show any kind of motivation to become farmer-citizens. One agent reported that they did not seem to be making any progress in civilization, farming, or education.[27] He believed, and rightly so, that the government was throwing away its money and time by stressing the Dawes philosophy under adverse conditions.

All the difficulties connected with the surveys, the allotments, and the settlers were magnified because the administration of Jicarilla affairs was handicapped by the lack of an agency headquarters and by the subsequent appointment of corrupt agents. For fifteen years the Jicarillas had only a temporary agency. In 1887, Governor Ross of New Mexico had suggested that the Jicarillas be temporarily attached to the Southern Ute Agency in Colorado, instead of to the Pueblo

Agency at Santa Fe.[28] This was acceptable to the Indian Office, partially because of its own reluctance to give financial aid to the Jicarillas without congressional approval, especially in light of the political circumstances surrounding the resettlement of the reservation. Senator Henry M. Teller of Colorado, New Mexico Congressional Delegate Antonio Joseph, and powerful ranchers in northern New Mexico were still trying to curtail appropriations for Indian affairs. These were the men who had tried to prevent the reoccupation of the reservation. They were certainly not eager to see the Jicarillas succeed. It was financially beneficial and politically more expedient to attach the Jicarillas to the Southern Ute Agency rather than to push for more funds to build a separate Jicarilla Agency. Another consideration was that the Jicarilla Reservation touched on the southeastern corner of the Ute Reservation. Since the Colorado headquarters was closer than Santa Fe, traveling expenses would be saved. Thus, from 1887 to 1891 the Jicarillas were under the jurisdiction of the Southern Ute Agency. Then they were transferred to the Pueblo Agency in Santa Fe.[29] They did not have a regular agency of their own until 1902.

During this period, Dulce, New Mexico, located in the northern part of the reservation close to the Southwestern and Rio Grande Railroad line, was the site of their subagency. In 1887, a settler who had built some houses and made other improvements on the land was bought out, but the construction of agency buildings did not get under way because the resolution of settlers' rights was pending. For five years, Agent Bartholomew of the Southern Ute and Jicarilla Agency conducted the subagency's business in shanties near the railroad right-of-way.[30] Finally, in 1892, a building and a warehouse were built. In the subsequent years more buildings—a physician's office, employee cottages, a wagon house, and a farmhouse—were added for the use of the subagency and its employees.

The administration of Jicarilla affairs was hindered not only by the lack of a regular agency, but also by the corrupt men appointed to the position of agent. The first case of graft occurred during the reoccupation of the Jicarilla Reservation, and involved the Southern Ute agent, Christian F. Stollsteimer, who had been charged with overseeing the administration of affairs at Dulce.

When Stollsteimer was notified by the Indian Office of his additional assignment as agent for the Jicarillas, he was irate. These duties created a conflict of interest for him, which, however, he soon turned to his own advantage. If he was angry at the news, the Jicarillas were even more so. They knew Stollsteimer did not have a reputation for honesty. He had not faithfully carried out his responsibilities as Ute agent, and the Jicarillas, through contact with their Ute relatives, were aware of it. At one time the Ute agent had profited from his position by selling Ute rations, awarding questionable contracts, and purchasing goods and services at excessive prices.[31]

On July 4, 1887, Welton arrived at Dulce to find several hundred angry Indians assembled to protest Stollsteimer's appointment. The Indians not only felt a grievous wrong was again being inflicted upon them; they also disliked Stollsteimer's appointment of Augustine Vigil as the chief of all the Jicarillas, since he only commanded a small following. Evidently, Vigil got along well with Stollsteimer, who supplied him with three hundred pounds of flour for a feast that Vigil held on July 3. Some Jicarillas also failed to appreciate Vigil's lack of contribution to the labor force formed under Welton's orders to build roads and bridges. Their major complaint, however, was that they did not want their interests subordinated to those of another group, the Southern Utes. They had had enough of that at Mescalero.[32]

Colonel Grierson charged Stollsteimer with using his official influence to retard the removal of illegal settlers from the reservation. Stollsteimer was in no position to protect Jicarilla interests. J. M. Archuleta, business manager of the Archuleta Mercantile Company and owner of a large livestock operation in southern Colorado and northern New Mexico, was his son-in-law. Naturally, a man of this economic stature was called upon to protect the interests of his neighbors. It was through the partial influence of this family that the Jicarillas had been removed to Mescalero in 1883, and it was this same group that sought the advice of Stollsteimer when protesting the return of the Jicarillas. Stollsteimer stated that he could not afford to offend the squatters; that he had much property; and that if he attempted to aid in their removal, they would prosecute him for damages. Furthermore, he expected to make his home in that section after he ceased to be Indian agent.[33] He also openly favored the removal of the Jicarillas to the Ute Reservation and removal of the Utes to Utah.

Stollsteimer opposed the construction of a sawmill for building an agency and homes for the Indians. When Welton confronted him, he denied the charges and informed the Indian Office that Welton's "envy" caused misinterpretation of his actions.[34] Grierson and Welton had more charges against Stollsteimer. They claimed he was opposing government policies with regard to the Jicarillas: that he was illegally grazing sheep on the reservation and instigating plans to prevent the Jicarillas from reoccupying it. They both recommended his suspension.

In October 1887, the commissioner appointed T. D. Marcum to investigate the charges. Marcum concluded that Stollsteimer should be removed from office, but the Indian Office took no action. During an inspection visit to the Southern Ute Agency, Marcum found Stollsteimer's farmer guilty of signing certificates for vouchers he knew to be false. This indirectly implicated Stollsteimer. In June, Marcum finally had sufficient evidence to file the following charges against the Southern Ute and Jicarilla agent: awarding contracts to higher rather than lower bidders, making open market purchases at excessively high prices, purchasing old buildings for five times their true value, making questionable distribution of annuity goods, and violating other departmental regulations. On June 20, 1888, Stollsteimer lost his job, but through his political connections he obtained the position of clerk for the Jicarilla Agency in 1889.[35] Stollsteimer's corrupt practices gave the Indians little cause to respect the government and its representatives.

Not all government officials were corrupt. There were actually a number of agents and inspectors who realized at an early date that the land was not fit for agriculture. One such person was Special Agent S. L. Taggart, who proposed an alternative to farming that would start the Jicarillas on the road to economic independence. There were two resources in abundance on the reservation: pine timber and excellent grazing lands. On the basis of conversations with Jicarilla leaders, Taggart was certain that all the Jicarillas would be willing to waive their rights to timber, on both allotted and unallotted lands, which could be cut and sold, with the proceeds going into a common fund. This would give the Jicarillas the necessary funds to purchase live-stock, and thus to use their grazing lands to good advantage.[36]

Another inspector, W. J. McDonnell, in 1896 supported and added a corollary to the Taggart proposal. He felt that because of the harsh winters and the inability to raise food, a southern range was necessary to ensure the success of the livestock plan.[37] Like the requests to buy out the settlers, these suggestions received scant attention from the Indian Office. Meanwhile, the Jicarillas were subsisting on meager rations because they experienced crop failures. Some even left the reservation for fear of starvation.

When the Indian Office was finally convinced of the feasibility of

Taggart's proposal, it began planning the sale of timber on the reservation. No complications were anticipated since it was only a matter of finding buyers for the timber. On August 15, 1894, Congress passed an act enabling the Jicarillas to sell $20,000 worth of timber to raise money for the purchase of livestock. Agent John L. Bullis of the Jicarilla Subagency was authorized to sell that amount of timber from the unallotted lands.[38] Advertisements for bids were sent out, but no bids were received. Bullis set out to investigate this unexpected problem.

Bullis found that the best timber was growing on allotted lands. The timber on the unallotted lands was so sparse and scattered that it would not be profitable for anyone to contract to cut it. Another problem was the twelve-month time limit set by the Indian Office for cutting and removing the timber. When no bids were submitted, the time was extended to eighteen months. This was still not sufficient. The preparations alone for the operation would take time: roads had to be built to gain access to the timber, and the sawmill that was being considered for purchase by the government was not bought. The revised time limit lapsed, and the timber was still standing.[39]

Jicarilla chiefs and headmen were understandably concerned. They presented a petition to the Indian Office, noting that the tribe was willing to have the timber on the allotted lands cut without regard to who owned the allotment. All agreed that the proceeds should be placed in a common fund. Livestock would then be purchased for everyone and distributed on an equal basis. While this solution was still in the discussion stage, high winds, lightning, and fire destroyed some of the timber, making the lumbering project even less attractive to contractors.

Obstacles to the sale of timber, as well as the chaotic allotment procedure, continued until 1900. Apparently the attitude of the department had changed, because it then favored allowing the timber to be harvested from the allotted lands. It could not ignore the reports advocating this change with which it had been bombarded. Once the consent of all the allottees was obtained so that the proceeds could be placed in a common fund for the benefit of the tribe,[40] the commissioner approached the secretary and presented supporting documentation for this proposal.

In January 1901, the commissioner urged the Senate Indian Affairs Committee to propose legislation providing for the sale of not more than ten million board feet of timber from both allotted and unallotted lands and for the purchase of livestock.[41] Unfortunately, it failed to become law, though this did not stop reservation officials from putting pressure on the Indian Office.

In March 1905, the commissioner again submitted a report to Congress, emphasizing the dire conditions prevailing on the Jicarilla Reservation, and focusing on the allotment confusion characterizing the surveys, the unsuitability of the land for farming, and the urgent need to purchase livestock to provide a means of livelihood for the Jicarillas. This approach was successful. On March 28 of the following year Congress passed a bill authorizing the secretary of the interior to sell timber on the allotted and unallotted lands with the consent of the allottees. The funds were to be spent for the benefit of individuals and not for community interests. Just when it looked as if the last hurdle was out of the way, another loomed up. The allottees could not give their consent without proper identification of their assignments,[42] impossible in many cases because of the allotment mix-up.

Finally, on March 4, 1907, a bill was passed to quit all titles to lands on the Jicarilla Reservation. The secretary was authorized to make a new assignment of allotments and to dispose of the salable timber. On November 16, 1907, the secretary accepted the Jicarillas' relinquishment of their old allotments and reassignment began. Allotment was expanded to include 160 acres of agricultural land and 640 acres of grazing land.[43] This was possible because the president issued an executive order on November 11, 1907, which nearly doubled the reservation, by adding twenty-five townships to the south.[44] A minor correction was made in 1908 due to conflicting claims with a small portion of the Navajo Reservation to the west.

This addition afforded a satisfactory solution to the problem of year-round grazing. The northern part of the reservation was to provide summer grazing for the stock (that still had to be bought), while the southern part was to be used as a winter range. The altitude of the southern area varied from 6,000 to 7,000 feet and winters were not particularly severe, with snowfall averaging about eight inches per year.

The reallotments were completed and approved by the Department of the Interior in 1909. Patents were issued to the people, and this time they contained proper names and descriptions. The first logging operation began in the winter of 1908–9. Eighty thousand feet of timber was cut. A sawmill with a capacity of 5,000 board feet was purchased and began operation in 1910. The sawmill produced railroad ties, most

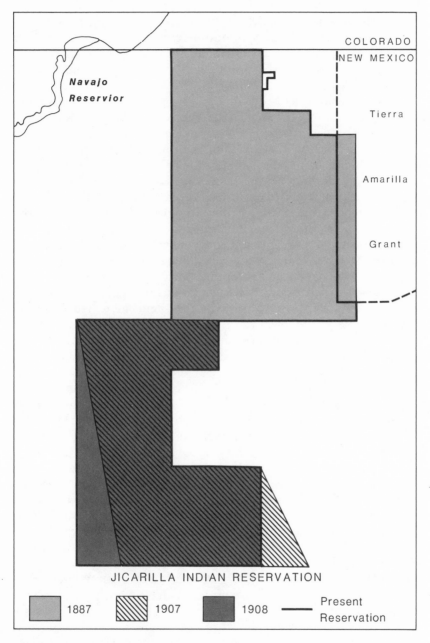

COLORADO
NEW MEXICO

Navajo
Reservior

Tierra

Amarilla

Grant

JICARILLA INDIAN RESERVATION

1887   1907   1908 —— Present
Reservation

The 1887 Reservation and Later Additions

of which were sold to the Rio Grande and Southwestern Railroad, which was constructing a spur on the reservation for the purpose of moving the timber out. The remainder of the lumber was used by the agency and the people. This new industry also provided some jobs for the Jicarillas.

With the reallotment of land, the enlargement of the reservation, and the sale of timber, it seemed that the Jicarilla economy was on the verge of a complete transition from farming to livestock-raising, but this proved illusory. The government slumped back into its former attitude of unresponsiveness and irresponsibility, which halted progress—one of the most treacherous acts that the government could possibly have perpetrated against the Jicarillas.

The intended livestock distribution did not occur. Stock for the individual members was not purchased; instead, the timber proceeds were deposited in the United States Federal Treasury in the name of the tribe. Congress, however, did approve a reimbursable government loan from which a flock of sheep and a herd of cattle were purchased. In 1914 a tribal herd of sheep was purchased for $23,477.50 and in 1915 a cattle herd was bought for $65,000. Both herds remained under the management of the agency.[45] Apparently the government did not believe that the Jicarillas individually were competent to care for the livestock, although there were a number of Jicarillas who already owned sheep and cattle.

The southern addition to the reservation, which was to be used for the planned livestock, was leased to non-Jicarillas for a very nominal fee with the understanding that the lessees were to develop the water resources. What resulted was not any development of the water resources, but overgrazing, which made the range less attractive to other potential lessees. Consequently, all that the agency could get were low fees. The Jicarillas could not use their own lands, with the exception of the three and one-half townships set aside for the use of tribal herds. On November 2, 1915, Special Agent O. M. McPherson indicated that the Jicarillas were losing revenue because of the low rates charged to the stockmen. He revealed that there were 108 short-term grazing leases on 509 allotments of 226,225 acres that yielded $6,837.47, and twelve grazing permits on 275,000 unallotted acres that amounted to $4,343.00.[46] Without water, it was not possible to increase the rates.

In addition, there were further problems: trespassing of livestock belonging to the lessees, predatory animals, and the failure to collect the fees. The southern addition, instead of helping to solve the economic problems of the Jicarillas, only intensified it.

The impounding of tribal funds derived from timber sales was a glaring example of the government's malfeasance as trustee for the tribe. Mismanagement of tribal funds was nothing new; but in the period 1908–20, when the tribe was in greatest economic need, the government chose to tie up its funds. While the funds were lying idle, the Jicarillas were suffering unnecessarily from the ravages of poverty. In 1917 Congress learned that "members of the tribe were starving while their funds lay in non-interest bearing accounts enriching the federal treasury."[47] It was later discovered that the Jicarillas had neither the use of the principal nor the benefit of the interest from their moneys. The senseless stupidity of this whole situation was described by United States Representative Hernández of New Mexico to the House of Representatives in 1919: "The Jicarilla Apaches with 750,000 acres of land, with a tribal flock of 8,000 to 1,000 head of cattle, have not enough food or clothing to keep them in good health. There is something wrong about that. . . . The tribal flock in the last eight years shows a profit of $143,000 over and above expenses."[48]

There was indeed something wrong, and, unfortunately, the power to change it rested solely with the government. The funds in the Treasury continued to increase. For example, in March 1912, the sale of 130 million board feet of timber netted $178,500—certainly an amount sufficient to provide relief for the people.[49]

After 1918, when the decision was made to distribute the livestock, the conditions prevailing on the reservation were at best deplorable. Poverty pervaded every aspect of the Jicarillas' lives. Their future was grim because economic privation, social dissipation, and disease were taking a heavy toll of the population. By 1918, conditions had become so serious and critical that the government could hardly continue to ignore them. With the appointment of Chester E. Faris to the Jicarilla superintendency, the trend of events was gradually reversed. Apathy was replaced by optimism and a program of affirmative action. Faris was truly optimistic when he accepted the challenge. He wrote, "It may be said that notwithstanding the clouds of pessimism, superstition [and] indifference, together with tuberculosis, general debility, and an excessive death rate, there are yet rays of encouragement."[50]

Under his leadership, a plan for economic improvement and health rehabilitation was begun that put the Jicarillas on the road to recovery. Actually, the plan had been formulated long before, but only when a critical stage was reached was the government forced to act. Basically this program involved setting up the Jicarillas in an industry where they could make a decent living from their lands. Stock-raising was of course the answer. In 1919 Faris was authorized to distribute the 8,000 head from the tribal sheep herd, and to purchase more sheep with funds from the timber account. A year later, in April, the first distribution was made. Each Jicarilla participant received twelve sheep. In December, nine more were issued to each individual. A third issue of fifteen head was made in November 1921. For the majority of the Jicarillas this distribution put them in business, though for the minority it simply increased their livestock holdings.

After the allocation of the livestock, the Indian Office began to worry about the possibility of overstocking, but it soon learned that the reservation had a grazing capacity of 100,000 sheep. As of 1921 there were slightly more than 8,000 sheep and fewer than 1,000 head of cattle. From 1920 to 1929, the people grazed their sheep on their northern allotments, but during the winter they shared grazing ranges in the southern townships. The Indian Office decided that the whole reservation should be used entirely for the benefit of the expanding industry as initially intended and the leases and permits of the non-Indian stockmen were not renewed upon expiration.

As expected, the industry grew, and by the end of the decade there were 28,000 head of sheep. In the fall of 1929, the Jicarillas received $37,644.12 from the lamb sale alone, and in the following spring, the wool sale receipts totaled $13,999.[51] These returns might have been higher had it not been for the stock market crash of 1929.

The cattle industry did not flourish as the sheep industry did, in terms either of financial benefits or of generating Jicarilla enthusiasm. In 1919 the operating costs exceeded the value of the entire herd by $2,000; because of this, the Indian Office did not think it was feasible to issue the cattle and the herd remained under the management of the agency. There were some tribal members who did exchange a few of their sheep for cattle, and by 1928, 500 head of cattle were individually owned. In 1930 when more of the southern range was becoming available, four townships were designated for the tribal cattle herd. A cattle ranch was established at Otero Ranger Station, forty miles south of Dulce, and a stockman was put in charge of its operation. It later became a kind of winter headquarters where the people congregated, and a branch trading post was established there about 1936. The main purpose of the cattle ranch seemed to be to produce bulls to sell to other agencies. Whether the herd remained as large as it was in 1921 cannot be determined, but speculation is that it was reduced in size. The livestock industry obviously did much to improve the Jicarillas' morale. It added a new dimension to their lives, and engendered a new feeling of confidence and a greater sense of self-worth. As a result, economic conditions improved and, consequently, so did social conditions. There was a complete transition from a bare subsistence agricultural economy to a thriving livestock economy—a transition that could and should have occurred much earlier.

Although the distribution of sheep had positive effects on the people and the economy, the tribal funds that accrued from the grazing fees on both individual and tribal lands and from the timber sales continued to be mismanaged and misused. Since about 1920, when the timber funds were released from the Treasury, a good portion of the money had been used for agency purposes. The Interior Department appropriations bill for 1925 made available $75,000 from the trust account to the Jicarillas. Of this amount, $25,000 was used for agency supplies and $2,500 for miscellaneous purposes. This same pattern continued until 1934. This meant that the Jicarillas were not getting the total benefit of their moneys during this period, moneys that would have hastened recovery.

The mismanagement of funds became evident during 1928–33 when a Senate subcommittee was holding field hearings on the condition of Indian tribes. At the hearing held in Dulce in 1933, Senator Burton A. Wheeler of Montana summarized what the Bureau of Indian Affairs had done with a part of the Jicarilla tribal funds. He stated: "What has been done to these Indians is that the timber resources have been depleted and all that money has been spent practically for agency purposes."[52] He felt that every dollar that was left in the federal Treasury should be protected so that the Indians could use that money to buy sheep and cattle, which would put them on a solid, self-sustaining basis, and that if the department did not do that, it would certainly be derelict in its duty.

Senator William H. King of Utah, in a speech on the "Conditions of the Indians in the United States" before the Senate on February 8, 1933, revealed that the Bureau and the Interior Department were mismanaging tribal funds to an unbelievable extent. He stated that the Indian Bureau had dissipated Indian tribal funds in the amount of hundreds of millions of dollars in excess of $110,000,000 since 1900 (that is, in addition to the large appropriations made as gratuities from the Treasury of the United States); and that in the fiscal year 1932 it used for its own maintenance 76 percent of the total tribal income of all Indians of the United States.[53] The supporting documentation for this speech pointed out that a draft was made against Jicarilla tribal funds for Bureau employees in the amount of $30,000, but the total draft on tribal funds was $78,886.[54]

Also at the hearing on the Interior appropriations bill for 1934 it was revealed that the "tribal funds of these Indians [Jicarillas] were exhausted, with future income uncertain, the amount they withdrew during the past year being approximately $13,000."[55] This had not been sufficient to administer their affairs and, therefore, the Bureau was requesting an increase of $25,000 in gratuity funds. One reason for the exhaustion of tribal funds was that practically all the timber had been cut. It was anticipated that within two years the cutting would be completed.

There was no legal basis for allocating tribal moneys for the expenses of operating Bureau of Indian Affairs–administered offices—especially for salaries or office expenses. There were some expenses specifically allowable by law, such as the administration of timber sales, and the agency could deduct a percentage of the total receipts. As a rule, however, the government was not supposed to deprive the tribes of their private property (i.e., moneys) without their knowledge and consent and without due process of law. Mismanagement of tribal funds and the unsuccessful Dawes policies eventually led to the reform of the Indian Service and the change in Indian policies embodied in the Indian Reorganization Act of 1934. The unsuitability of lands, the unfavorable climate, the inefficiency and incompetence of the Indian Office, and the neglect of trust responsibilities ensured the failure of the Dawes policies. Far worse was the effect the administration of these policies had on the lives of the people.

There was a bit of irony to all this. Although the Jicarillas suffered considerably from these unnecessary wrongs perpetrated by the government, in the long run they gained from the government's irresponsibility and neglect. While other Indian tribes and groups were losing vast amounts of land, Jicarilla land holdings increased. The chaos surrounding allotments of land for a long time prevented the issuing of patents; in the interim, the allotment laws had changed, providing for the addition of grazing lands. By that time, the government had realized that livestock-raising was the only occupation that would put the Jicarillas on a self-sustaining basis and so increased their reservation by the southern addition. It was primarily the southern addition that was eventually to produce oil and gas—resources that would provide the Jicarillas with a substantial income.

It is also ironic that the government, in making an exception to the Dawes policies by adding more trust lands to an Indian reservation, was committing an act contrary to severing its guardianship over the Indians. Had the same reasoning that supported the southern addition been applied to the other problems, the government would have had an excellent chance of accomplishing its objectives. Nonetheless, in spite of future compensations, these policies served only to make life miserable for the Jicarilla Apaches from the time they returned to their reservation in 1887 until the mid-1930s.

Chapter 6
The Twilight Years: Reservation Life, 1887–1934

The optimism that permeated the Jicarilla Apaches' tribal character persisted into 1886 when the tribe migrated back to its old northern reservation, despite the portents of an unpromising future. The desolate and ominous landscape was dotted with impoverished and inhospitable settlers who themselves had been victimized by their struggle to survive in a harsh and rugged climate. Their experience alone would have driven most people away. For the Jicarillas, however, this was home, where they would confront the challenge to rebuild their tribal society, compromising between the old and the new.

In this hostile environment a handful of Jicarillas, who had escaped the removal in 1883, staged a warm welcome for their returning kinsmen.[1] In the interim, these escapees had lived in the more remote areas of the old reservation evidently without much public notice. Approximately 850 Apaches returned to begin the task of rebuilding their homes. The 500 Llaneros banded around Santiago Largo, Juan Julián, and Elote. The smaller band of 350 Olleros grouped around their leaders, Garfield Velarde, Augustín Vigil, Vicentito, and Augustine Velarde.

These leaders staked out homesteads on the reservation for their families, relatives, and followers, establishing a residential pattern that remained unbroken for the next half-century and to which the allotments of land would later conform. All the homestead sites were not the choice agricultural areas—the arable regions had already been preempted by the non-Indian settlers.

The lingering animosity over the recent removal experience continued to cause friction between the two bands, so they segregated themselves from each other, putting as much distance as possible between their campsites. For example, the Llaneros who were close relatives of Largo settled the Horse Lake area in the east central part, while the Pesata Llaneros settled the northwestern canyon regions off the tributaries of the Navajo River. The Olleros under Vigil homesteaded the La Jara Valley. The pitching of their tepees and tents on these lands marked the beginning of the establishment of their permanent homes.

In the first decade and a half after the homecoming, the Jicarillas were like pensioners at the mercy of the government, looking to their benefactor for subsistence. In 1887 the commissioner of Indian affairs offered assistance and a plan that would have provided comfortable homes, a resident physician, a farmer and his assistant, a carpenter, and a blacksmith, together with farming utensils, stock fence materials, and so forth, as required by the Jicarillas. An industrial school was also a part of the plan to help them along the path to civilization and self-support.[2] It took fifteen years to complete the building of the agency, recruit the personnel, appoint the physician, and construct the school. Had it not been for the Denver and Rio Grande Railroad, which had laid its tracks in 1881 across the northern portion of the reservation, it would have taken even longer. This railroad line tied this area to the rest of the country, and freighted in the building materials, agency supplies, annuity goods, and the mail.

As in any locale, the founding of a community takes time and patience; but on the Jicarilla Reservation, the building of the agency was inordinately slow. Unlike most communities, the Jicarillas were in no position to help direct the growth of their core community, the agency site. The federal government was the sole architect, and it acted with no deliberate speed. Not surprisingly, the government policy of trying to make citizens out of the Indians did not include involving them in the building process, an action that would have been an exemplary lesson in citizenship and community action.

Despite the lack of involvement in building the agency, the Jicarillas were busy—reestablishing their homes and trying to create an atmosphere of normalcy after the past tumultuous decades of being uprooted. The task of the 1890s was to lay the foundations for a new tribal community by forging the old with the new. While the agency was being constructed, the most it had to offer its clientele was food rations supplemented by annuity goods such as clothing, shoes, blankets, cooking utensils, small farm implements, and seeds. For the majority of the people, these issues constituted their only material possessions.

The first winter was one of merely surviving the cold weather, but when spring came, families began clearing fields to plant crops. Children helped with the planting as there were no local schools to attend until 1903. Agricultural pursuits were nothing new to the Apaches: they had a long history as agriculturists.

When the crops were planted there were other matters needing attention—the pending selection of land allotments, picking up the biweekly rations, hunting game, assisting with religious activities, and searching for ways to supplement one's income. The men attended to this business, while the women were occupied by their duties of keeping the camp in order, cooking, sewing, and caring for the children.

Within a short time the women had surveyed the countryside for vegetal foods, to vary the ration diet, and for useful medicinal plants. On the mountains and hillsides were berries of various kinds, wild celery, herbs for tea, wild spinach, edible roots, and a host of pharmaceutical plants. The women were able to renew their age-old activity of gathering; but like crops in the field or game in the mountains, this natural storehouse was dependent on weather conditions.

A Jicarilla family's main source of sustenance was government rations, supplemented in a few cases by small herds of sheep or goats. Several families owned fairly large herds, notably Augustín Vigil and Garfield Velarde. It seems that while the Jicarillas were on the southern reservation, sheep had been acquired, possibly through a distribution from the government. Due to the nature of the exodus in 1886, sizable herds had been left behind. After the tribe's relocation in 1887, Vigil and Velarde returned to the Mescalero Reservation to fetch livestock, thus establishing an economic advantage over their fellow tribesmen.[3] Perhaps more Jicarillas could have done the same, but the risk and expense entailed were too great. It was not only livestock that had had to be abandoned; many household belongings had been left behind because there were so few wagons to carry them. Only those items that could readily be packed on horses were transported. In proportion to sheep and goats, more horses had been brought along because they could be herded at a faster pace than the smaller animals.

In addition to the mundane tasks of trying to make a living, during the summer months the Jicarillas busied themselves with religious matters such as feasts and Bear Dances, which provided the opportunity to socialize. Most feasts were simple, for the people could not afford the expense of more elaborate ones; but with communal cooperation, it was still possible to carry out religious obligations.

The summer and fall seasons found some Jicarillas off the reservation. Not entirely cured of their nomadic habits, they wandered off either to trade with the neighboring communities, visit old and new friends, or just to have something to do. The Jicarillas could scarcely afford the fares on the railroad, but this didn't stop them from hopping the freight cars. Horses, however, continued to be the common means of transportation. Mostly, the Jicarillas visited the small villages of Lumberton, Monero, Chama, and the bordering Colorado mining towns.

The main objective in leaving the reservation was to trade. A trading post was not established until 1889, when Emmitt Wirt, an emigrant from Michigan, settled near Amargo and acquired a license from the government to trade with the Jicarillas. Nonetheless the Jicarillas maintained their commercial ties with merchants in the area.

By and large, rations were the mainstay for all Jicarilla families, with the exception of those fortunate few who owned livestock. To exist merely on rations was unacceptable to them, but up through the turn of the century the alternatives were severely limited. The Jicarillas were placed in an environment that fostered dependency on the government. The few rural communities bordering the reservation offered virtually no employment for the Indians. When there were jobs, such as those offered by the coal mine in Monero, or by the railroad company, they were so few in number that the competition automatically eliminated the Indians.

The government provided a few short-term menial jobs, such as hauling construction materials for bridges or digging ditches. Only a few Jicarillas were occasionally employed at the agency site since government contractors brought in their own labor crews. Ironically, the government complained about doling out rations to lazy Indians while refusing to provide employment for them on construction work that required no more than muscle power. Admittedly, not a single Jicarilla was educated enough to hold even the lowest-paid permanent job, but this was a poor excuse. A good part of America was built by non-English-speaking peoples with no formal education. The only permanent position open to a Jicarilla was that of tribal interpreter, which required knowledge of Apache and English. This single prerequisite virtually eliminated most Jicarillas; they had a functional command of Spanish, but English was still a foreign language. In 1892 the Jicarilla Apache Police Force was organized by the agent, but it offered only eight jobs paying ten or fifteen dollars a month. Also, the appointment of two tribal judges provided small stipends for two Jicarillas.

Although opportunities for earning wages were few, on some occasions the Jicarilla artisan could sell or trade handcrafted articles such as baskets, buckskin moccasins, beaded accessories, bows and arrows, and pottery. The market for Jicarilla arts and crafts was limited due to the remoteness of the reservation (despite the railroad line). No major roads led to or through Jicarilla land, so commercial relations with the rest of the country were inhibited. One outlet for Jicarilla goods was the annual celebrations held at the various Río Grande Pueblos, the Ute Reservation in Southern Colorado, and the Navajo Reservation, where exchanges were made.[4] The ability to take advantage of these markets was contingent on whether or not the expenses for the long trips could be raised and whether or not the would-be traveler would receive permission to travel from the agent.

Not only were there limited opportunities for employment and supplementing one's income in rural northern New Mexico; the outlook for developing a self-sufficient agricultural economy was even more unpromising. The government stubbornly and ill-advisedly persisted in trying to implement the Dawes policies. This single-track attempt to turn Indians into farmers in a wholesale fashion was bound to engender problems. It was no easy task for the Jicarillas to follow the paths charted by the white man, despite their adaptable tribal disposition. The overriding factors blocking the government's utopian plan were the sterile land and the harsh climate.

The Jicarillas were well aware that the land was not suited for farming, but in good faith tried to cultivate it, only to be discouraged. The increase in livestock from 1887 to 1896 was proof enough that stockraising was the only business that promised success in this part of the country. In this same period, forty dwellings were built from logs, some of lumber. To this the agent proudly pointed in his 1896 agency report.[5] To him it meant that the Jicarillas were making some progress. He did not, however, specify which Jicarillas owned the houses. It is not unreasonable to assume that the houses built with lumber were the homes of the livestock owners and not the "ration-farmers." The growing disparity between the haves and the have-nots did not go unnoticed among the Apaches.

The unproductive lands plus the inability to acquire livestock discouraged and alienated a substantial number of Largo's and Pesata's followers. Underlying their dissatisfaction was their past opposition to leaving their beloved Cimarron country. They still blamed the Ollero leaders for this move, especially since the latter, in contrast to the average Apache, seemed to be fairly well off.

The Largoites expressed their discontent by filing a petition with the commissioner on April 29, 1892, listing their grievances.[6] Evidently this was accomplished with the assistance of Severiano Martínez of Mora, who in turn briefed Antonio Joseph, delegate from New Mexico, about conditions on the reservation as related by Largo.[7] The petition pointed out that the Jicarillas could not produce crops, or rely on the irregular and insufficient rations, or cope with the favoritism toward the Olleros shown by the agent. The request for the redress of grievances led to the investigation of agency affairs, but did little to alleviate the real problems.

Upon receipt of the petition on May 28, the acting commissioner sent an inspector to look into the situation and report his findings as soon as possible. Coincidentally, a letter from Jicarilla agent John H. Robertson to the Indian Office reinforced the need for an urgent investigation. Robertson had accused Largo of murdering an Indian woman and labeled him a desperate renegade, claiming that Largo had fled the reservation for fear of revenge and had persuaded his people to leave with him. Largo and other aggrieved Jicarillas had in fact left the reservation by May. Robertson also wanted the "ringleaders," Julián, Pesata, and Elote, arrested and imprisoned. The commissioner received still another letter, from David S. Keck, superintendent of education at Fort Lewis, charging Robertson with lack of control over the Indians, who were, in his opinion, socially regressing rather than progressing. In essence, Keck implied that Robertson was an ineffective administrator who was letting things get out of control.[8]

By June 3, Inspector James H. Cisney was on his way to Dulce. In one of his reports he verified that a deplorable state of affairs did exist at the Jicarilla Agency due to the dishonesty and peculation of the employees. Cisney found that the Jicarillas were credited with having received 27,338 pounds of beef, which had not been distributed to them. Unknowingly they had signed vouchers acknowledging receipt. The employees had also conspired to defraud the Jicarillas of annuity goods, which were seen on sale at the Archuleta store.[9] Numerous Jicarillas had seen the agency team hauling a loaded wagon to Amargo during the night on several occasions. Robertson was alerted to this suspicious activity, but he ignored it. Cisney tried to obtain testimony from J. M. Archuleta, Jr., but he managed to avoid the inspector.[10]

Cisney cleared Largo of the false murder charges levied against him by Robertson. Largo was in fact not the culprit. Furthermore, the assailant had made ample restitution to the injured family. The investigation was completed by August and Robertson and his employees were charged with dishonest conduct. With all this evidence before the commissioner, he had no choice but to ask Robertson to resign.

While the Cisney probe was being conducted and a search for a new agent was pending, the two disgruntled bands lived off the reservation. Largo's band had gone to its old haunts near Mora; Pesata and his followers had returned to Taos country. Wanting as little publicity as possible, the Indian Office made cursory efforts to compel their return, once by delegating the responsibility to Garfield Velarde. Velarde was not in the habit of telling other bands what they should or should not be doing, nor did he have the power to make them comply.

Almost a year later, on September 14, 1893, Largo informed the commissioner that reservation conditions justified not returning. He asked permission for himself and his band of 200 people to spend the winter in Mora. Evidently only three families, the only ones with horses, returned to Dulce. There was no chance that the commissioner would agree to this proposal. The new agent, Captain John L. Bullis, was to make sure that all the absentee Jicarillas were back in the very near future. Bullis managed to meet with the leaders later in the month, again to hear their complaints about reservation life. One salient complaint was the alleged favoritism shown by the previous agent toward the Olleros in the assignment of good lands and in their representation on the police force. Largo's proposed solution to all their problems was a separate reservation near Fort Union, in Cimarron country,[11] so that his people would not have to associate with the other band. Bullis was not able to get commitments on when the bands would start home.

Out of patience, Bullis sent a message to Pesata warning him to return to Dulce unless he wanted the military to boost him along. Pesata must have figured it was in the best interests of his band to comply and notified Bullis of his decision. He and his twenty families reluctantly trekked back toward the reservation. Bullis was so pleased that he even supplied Pesata with rations for the homeward journey.[12]

Largo had sent word with Pesata that he would not be back until the following spring, but he obviously had second thoughts, for he, too, headed home. On November 8, 1893, all the Indians were back on the reservation. This was to be the last time that these Jicarillas returned to the Cimarron area with the intention of remaining there. It marked the end of the long struggle to go back to the old country and the old ways. After this, Cimarron became only a nostalgic and treasured memory for most of the tribe.

Curiously, as a result of the absence, the Llaneros were treated more fairly by the new agent. Largo was appointed by the commissioner as lieutenant of the police force. The Indian Office did not want to give this reconciled band another excuse for leaving the reservation. Largo and the other Llanero leaders, however, were not content with these few concessions and they continued to press for changes.

The Jicarilla leaders were not only instrumental in organizing protests, but served in the greater capacity as liaison between the past and the future for their people. No formal governmental body existed. The federal government's policy was to break down tribal entities; it gave no formal recognition to traditional leaders, nor, in order to play down tribal sovereign powers, did it encourage the establishment of tribal governments. This undermined the only means it had to ensure the success of its ill-conceived policies. How it expected to make citizens out of Indians without inculcating the rights and responsibilities of citizenship is truly incomprehensible. As the International Council of 1887 explained:

Like other people, the Indian needs at least the germ of political identity, some governmental organization of his own, however crude, to which his pride and manhood may cling and claim allegience, in order to make true progress in the affairs of life. This peculiarity in the Indian character is elsewhere called patriotism, and the wise and patient fashioning and guidance of which alone will successfully solve the question of civilization. Preclude him from this and he has little to live for. [13]

Irrespective of recognition or encouragement, the Jicarillas, like most other Indian groups, maintained their informal governmental bodies. Traditionally the Jicarilla leadership consisted of chiefs and headmen from the various bands within the tribe and in the 1890s the political system was still structured around these leaders. Largo and Julián retained their positions uncontested well over three decades and, although they were joined by Pesata and Elote, a problem of succession arose when these powerful elderly men passed from the scene in the early 1900s, leaving almost a void until the 1930s.

As for the Olleros, the most prominent leader, Huerito Mundo (who died in 1885), was succeeded by his next oldest brother, Garfield Velarde, who provided stability for the Ollero leadership. He held that position off and on until the 1930s, when a regular council was elected and he was one of the representatives. Velarde had the advice of the wise and respected Vicentito and the capable assistance of the younger headmen, Augustín Vigil and Augustine Velarde. The age distribution and points of view among the Olleros made it easier for them to make a transition into the twentieth century, unlike the Llaneros, who were more traditional.

In establishing the new tribal community, the tribal leaders were active in providing direction for the people. Velarde, for example, constantly pressured the agent to rid the reservation of the settlers so that the Jicarillas could have the benefit of all the reservation lands. The education of the children was another issue in which he was deeply involved. The Ollero leaders demonstrated their recognition of and support for the need to educate the young by sending their own children to off-reservation schools.

The Llaneros seemed less interested in education, but were just as concerned about the status of the economy as were the Olleros. The protest staged by Largo and Pesata was directed at focusing attention on economic problems. When the allotment assignments were in a chaotic state, complicating the sale of timber and the purchase of livestock, leaders from both bands got together and offered their solution, illustrating that there was a consensus in common issues.

Although the government professed a dislike for traditional leaders, inevitably when there was an investigation of tribal matters, as in 1892, when affidavits were taken by Cisney on fraudulent handling of Indian goods, or when inspection tours were conducted, the traditional leaders were called upon either to testify or to express their opinions.

While the leaders were progressive in their outlook, they retained a portion of their native dress, symbolizing their respect for their Apache heritage. This cultural carryover was manifested especially in their religion. Rarely did the leaders separate their roles as political and religious authorities. This dual leadership was possible only because the Jicarillas were a devout people. As in the period before 1883, they continued to practice their native religion, in part due to their geographic isolation and the lack of attention from either the government or missionaries. Not until about 1892 did two women from the Women's Home Mission Society of the Methodist Church begin proselytizing among the Jicarillas, with little success. These dedicated women managed to get only a few followers. They were able to persuade only three families to bury their dead in the Christian way.[14] The Apache practice was to dispose of the dead in a remote spot in the mountains. Only the medicine man and his helper attended this burial.

The period from 1887 to the early 1900s was the last era in which the traditional leaders exercised their influence; their powers had decreased considerably, although one superintendent observed in 1914: "About eight men are recognized leaders, each representing a group of families. These men seem to have been wisely chosen and in most instances use good judgment in their councils. There is a factional feeling existing, however, but it is not of sufficient importance [to cause problems]."[15]

By the second decade of the 1900s, the government revitalized its policy of deemphasizing tribal culture, and began to suppress Jicarilla leadership. It was during this period that the Jicarillas were on the verge of becoming extinct and it did not seem to matter much whether there were any leaders. The superintendent made very little use of the leaders, but frequently played on factional differences. In one case when the Olleros were attempting to get the attention of Washington officials for relief of their distressing problems, the superintendent agitated the factional conflict and no consensus was reached on how the Indian Office should be approached. The superintendent consistently tried to undermine and cripple the leadership. As a result, the importance of the role of the interpreter increased. The interpreter was a vital link in the communication process; unfortunately, he often used his position to assume political power and was therefore often perceived as being an agent for the government in its attempt to suppress Jicarilla native ways. One interpreter was killed by an irate tribal member who evidently felt that the man had caused harm to his family and his reputation by abusing the power of his position. Understandably, the job was dependent on an interpreter's cooperation with the agency officials and not with the tribal leaders.

Also responsible for eroding the power and influence of the traditional leaders was the post trader, who not only had a monopoly on trade, but also exerted a powerful influence through his economic stranglehold on the Jicarilla livestock economy. He had the means to determine who would get credit, at what interest rates, and to set prices for his goods and services. In an era when morale was at its lowest and poverty was a way of life, it is no wonder that he was able to exercise so much control.

While agents came and went, the post trader provided the people with a sense of continuity and stability. His familiarity with the families and their problems directly affected his business. It was not uncommon for him to set up young Jicarillas in the livestock business, thus establishing the kind of relationship that existed between a frontier banker and his borrowers. All these factors added up to make him the titular father figure for the Jicarillas in the period up through the late 1930s.

In addition to the recognized leaders, the Indian police played a useful, indeed valuable role in the social changes of the 1890s, serving as peace officers and employees of the Indian Office. The police force became an important institution because of its prestige and because of the employment opportunity it provided. The salary of the captain was fifteen dollars, while the privates received ten dollars a month.[16] Factions within the tribe lobbied with the agent to get their men on the force and since the factions were ruled by the chiefs and headmen, the police remained partially under the control of the leaders.

Five police patrolled the agency at all times, and the other three were stationed at outlying posts on the reservation. These law enforcement officers maintained peace, protected agency property, helped the agent in carrying out his duties when necessary, and suppressed the liquor traffic. It was their duty to arrest disorderly persons, those possessing liquor, showing evidence of criminal behavior, or those guilty of fomenting civil disorder.

The suppression of the liquor traffic was one of the more important duties of the Indian police. This involved keeping the non-Indian settlers from carrying on illegal liquor operations—a task that was especially difficult since the whole business was cloaked in secrecy by both the non-Indians and the participating Jicarillas. Even the police were accused—justifiably—of not performing their duties with complete sincerity. Social pressures exerted upon them by their fellow tribesmen perhaps contributed to this occasional lack of effort. The Indian police did succeed in bringing some cases to court, but the agent was the only person who consistently tried to bring transgressors, both Jicarillas and non-Indians, to justice. Because it was a federal crime to sell liquor to Indians at this time, offenders were brought before the United States marshall in Pueblo, Colorado. Almost every effort by the agent to obtain convictions for guilty parties ended in failure. In only a few cases was the agent even successful in getting the accused to trial.

The Jicarillas continued to go off the reservation to trade, sell, and purchase their goods. The town of Lumberton just east of Dulce was the nearest trading area, which the agent described as being distinguished by the presence of a man (whose name was withheld) who was notorious for selling liquor to the Indians.[17] This man owned a general store where he took anything from the Indians in exchange for liquor. He even had sales representatives on the reservation, who bartered with the Indians, thus saving them a journey to town. One of the store owner's bartenders who actually was caught violating the federal law was brought before a grand jury; in typical frontier fashion, he was acquitted because the merchant had managed to secure enough witnesses in his own behalf to convince the jury of his innocence. The agent was furious with the decision and proposed to the Indian Office that it employ a detective who was familiar with the frontier and who could work with him to set up a scheme to prosecute this merchant. The Indian Office, of course, was not interested and took no action.

The Indian police, thus, were appointed government agents who were expected to suppress the cultural practices of their people. One historian had suggested that the Indian police served as "agents for civilization" in the acculturation process that was taking place on the reservations and aided the breakdown of tribal leadership and culture.[18] But the Jicarilla tribal leaders were powerful enough to keep the police attuned to tribal ways. Jicarilla police were agents for their own people rather than for the government.

Although there were reports of "immoral practices"—such as plural marriages, destruction of property at the death of relatives, and medical treatment by the medicine men—in many such cases the Jicarilla police paid little attention to the rules and regulations.[19] By the time a man was eligible for employment on the police force, he was well versed in the customs and mores of his society. Chances were that he knew that Jicarilla society was better able to prevent crime than were the laws of the dominant society. Also, it was difficult for the police to report practices that whites labeled immoral: it was more important to them to be accepted by their people than to enforce rules that could be evaded and dealt with internally. The agent, however, concentrated his efforts on trying to eradicate the traditional customs of the Apaches. By doing this, he unknowingly added more problems to reservation life than he could have anticipated.

Life on the Jicarilla reservation during the 1890s was hard, but the Indians were determined to make it easier and more comfortable. For a short span of time, deceptive signs pointed toward better days. In 1896 statistics showed that thirty-four more homes had been built and that livestock holdings had risen to a record high of 3,000 sheep and 500 goats. Even the arts and crafts were selling well and bringing in good profits for the craftsmen.[20] This spurt in economic growth proved short-lived, reversing itself and continuing its downswing well into the early 1920s. A drought hit the country in the summer of 1896, seriously affecting the economy and dealing a serious blow to the morale of the Indians. To offset losses, the sympathetic agent requested an increase in the ration supplies, but to no avail. This experience added an extra burden to the uphill struggle to make a living and it was so dispiriting that the people began losing their desire to go on. The pessimism that ensued engendered a depression from which the Indians did not recover for the next two decades. The Jicarillas entered the twentieth century with a loss of spirit, which was certainly uncharacteristic of their nature.

The grimness of their plight could not be disguised. In 1897, Hamlin Garland, the American novelist, spent time traveling among the Indians of the Southwest, including the Jicarilla Apaches. The experience left him very depressed. He described one of the days of his visits as "perfect, but the land was distressingly bare and dry. The beautiful valleys had no streams. The hay in the lowlands was scant and yellow, and the people seemed dispirited and silent. . . . They seemed to be making a desperate attempt to secure a living in conformity to the law of the awe-compelling white man."[21]

Garland surely must have felt sorrow as he wrote:

The cabins are in the valleys and quite widely separated. The loneliness of the families was almost civilized in its painfulness. . . quite unlike the cheerful village settlement of the Pueblos. It is hard to be so poor and so lonely too. . . . They are more sorrowful than the Navajos, for their lives are solitary. . . . These poor people are as lonely as the settlers on the Kansas Plain, and even more poverty stricken and drouth accursed. They endure because they must, also because they can. May their dreams of the Happy Hunting Ground all come true.[22]

Garland indeed saw the harshness of life on the reservation. But the Jicarillas, although poverty stricken, tried to maintain their courage by clinging to their native ways. The government, through the "process of acculturation had reduced him [the Jicarilla] to the lowest Anglo denominator, the poor white."[23]

If life seemed grim at the turn of the century, it must have been considered the "good old days" by those who lived to see the near extinction of their people in the following two decades, the "twilight" years that brought the Jicarilla Apache Tribe to the brink of complete disaster. The combination of economic deprivation and social dissipation that had built up since 1887 could no longer be suppressed.

The rapid decrease in the tribal population from 815 in 1900 to a low of 588 in 1920 serves as testimony to this story with its near-tragic ending. Tuberculosis was the main cause of the decline, but other diseases such as trachoma, measles, and influenza also took their toll. The following statistics illustrate the decline in the population.

Year	Population	Year	Population	Year	Population	Year	Population
1891	824	1902	802	1913	669	1924	616
1892	844	1903	774	1914	659	1925	635
1893	842	1904	782	1915	642	1926	638
1894	842	1905	795	1916	642	1927	627
1895	845	1906	784	1917	645	1928	636
1896	853	1907	776	1918	621	1929	639
1897	841	1908	776	1919	600	1930	647
1898	845	1909	791	1920	588	1931	652
1899	831	1910	743	1921	594	1932	664
1900	815	1911	720	1922	596	1933	664
1901	813	1912	723	1923	608	1934	680

The Jicarilla Apaches were not the only Indians in the United States to suffer from a high morbidity rate, a situation that prompted the commissioner to order a comprehensive health survey in 1903.[24] Abstracts from this survey indicated that the Indian morbidity rate exceeded that of whites in any given region throughout the United States. The study identified tuberculosis as one of the two diseases most prevalent among the Indians. It was caused primarily by poor and unsanitary living conditions, lack of proper nutrition, and inadequate health care, which made the Indians highly susceptible to the disease. These conditions were concomitant with the poverty on the Jicarilla Reservation.

Although there was clear evidence that something had to be done about the disease and the general economic conditions among the

Indian tribes, a campaign to wipe out the dreaded white plague did not begin in earnest nationwide until 1908.[25] The campaign was directed against the spread of tuberculosis and trachoma in the Indian schools, a nucleus from which the contagion spread to entire Indian communities. Gradually it was recognized that tuberculosis could be controlled only if homes were included in the fight, so the Indian Health Service began, on a limited basis, an inspection of homes, appointing field matrons to educate the Indians in the basics of sanitary living and nutrition, and instituting other programs of preventive health measures. This war on tuberculosis did not reach the Jicarilla Reservation on a tribal-wide scale until about 1912, although there were several efforts made to establish tuberculosis camps before 1901. These elicited little response from the Indians, and the agency staff was less than enthusiastic about the program, which ended in failure.[26]

In 1912, more attention was given to the Jicarilla Apache Reservation because of the alarming statistical information that was reaching the bureau, indicating that the Indian morbidity rate was rising. The bureau intensified its campaign, but this time directed efforts toward increasing congressional appropriations for the improvement of health conditions on Indian reservations. Congress, not convinced of the validity of the Indian Office's reports on health conditions, ordered the Public Health and Marine Hospital Service to conduct an independent study of Indian morbidity in 1912. For this study, thirteen physicians covered twenty-five states and examined 39,231 Indians; they refuted the claim that the rate of tuberculosis as of 1912 was 3.54 per 1,000 population. Instead, they found that the rate far exceeded this figure. The highest rate was 32.7 among the Paiutes of the Pyramid Lake Reservation in Nevada; the low was 6.92 among the Coeur d'Alene in Washington. For the Jicarillas, the rate was 9.45.[27]

The physician assigned to the Jicarilla Reservation was Dr. Ferdinand Shoemaker, who made his visit in March 1912. He reported: "These Indians are largely affected with tuberculosis in its various forms from which the annual death rate is necessarily large. It is estimated that at least 75% of the population is obviously affected with tuberculosis, and that 60% of the death rate occurring on this reservation is due to this cause."[28] Dr. Shoemaker drew a direct parallel between the health of the tribe and housing conditions, which he described as "being as bad as can well be imagined."[29] George Wycoff, the agency doctor, felt that even the tepees were infinitely preferable from the sanitary and ventilation standpoints to the houses that held a family to one spot, with disastrous results to their health.[30]

The Jicarillas were encouraged to obtain lumber from the agency sawmill to improve their homes, but few families were able to take advantage of this suggestion for various reasons, mainly the inability to pay for the lumber. To the chagrin of the government employees, the Jicarillas continued to practice the abandonment of their homes when a death occurred in the house. One man who was considered quite "progressive" had built a rather nice multiroom adobe house with windows and wooden floors, but he moved into a tepee when his wife died.[31] This custom annoyed the agency personnel, but one superintendent found it reasonable. He commented that "it is more of a blessing than an affliction when a death occurs in a house and it is abandoned, especially if it is a detriment to the health of the occupants to begin with."[32]

In addition to the poor housing, Dr. Shoemaker noted that there was a general lack of adequate nutrition among the people, which contributed to their low resistance to tuberculosis. He wrote, "Many . . . hardly know what it is to have a full belly. . . . Their staple diet is tortillas and black coffee. A Jicarilla is so poor that meat is a luxury that he can seldom afford."[33]

In 1906 the government had invoked stringent measures for the issuing of rations: they would go only to the old and needy, which meant the Jicarillas' ration rolls were severely cut.[34] This new policy was to distribute rations to the able-bodied heads of family only in lieu of labor. The policy was badly timed and detrimental to the Jicarillas.

As a result of the labor-in-lieu-of-rations policy, conditions deteriorated to the point of near starvation. In 1911 Superintendent C. A. Churchill informed the commissioner:

The whole tribe is in a very destitute condition. . . . This year their poverty is unusually accentuated. Not only were their pitifully inadequate crops a total failure, but their allowance of subsistence supplies for issuance of rations has been cut in half of what it was last year on the supposition that a large amount of work in the timber would be available this fiscal year for irregular Indian labor [and actually it] is considerably less than half of what it was last year. Only for the mild winter with which we have thus far been favored with, the neglect of these Indians would have resulted disastrously. Even yet we will probably have a couple of months of severely cold and stormy weather and additional subsistence supplies will be required to relieve their distress.[35]

The government had reduced the rations before the work was available. In 1909 a sawmill had been purchased for the agency. It was installed the following year, but not until March 1912 was the Navajo Lumber Company contracted to purchase 130 million board feet of timber.

Living conditions were so bad and so disturbing to visitors and missionaries that they felt compelled to publicize the plight of the Jicarillas. On February 25, 1911, the *Albuquerque Morning News* and the *Denver Post* carried stories of the deplorable situation on the Jicarilla Reservation.[36] The *Post* article had the title "Starvation of Jicarillas National Disgrace."[37] The article, perhaps without really knowing it, put its finger on the underlying cause for the misery, as is indicated by the following excerpt: "Unlike most reservations, this one will not provide a living for Indians, or white men either, if they have to depend upon the cultivation of its soil."[38]

Stories of this nature continued to appear in newspapers throughout the nation until the 1920s. Joseph A. Dixon wrote an article for the *Chicago Tribune* on November 21, 1912, accusing the government of causing starvation among the Jicarilla Apaches.[39] Missionaries like James Bell published observations similar to the one that appeared in one of the Philadelphia papers.[40] Several letters reached congressmen, who sent inquiries to the Indian Office. The newspaper stories were often exaggerated accounts, but they were not far from the truth.

Not until this type of publicity hit the media did the bureau take action. Shortly after the barrage of stories in 1912, the bureau sent an inspector, William Peterson, to check out affairs at the Jicarilla Agency. His main task seemed to be to rebut the charges about starvation and to show that there were ample employment opportunities for all Indians willing to work. Peterson found that there were no actual cases of starvation and that there were jobs available in the timber industry for tie cutters. According to the inspector, there was no reason for anyone to starve with this kind of labor. He admitted, however, that the work was only temporary in nature. Out of 680 Jicarillas, 160 were able-bodied: they were supporting 242 individuals besides themselves, and of this number, 73 were children under the age of five. Peterson estimated that the average annual income was about $271, but since the Jicarillas did not have to pay rent or fuel costs, their income compared favorably with that of most unskilled laborers throughout the country.[41]

Regardless of the government's attempted cover-up of actual conditions, it could not deny that employment opportunities were severely limited. Neither could it claim that the Jicarillas were not trying to make a living. The agent had reported in 1910 that "they seem to take advantage of every available means at their command by which to gain a livelihood, except that they seem prejudiced against leaving the reservation to secure employment."[42] He also reported that there were 226 Jicarillas who were incapacitated and who could not perform manual labor, and that a force of only 140 able-bodied men existed. The incapacitated not only included the elderly, but also those who were suffering from the debilitating effects of tuberculosis or some other disease.[43]

There may have been enough temporary jobs, but it appeared that the Indians did not receive wages equal to non-Indian employees. Peterson had indicated that the Jicarillas were being paid $1.22 per day for cutting ties. Evidently this wage was below what non-Indians were receiving, because the agent complained to the commissioner that there was no reason for the Indians to get lower wages than other men doing similar work.[44]

Arthur Brown, a government employee, reported in 1914 that there was employment available for those who wanted jobs, but in many cases preference was given to Mexicans living in that locality. It seemed the employers felt that the Indians were undependable and demanded much higher wages than the Mexicans did.[45] At the sawmill site a few unskilled jobs were given to Jicarillas, but the pay was not regular and the "Indians disliked work that promised pay in the indefinite future."[46] For a time in 1913 part of the sawmill machinery was destroyed by fire and workers were laid off until replacements were made. All in all, according to Brown, "taking into account the wages received through labor, the sale of some articles, crop sales, and returns from leased lands, the earnings of the tribe amounted to less than fifty dollars per year per head of family . . . a sum not sufficient for comfortable support in so cold a climate."[47]

Another government inspector who assessed the employment picture on the Jicarilla Reservation in 1917 came to conclusions similar to Brown's. This inspector stated that "there were very few Indians among the tribe that might be considered able-bodied or who are capable of enduring a hard day's work so that it is a difficult matter for them to earn sufficient money by their physical labor to properly equip themselves with sanitary homes and supply their families with proper food."[48] By 1920 only twenty Jicarillas were holding part-time jobs in the timber industry.

Thus means of making a decent living were circumvented both by limited jobs and by the inability of the work force to cope with hard labor due to failing health. Moreover, the community of Dulce did not have adequate medical care, although there was an agency physician who had been in residence since 1892. He devoted a large portion of his time to the non-Indians in the area, in part because the government was unwilling to pay him a living wage. Working with outdated equipment and insufficient supplies of medicine, the understaffed personnel were confined to the school hospital, which gave priority to the children in the boarding school.[49] Adults were admitted as bed patients only in emergencies. A regular reservation hospital with a twenty-four-patient capacity was not completed until July 6, 1917. By then tuberculosis was widely disseminated among the Jicarillas. Dr. Shoemaker, who revisited the reservation in the fall, advised that if the disease were not checked, it would have the effect of annihilating the entire tribe in a few years.[50] Since his first visit in 1912, the situation had gone from bad to worse.

The tribal health picture obviously had interlocking pieces, including cultural factors. The people looked upon the doctor with suspicion and sought out his services only on rare occasions, when a sick person reached a critical stage. Medicine men were still highly regarded, but as the death rate climbed, pragmatic notions overcame cultural beliefs. Help from the medical corps was sought out, but, more often than not, it was hard to get. Thus the Indians had no choice but to fall back on the medicine men. Resorting to Indian medical practices because of lack of modern medical services was often interpreted by non-Indian observers as an indication of ignorance and superstition.

By far the greatest danger seemed to be the psychological impact of the vicious circle of poverty and the increasing number of deaths. The atmosphere of pessimism was reinforced by the newspapers, agency personnel, and neighbors, who constantly reminded the people of their excessive death rate, but at the same time offered neither assistance nor hope.

The adverse circumstances with which the people had to deal were overwhelming, and moreover, the Jicarillas had little knowledge of how to help themselves. "The combined effect was like an insidious poison."[51] Several extreme cases of this apathy and pessimism were cited by the superintendent to explain the extent of the situation in his 1919 annual report:

For five years Alonzo Garcia, a confirmed pessimist, half deaf, rheumatic, and tubercular, lived in a mere hovel and for two years of that time there was within one hundred feet a new log house constructed for him. . . . Less distant from the agency . . . a larger house was constructed for a family of three who were in a condition no less pitiable and of equal duration. The hovel occupied by this family was not to exceed eight by ten feet and had no light save by the open door. The palsied father was helpless, the mother was almost blind of trachoma, and their only son at thirty-six years of age was bedfast before them, rheumatic, tubercular, and entirely helpless. Every reasonable effort was made to relieve this condition until death brought relief July fourteenth last. No reason was given for the extreme obstinacy and none can be deduced except that it indicates one of the underlying principles of pessimism . . . what's the use. Moving to a new house would have afforded some relief. Immediately following the death, however, the old couple moved to other quarters and burned the hovel. It is a tribal custom to vacate any premises visited by death and often such houses are burned. Jicarilla hypochondria has manifested itself in another extreme. A few years ago there was on the roll of agency employees a model policeman . . . active and resolute. He knew the condition of his tribe. He had seen friends sicken and die, the disease found his family and claimed his wife. The singular delusion of witchcraft struck the bereaved man and he suspected a neighbor woman as being in league with evil spirits and instrumental in his loss. The thought of it coupled with a stupefied mind under the influence of alcohol led to murder and today a lone Jicarilla is serving a life sentence in the United States Penitentiary at Leavenworth. Frequent letters from him show his deep interest in his tubercular children who are now being cared for by near relatives.[52]

These were extreme cases, but the depths of despondency permeated every aspect of Jicarilla life.

With disaster imminent in 1920, the government belatedly realized that economic well-being was directly related to good health, and it designed a program to rehabilitate both the economy and the health of the people, mainly by distributing livestock to individual families.

TABLE I

Birth and Death Rates and Tuberculosis Mortality
on Reservations Visited: Jicarilla Apaches

Year	Pop.	Births	Deaths	Tuberculosis Deaths	Indians Examined	Tuberculosis Latent	Active	Estimated
1913	669	43	51	22	324	42	28	73
1914	659	23	34	14	340	33	22	67
1915	642	19	8	15?	370	26	17	70
1916	642	23	23	13	401	9	34	43
1917	645	35	32	16	413	15	32	66
1918	621	17	41	13	465	40	68	151
1919	603	39	57	42	490	55	85	260
1920	588	27	45	9	500	95	42	452
1921	594	26	20	10	270	20	11	—
1922	596	28	26	11	137	9	11	78
1923								

SOURCE: "A Study of the Need for Public Health Nursing on Indian Reservations,"
Report for the Bureau of Indian Affairs by the American Red Cross, pp. 4–5.

While the standard of living shifted upward, the health situation
only slowly improved. In 1923 a team of nurses was sponsored by the
American Red Cross to conduct another health survey of the Jicarilla
Reservation. Their findings indicated that the Jicarilla birth rate was
43.8 per thousand population, compared to other southwestern tribes
with a birth rate of 30.4. Both figures were greater than those for the
entire United States, 24.3. The death rate, on the other hand, was 33.7
for the Jicarillas, 20.5 for other southerwestern tribes, and 11.7 for the
United States in general.[53] The survey indicated that the tuberculosis
rate was 16.8. While the disease was still a menace, some progress was
being made in conquering it. This survey was the most comprehensive that had been made up to this time.

The gradual growth of the tribal population throughout the 1920s
reflected the improvement in the economic sector and in the health of
the Apaches. Psychologically, they were experiencing a new sense of
confidence by working for their own benefit and welfare. The sheep-
raising endeavor had positive effects on the Jicarillas. There was one
man who, before receiving his share of the sheep, made a scant living
by selling war clubs and other items at the railroad station. Afterward,

he was able to pay off debts to the local trader. There were others who used their new income to supplement their existing resources. One used the stock to supplement his yearly wage income of $300, which had been scarcely enough to feed and clothe his family of eight. The sheep, together with his garden crops and the returns from his wife's handicrafts, increased the family income by 140 percent.[54]

Other changes were also evident. Living conditions were better and there was a new interest in farming; what had been frustrating became challenging. An increasing number of families were growing garden vegetables, and there seemed to be a greater acceptance of vegetables in the diet. Surplus oats provided enough feed for the animals during the winter, and wheat was sufficient to grind into meal at the agency flour mill. Improvements on the allotments were noticeable—including new log houses, barns, corrals, and stacks of winter hay. More wagons and teams were purchased for use on the family plots and as a means of general transportation. Most of the newly built homes had windows, wooden floors, and several rooms. They were better than the homes described by Dr. Shoemaker in 1912, but still substandard compared to most American homes.

Progress was so visible that in 1922 the superintendent wrote in his annual report:

Proverbialisms common to former correspondence from this agency as "idle Indians," "dying race," and "starving Apaches," have been effectively silenced by the definite industrial effort which in time will make full utilization of all labor and resources of the reservation with reasonable certainty that the Jicarillas can win and maintain an enviable distinction among producing Indian people of our nation in the move to self-support and independence.[55]

The social progress brought on by the expanding economy had other benefits. With the increase in prosperity, there was a return to some of the old practices the agency thought had been abandoned. Religious ceremonials regained their former stature. There had been a decline in some of the ceremonials because of the poverty and sickness, but better days brought back the Bear Dances and Puberty Feasts since the families were able to afford the expenses incident to such events. There was a belief on the part of some non-Indians that the young men were no longer taking up shamanism or engaging in the Indian medical practices, but this was perhaps more wishful thinking than actuality.

This pattern of cultural revival, improved health, and economic progress continued throughout the late 1920s. By 1934, the Jicarillas had basically recovered from the disaster of the past two decades, proving that they were more than capable of helping themselves when given the opportunity.

The standard of living and the quality of life on the Jicarilla Apache Reservation from 1887 to 1934 was intrinsically related to the economic problems fostered by the Dawes policies. The Dawes philosophy had been erroneously formulated. It had attempted to reshape the Native Americans' way of life in the image of the American yeoman farmer, without proper planning and necessary tools. On the Jicarilla Reservation, the sterile lands were prima facie evidence that agriculture was not feasible. Although this should have been convincing enough, the government ignored it and continued to insist on the cultivation of the land. In the process, the means to a more practical route to a decent livelihood for the Jicarillas were severely curtailed, affecting their whole society in a most distressing manner. The ultimate disgrace, however, was the near extinction of the tribe. The government alone must bear the responsibility for this, because of its inefficient handling of its trust responsibility. Once the government provided the economic means (livestock), the Jicarillas, through their own individual and collective efforts, laid the foundation from which the Indian Reorganization Act of 1934 was able to launch its successful programs. In 1934, although on a comparative basis the Jicarillas were better off, there was still much catching up to do with the rest of the nation in the field of education, an area that had suffered from neglect because of the economic and social problems during the previous half century.

Chapter 7
The Search for Education:
1887–1940

At the beginning of the twentieth century, the majority of the adult Jicarillas were illiterate, and the school-age children were not receiving the benefits of a formal education, reflecting another consequence of the disastrous Dawes philosophy that helped to block Jicarilla progress since 1887. Like the land that precluded agricultural success, the manner in which the federal government educated the Jicarilla children ensured dependence.

Formal education had always been valued by the Jicarilla Apaches. Since the days when the Olleros lived in the vicinity of the Abiquiu Agency before the removal to Mescalero, there were requests made to the agent by the leaders to start a day school for the children, but the requests fell on deaf ears. Throughout the removal years (1870–87) tribal affairs were in such turmoil that schooling was an impractical goal. While in residence on the Mescalero Apache Reservation, however, the Jicarilla children attended the local government school. After 1887, due to the more pragmatic and pressing economic concerns, education was relegated to a secondary position, but within a few years the issue was raised and put before the agent. Throughout the 1890s the Jicarilla leaders persistently raised questions as to why a boarding school could not be built right on the reservation. Their inquiries did not spur the government to any immediate action. In 1895 the government finally made a preliminary site survey for a school on a tract of land belonging to Gabriel Lucero, one of the settlers. Purchase of this property was delayed and complicated by Lucero's lack of clear title to the land, but the bureau generously allowed him sufficient time to obtain title, at the expense of the Jicarilla children's education.[1]

The purchase agreement was negotiated, but in 1899 the school was still in the planning stages. The contractor finished the school in 1902. It was enthusiastically received by the Jicarilla parents, who enrolled 130 students on October 1, 1903.[2]

Before 1903 very few children went to school. Those few who did attended boarding school at Fort Lewis, Colorado, and the Ramona Indian School in Santa Fe, New Mexico. The figure for enrollment was not more than 35 all throughout the 1890s. In 1899 the agent reported that there were 251 children of school age who were not attending any school anywhere.[3]

How the government rationalized its negligence of the education of the Jicarillas is difficult to determine. Federal Indian policy clearly called for Indians to become citizens of the dominant society as soon as possible. Yet, for the Jicarillas, their only passport to a meaningful acculturation, education, was not available. Specifically, in the 1890 annual report of the secretary of the interior the general purpose of the government was defined as

the preparation of Indian youth for assimilation into the national life by such a source of training as will prepare them for the duties and privileges of American citizenship. This involves the training of the hand in useful industries; the development of the mind in independent and self-directing power of thought; the impartation of useful practical knowledge; the culture of the moral nature and the formation of character. Skill, intelligence, industry, morality, manhood, and womanhood are the ends aimed at.[4]

Despite this directive to secure education for Indian children, it took about twelve years—the time necessary to educate one entire generation—before the "noble" sentiment of the Indian Office took the form of a reservation school at Dulce.

Jicarilla parents, although they approved of educating their children, were not particularly eager to send them away to distant, off-reservation boarding schools. It was the distance they objected to, and the prolonged separations, which naturally had adverse psychological effects on both children and parents. This cruel separation surely affected the children, who were often sent home when they became ill. In one case, after suffering a serious illness at Santa Fe, a Jicarilla student was sent home. He died shortly thereafter, reinforcing parents' anxieties about the price of educating their children.[5]

The internal policies and practices at Indian schools found little support from Jicarilla parents. Indian schools demanded that a certain number of students be delivered to their institutions; they threatened retaliatory and legal measures against uncooperative parents. In the appropriation act of March 3, 1893, the secretary of the interior assumed the power to prevent the issuing of rations or the furnishing of subsistence of any kind to the head of any Indian family if its children between the ages of eight and twenty-one were not attending school. Unfortunately, there were no laws requiring the secretary to make sure every Indian child was given a fair opportunity to become educated.

As if this policy were not sufficiently intimidating, there was an active rivalry between the schools at Fort Lewis and Santa Fe for the Jicarilla students, in part because enrollment determined the amount of appropriations the schools received from Congress. Therefore, each school used several different tactics to boost its enrollment. For example, Santa Fe paid parents fifteen dollars per trip to bring in students, while Fort Lewis tried to convince the Jicarilla leaders of the benefits of attending its institution. One year, the superintendent at Fort Lewis invited Garfield Velarde to the school for entertainment to win over his support. Velarde was pleased with the entertainment but aware of the treatment students had received at Fort Lewis and made no tribal commitments. He did, however, enroll his own children.

Later, in a meeting at the Jicarilla Agency among Velarde, other leaders, and the superintendent of Fort Lewis, David S. Keck, the Jicarillas indicated that they did not want their children at Fort Lewis. This, of course, surprised the superintendent. He insisted that orders from the Indian Office made it clear that the Jicarillas were to attend only the Fort Lewis school. The Jicarillas vehemently disagreed. Keck was so angered that he said that the Jicarilla police ought to force the children to go to school, and if the police did not obey, "they ought to be shot down in their tracks."[6] Keck was so irate that he accused John N. Robertson of disobeying orders from the Indian Office by encouraging his charges to send their children to Santa Fe. Robertson later wrote that he himself preferred Santa Fe, but that he had not influenced the Jicarillas' decisions.

One practice most resented was that of keeping students in school during vacations. Parents traveled many miles to bring home their youngsters, often to discover that their children could not leave. The rationale for this, according to the school personnel, was that the parents could not be trusted to return the children following the vacation. This might have been true in some cases, but usually not without good reason. In 1890 such an instance occurred at the Ramona Indian School. Elmore Chase, the superintendent, claimed he had sole authority to determine the length of the summer vacation, if indeed any vacation was forthcoming. Earlier, Chase had promised the parents that their children's vacation would begin July first. When the parents showed up, Chase arbitrarily decided that vacation did not begin until August first, ending on September first. This led to much argument between the parents and Chase. As Chase would have predicted, the Jicarillas did not return their children in September.[7] Chase wrote the commissioner requesting the aid of troops, and accused Bartholomew of noncooperation. Bartholomew reminded him of his broken promises to the Apaches.[8]

Parents also disliked the disciplinary measures taken against their children and they disapproved of the general living conditions at the schools. Some Jicarilla students ran away as a result of harsh treatment. On one occasion, a student, Guernsay Vigil, wrote the Jicarilla agent about the treatment some of the boys were receiving at Santa Fe, which was his excuse for running away.[9] Fortunately, the agent did not compel him to return to Santa Fe, but instead suggested Fort Lewis—the lesser of two evils.

The Indian schools did not meet with the approval of the Jicarillas over the years, and as a result, many children did not receive an education. For a few who were fortunate enough to be schooled in this era, the experience proved beneficial. These included men like John Mills Baltazar, who became chairman of the Tribal Council in 1937, and Albert Velarde, Sr., Grover Vigil, and Edward Ladd Vicenti, who qualified for Bureau employment in the years from 1910 to 1930, when it was rather difficult to obtain work. These were also the men who consistently urged the government to build a school at Dulce.

When the government built a boarding school in 1902 on the Jicarilla Reservation, students were no longer sent to Fort Lewis or Santa Fe unless they volunteered to go, which rarely happened.

The education provided by the off-reservation boarding schools proved to be so inconvenient and inadequate that the government was compelled to establish the local boarding school it promised in 1887. It opened its doors in 1903 and was greeted with an overwhelming response—130 students. The Jicarilla Apache boarding school was

built about one mile north of the agency site, occupying a commanding position at the edge of a pine grove on gently sloping ground, near
the foot of abrupt cliffs. There was a large two-story dormitory that
housed 125 boys and girls, a classroom building, employees' quarters,
a principal's cottage, and some playground equipment.[10] Over the
years the plant grew as more buildings were added, including the
small school hospital, which was built in 1905.

Room and board for nine months (from September to May) was
provided for all able-bodied children of school age, whose attendance
was compulsory. The grades that were taught were primary or pre-first
to the sixth. In the first years, most of the students were in the first
two grades, except for the few who had previously been to off-reservation schools. The personnel consisted of a school superintendent,
several teachers, matrons, cooks, janitors, and maintenance men.

In addition to the plant itself, the school had the use of 160 acres of
land adjacent to the agency farm where oats, wheat, alfalfa, and other
grains and vegetables were planted for part of the school food supply.
As part of the vocational training program, the farm was operated by
the older boys, while the girls were to learn the domestic arts by
helping with the cooking, laundry, and housekeeping. This emphasis
was in keeping with federal Indian policies, which dictated that
Indians must be assimilated and learn the skills necessary for agricultural pursuits.

Half of a student's day was devoted to chores for the upkeep and
partial support of the school, the other half being spent in the classrooms. The duties were to provide them with vocational training
since the school did not yet have a regular industrial training program.
In 1913 funds were allocated for a school farm, complete with a dairy
herd, a small barn, and chickens and hogs. A domestic cottage was
also built.[11]

The academic curriculum consisted of the regular courses common
to all American schools of the period—reading, writing, arithmetic,
history, and English. The Indian schools had their own curricula, but
in 1911 the Jicarilla school adopted the New Mexico course of instruction,[12] which concentrated on English as a spoken language. Most of
the students upon entrance could not utter a word of English and
those who subsequently learned it were reluctant to use it outside the
classroom. A constant effort was made by the teachers to get the
children to practice their English. They were threatened with punish-
ments if they did not do so.

Time and time again the teachers and boarding school employees
were reprimanded by the Indian Office for their inability to enforce
the use of English among the Jicarillas. One Jicarilla superintendent
defended school personnel by tactfully informing the Indian Office
that the schools alone could not solve the problem in an isolated
community, surrounded by only Spanish-speaking people. Jicarilla
parents and grandparents did not speak English, though they spoke
Spanish well enough to conduct their business.

The girls seemed most unwilling to use English. One Indian inspector noted that "they do not pretend to speak anything but Apache."[13] A
distressed employee commented that "immediately upon returning
from school the girls reverted to their native dress and refused to utter
a word of English unless compelled to do so."[14] In many instances,
women and girls were viewed as the invincible obstacle to advancement because they insisted on maintaining native customs and traditions. In contrast, the men and boys were seen as the only hope for the
tribe's acculturation. The males were usually more inclined to use
English; but they also had more opportunities to use the language
through business and trade. Their mode of dress after they left school
was often a mixture of "citizen's clothing," but they wore long hair
and preferred blankets to overcoats.[15]

Academic progress was slow, but the teachers and administrators
were not easily discouraged. In 1910 the superintendent commented
on how far behind the Jicarillas were in comparison to other tribes. He
wrote: "Naturally the younger generation is not nearly so far advanced
in learning as are the second and third generations of children on
reservations where schools have been in operation for fifteen, twenty-
five years . . . It is remarkable, though, what progress has been made by
the pupils who have attended the reservation school since it has been
in operation a few years."[16]

The Jicarillas' desire to have their children educated was severely
stifled by the terrible experience with illness and death from 1903 to
1918. These years reflected the experiences of other Indian boarding
schools throughout the United States. During Commissioner
William A. Jones's term in office (1897–1904) a policy of high student
enrollment was strictly enforced, despite the lack of adequate housing
facilities.[17] At the local level, any and all means of acquiring students
were employed. Eventually the policy and practice led to the rapid
spread of tuberculosis, trachoma, and other diseases in the boarding
schools. Report after report, especially those filed by Inspector
William J. McConnell, told of poorly ventilated, overcrowded, and

unsanitary conditions that existed at boarding schools across the country and that led to sickness and death. In 1901 McConnell even assembled testimony from physicians, who concluded that "tuberculosis was contagious, infectious, and unchecked in the Indian schools."[18]

Frustrated by the uncaring commissioner, McConnell resigned, but not until having compiled irrefutable data that proved an unhealthy school population was living in an unsanitary environment, daily spreading the terrible plague that was exacerbated by the school enrollment policy. Jones for the longest time believed that tuberculosis was hereditary; that Indians were simply predisposed to succumb to the malady; and that there was little the Indian Office could do to eradicate the disease.[19]

Fortunately, the secretary was not as ignorant as the commissioner. He directed Jones to answer McConnell and other Indian Service physicians who constantly bombarded his office with charges that tuberculosis was prevalent in the Indian schools. Unable to withstand the onslaughts and growing statistical information, Jones, to comply with the secretary's request, ordered the 1903 health survey. This study produced irrefutable evidence that tuberculosis was ravaging the young student population in the Indian schools.

Just before the opening of the Jicarilla Boarding School, the Bureau was totally aware and convinced of the incidence of tuberculosis as well as conditions that promoted the dissemination of the tubercle bacilli. Since the Jicarilla children were basically free of the disease, all efforts should have been made to maintain that status quo; instead it was as though the local government agency knowingly and deliberately led the young Jicarillas into a death trap.

In September 1903, a month before children were brought to the boarding school, the commissioner emphatically prohibited overcrowding in the schools, and especially in the dormitories. In his enlightenment, he warned the Bureau agencies that "Indian children should be educated, but should not be destroyed in the process. Health is the greatest consideration. Therefore if you cannot accommodate your present enrollment, without lowering the vitality of the students, a decrease should be made."[20]

Rules guarding the health of the students were to be strictly observed. Physicians were to examine students before they entered school, and all who were not medically sound were not to be admitted. During the course of the year, if students showed signs of tuberculosis, they were to be sent home.[21] With this policy clearly outlining the importance of safeguarding the health of children, there was little reason for the Jicarilla boarding school to have become a tuberculosis asylum.

The Jicarillas fully cooperated with the government by enrolling 130 children, but the dormitories accommodated only 125. An average of approximately 79 school-age children were not attending for various reasons, including ill health.[22] There was no enforcement of compulsory attendance so long as the dormitory was filled beyond capacity.

From 1903 to 1906 student enrollment increased from 130 to 165, 40 more than could be safely accommodated. A resolution to the problem of overcrowding was badly needed. Since 1903 the school had been subjected to hard use and had been poorly maintained.

Three years after the boarding school opened, the superintendent informed the commissioner that additional buildings were needed, especially sleeping quarters. Only 250 cubic feet of the 400 required of air space per student existed, making ventilation a serious problem. The acting commissioner, who was not kindly disposed toward the request, advised the superintendent that "the office advises you that at present it does not care to put up another building for your school. If pupils are overcrowded to the detriment of their health, the remedy is easy; reduce the enrollment."[23] The commissioner, however, suggested that he check into day schools to absorb the surplus.

In 1906 a trend developed within the ranks of the Bureau favoring day schools over boarding schools.[24] Day schools were a better testimonial to the Bureau's effort to sever the federal-Indian relationship, but they also helped to relieve the congestion at the boarding schools. The Bureau approved the establishment of two day schools on the Jicarilla Reservation. One, located near the agency in Dulce, had a capacity of twenty-five students; the other, which could accommodate about twenty, was located about eighteen miles south of Dulce at La Jara. They were opened in 1908 and 1909. Plans for a third day school at Horse Lake fell through because the local agency did not feel it was necessary, despite the fact that too many children were not in school for lack of space. The Horse Lake school could have served the large permanent settlement of about twenty Jicarilla families who lived nearby.

The day schools accommodated fewer than sixty students but they helped the congestion problem at the boarding school. By 1908, however, the deadly contagion had a grip on the student population. The overcrowded dormitories had helped to spread tuberculosis and caused other epidemics. The day schools only served as a radius of infection, which now reached into the community.

The Bureau had sent out voluminous numbers of circulars and memorandums pertaining to its tuberculosis campaign. Carrying out the directives was left to the superintendents, medical administrators, and boarding school personnel, who were often derelict in their duties.

Tuberculosis spread among the Jicarilla school pupils at about the same rate as it did among the general adult population. By 1912 it was a well-known fact that the Jicarilla students were living with the menace of the disease. In that year, a visiting member of the Tuberculosis Commission of the California State Board of Health reported that out of 116 Jicarilla children who were given a tuberculin test, in the age group from six to ten years old, out of forty-eight sixty-eight had been exposed to tuberculosis. Among the ten- to twenty-one-year olds, numbering sixty-eight in all, 95.5 percent had positive reactions. Among this same group there was also trachoma.[25] In a separate survey, Dr. Shoemaker found that 57 percent of all the children he examined (he did not specify the number) had tubercular enlargement, to some degree, of the glands of the neck. There were seven serious or advanced cases of trachoma out of the 85 students he examined for that disease.[26] It is quite clear that tuberculosis did not develop overnight and, therefore, that its rate of occurrence must have increased over the years.

In the years from 1903 to 1918, the lack of proper administration of the boarding school undoubtedly contributed to the spread of tuberculosis, although it alone cannot be blamed. The students were vulnerable from the moment they stepped into the school. From a background of poverty, parents sent their children to school hoping they would have a better chance of life. This was an illusion; the school became an accessory to misery.

Even if the school were efficiently managed, there was still the problem of economic poverty. As one nurse put it, no amount of technical skill and intelligent effort could have successfully supplanted the fundamental need of every human being for sufficient food and decent housing.[27] But by the same token, if the school had been more efficient and better funded, the tuberculosis problem would have been less devastating. Nonetheless, the school administration was negligent.

Contrary to policy, children were not always given physical examinations upon entrance. In 1911 the superintendent reported that "the general health condition at the school was not what it should have been, greatly caused by the Physician not making the required physical examinations of the pupils when entering school and not keeping in touch with their physical condition throughout the year."[28] Evidently the physican was more interested in private practice. This meant that the contagious students continued to roam freely among the well students, a situation that was not corrected as late as 1919 when a government inspector reported that "the first contributory cause of the spread of the disease was the association of the diseased with the healthy."[29]

The school plant never had adequate facilities to deal with the segregation of the afflicted. Dr. Shoemaker noted as late as 1917 that there were not facilities for segregating the sick from the well, as the hospital had only eight beds and there were no sleeping porches. Under these kinds of conditions, the medical staff was working at a great disadvantage.

The boarding school children were not getting proper medical attention, but it was even worse for the day school students, who were nursed in their homes. Medical care was so poor that in the spring of 1912, after a measles epidemic caused about fifteen fatalities, the La Jara school was closed for lack of students. Whatever children from La Jara wanted to go to school had to return to the boarding school.

The dormitory was constantly plagued with the need for repairs and inadequate space. During the first three years, overcrowding the building caused it to deteriorate. There was a chronic problem with the water system. The superintendent complained in 1910 that "our water system has been extremely unsanitary, muddy, and foul-smelling." Five years later it was reported that pupils were drinking unfiltered muddy water that frequently contained dead mice.[30] Dr. Shoemaker was not pleased when he found that the bathing facilities were so bad that the students had to use communal tubs for bathing. The toilets, he described as "impoverished."[31] He realized that it was these kinds of unsanitary living conditions that were often the source of the tuberculosis problem.

The lack of adequate staffing also contributed to the failing health of the children. The successful operation of the school depended on their help, and duties were imposed on physically weak children. The vocational training program was becoming a detriment to their health instead of being a positive learning experience for future self-reliant agriculturists. Girls were unable to carry the workload in the badly equipped laundry, and the boys often had to relieve them of their

Jicarilla men in ceremonial dress at the Ceremonial Relay Race held during the 1935 Annual Feast. Left to right: Alasko Tiznado, unidentified boy, Trucha Tafoya, and Jose Inez, all members of the Llanero band. Smithsonian Institution, National Anthropological Archives.

*1937 Jicarilla Apache Representative Tribal Council. Back row,
left to right: Antonio Veneno, Cevero Camarillo, Dotayo Veneno,
Juan Vigil, agency superintendent A.E. Stover, DeJesus Campos
Serafin, Garfield Velarde, Sr., Anastacio Julian, Norman TeCube,
Jack Ladd Vicenti. Front row, left to right: Agapito Baltazar,
Ramon Tafoya, Sixto Atote, Albert Velarde, Sr., Grover Vigil, John
Mills Baltazar, Sr., Laell Vicenti, Henry "Buster" Vicenti, Lindo
Vigil. Branch of Land Operations, Jicarilla Apache Agency, Dulce,
New Mexico.*

*An oil rig in the southern portion of the reservation, 1970. Oil has
been important to the tribe since the 1950s. Branch of Land
Operations, Jicarilla Apache Agency, Dulce, New Mexico.*

Recreation is a modern enterprise on the Jicarilla Reservation. Dulce Lake, 1962. Branch of Land Operations, Jicarilla Apache Agency, Dulce, New Mexico.

Typical Jicarilla home near Dulce, 1961. Branch of Land Operations, Jicarilla Apache Agency, Dulce, New Mexico.

Stockyards of Jicarilla Apache Livestock Enterprises, 1972. Branch
of Land Operations, Jicarilla Apache Agency, Dulce, New Mexico.

Tribal office building complex, Dulce, New Mexico, 1971. Branch
of Land Operations, Jicarilla Apache Agency, Dulce, New Mexico.

Jicarilla Apache tribal council in session, 1970. Jicarilla Apache
Chieftain.

A Dulce High School track team of the 1970s. Jicarilla Apache
Chieftain.

chores. Once an overzealous teacher decided some physically weak girls should take on ninety-minute cooking classes after school in the domestic cottage. The girls wisely complained to the principal, who decided that not only were the lessons too tiresome, infringing on their relaxation time, but that they were to learn to cook only during the regularly scheduled hours.[32] The doctor suggested that more employees be hired so the children could rest, but no new employees were hired and the students continued to labor.[33] In 1919 one inspector found that the conduct of the boarding school involved "the imposition of tasks that took heavy toll of health and life among a student body that was predisposed to tuberculosis."[34]

When the Jicarilla Agency was turned over to Chester E. Faris in 1918, a new era of hope began. The general health recovery program mandated that health be made a chief consideration, and that education be put in second place. By this time, at least 90 percent of all children of school age were considered tubercular and the remaining 10 percent were deemed physically incapable of attending.[35]

The dilapidated boarding school was closed for remodeling and was to be converted into the Southern Ute Mountain Sanatorium. The remodeling lasted from 1918 to 1921. During this period the children were sent home and were again without the benefits of education. This had its advantage because the marginally healthy children helped their parents set up the new family livestock businesses. This break gave the entire community an opportunity to make a start toward recovery from the devastating past.

The sanatorium was ready to receive patients in 1921. The government had entered into an agreement with the Dutch Reformed Church of America Mission to operate a school for the children. The government supplied food, clothing, school equipment, fuel, and the salary for one teacher. The rest of the personnel and the school plant were provided by the mission.[36] There were not more than five teachers at the mission throughout the 1920s and 1930s. Its dormitories could hold about seventy students. Students in grades one through eight were taught Bible studies, reading, writing, arithmetic, geography, and history. Domestic science was offered to the older girls, while the older boys received vocational training similar to that at the old boarding school.

There was no mad rush to take advantage of the sanatorium even though the vast majority of the children were in need of care. The previous years had seen nothing but despair and parents were not eager to place their children in another institution. Certainly the parents were ignoring their responsibilities, but the past experience had been too painful, and was not easily forgotten.

General enrollment was low in both institutions in the first two years, but the mission school enjoyed a rising enrollment because it was not associated with the old boarding school. In the eyes of the Jicarillas, it was not full of evil spirits and bad memories. In contrast, the sanatorium did not fill to capacity until 1928.

TABLE 2
Jicarilla Apache School Enrollment Figures, 1920–29

Year	Mission	Sanatorium	Total School Population
1920	30	0	174
1921	46	24	146
1922	50	30	155
1923	50	30	155
1924	46	40	145
1925	50	43	159
1926	64	54	171
1927	44	36?	178
1928	55	84	160
1929	48	85	169

SOURCE: Jicarilla School Census, Jic. Agency, *Narr. Annual Report*, 1920-29.

It seemed that doctors had little experience with running a sanatorium and treating tubercular patients. But this all changed in 1926 when Dr. Howard T. Cornell was hired at Jicarilla. Evidently he had more experience with tuberculosis than had the previous doctors.[37] With the hiring of Dr. Cornell, a serious regimen of annual medical examinations was instituted. Depending on the result of the examination, each child was assigned to either the mission or the sanatorium. As a result of this first examination, twenty-two children were transferred from the mission to the sanatorium and two were sent from the sanatorium to the mission.[38] This procedure marked the starting point for the arresting of tuberculosis on the Jicarilla Reservation.

In spite of the poor use that was made of the sanatorium, the superintendent did not force the parents to bring in their children for treatment. When the Bureau of Indian Affairs supervisor of education visited the facility in June 1922, he was surprised to find that all twenty-eight children were healthy, hearty, and well cared for. He inquired as to why healthy children were put in the sanatorium intended for tubercular children. Faris explained that so many children had died at the previous boarding school that the parents had a very strong prejudice against the place, and believed that, should the children be placed in the remodeled structure again, most of them would die. It was the psychology of the approach that concerned Faris. If the parents were forced to place their children there and the death rate again increased, this would only reinforce their fears and there would be no telling what this would do to any future educational efforts.[39]

Under the circumstances, Faris felt that the best strategy would be to accept the healthy children who enrolled on a voluntary basis and take the best possible care of them and build them up physically. This would demonstrate to the parents that the new institution was a good place for their sick children. This was a good strategy, and it showed a rare understanding of Indian reasoning, an understanding few superintendents had had up to this time.

Faris's plan must have been condoned—or perhaps nothing was done to the contrary because of the usual inertia of the Bureau. By 1925 more parents were convinced of the potential benefit of the sanatorium and they brought in more children.

The placement of students in either the mission school or the sanatorium was left completely up to the parents, but this voluntary and lax approach had its problems. The mission school was the preference, but as a consequence the healthy children were again exposed to children with tuberculosis, while the sanatorium was operating at half its capacity. This worried visiting medical authorities. They were possibly responsible for having Bureau directives sent out to the agency to enforce the attendance of all eligible children at either the mission or sanatorium, with orders to separate the sick from the healthy.[40]

The sanatorium not only provided medical care, rest, and proper nourishment, but it also carried out a primary educational program for children from grades one to four. Most of the patients were under the age of twelve and their length of hospitalization was between two and six years.

For the children who were not bed cases, the daily routine consisted of attendance in the classrooms from 8:30 to 11:30 A.M. After lunch, from 1:00 to 3:00 they were required to rest. Light work was assigned to the stronger ones, while the others participated in supervised indoor recreation. Dinner was served at 5:00. During the summer months, classes were not in session and the children spent the morning hours outdoors. In the afternoon all children underwent heliotherapy; that is, sitting or playing in the sun in bathing suits.[41] Once a month parents and relatives were permitted to visit. The visiting days usually coincided with the days rations were issued. If the young patients were not too ill, they were allowed a week's vacation at home in June.

The procedural administration of the sanatorium was well established by the late 1920s. But by this time it began to experience problems with the facilities; evidently the previous difficulties with the water system, worn out laundry, and so forth, had not been solved during the remodeling.[42] The structural problems hindered the staff and patients, but it seemed also that the staff had settled perhaps too comfortably into routine matters. Just as the old boarding school had been cited as contributing to the spread of tuberculosis, so the practices at the sanatorium were also questioned. In 1933 a woman employee who was a bit more concerned than her colleagues created a stir that received the attention of the national press and a few senators, and an investigation was ordered. She charged that the management of the sanatorium was encouraging the spread of the disease rather than curtailing it. She complained about the quality of care and food that the children were receiving, the unsanitary conditions, and the medical procedures used by the physician. The last involved the annual examinations given to all children: there were too many healthy children unnecessarily and capriciously placed in the hospital. She related one incident when a six-year-old girl was brought in for an examination. She was found to have a clean bill of health, but minutes before the final order was given, the father of the child remarked that he did not want his daughter put in the sanatorium. "Dr. Cornell put —— to bed as he did not want an Indian to dictate to him what he, the Doctor, could do."[43]

The woman employee had sent her letters to the commissioner and the vice-president of the United States. After the Bureau was called down, an inspector was sent to investigate and the complaints were deemed exaggerated.[44] In a letter from the commissioner to the vice-president, the charges were said to contain only a minor element of truth. The employee, from past experience, expected this would happen. Whenever there was to be an inspection or investigation, the employees were alerted and prepared for it. To this employee, the inspections were self-defeating.

This one incident may or may not have been exaggerated, but later reports and letters tended to support her charges. During May and April 1934, a health survey was taken in Dulce, specifically to determine the rate of tuberculosis among the Jicarillas. A total of 567, or 88 percent, of the Apaches participated in this survey. The Mantoux tests were administered to 226 children who were patients at the sanatorium, or students at the mission and public schools, as well as to 45 reservation children who were not in school. One of the more startling findings of this survey, which tended to support the employee's allegations, was that "only 39.4 percent of the sanatorium children had positive Mantoux reactions and . . . 53.5 percent of the patients in that sanatorium were found to be free from tuberculosis."[45] One reason for the number of nontubercular children at the sanatorium was that if children showed signs of fatigue, rapid pulse, malnourishment, or high temperature during the preschool examination, they were admitted.

The medical director in charge of the survey recommended that those patients who were eligible for discharge be sent to the mission, and that the sanatorium be conducted strictly as a hospital facility. It was imperative that only sick patients be admitted. If it were to serve as a "preventorium" as well, then at least there should be a separate ward.

It was also discovered that the mission school was filled to capacity and that children had been transferred to the sanatorium to relieve the overcrowding.[46] As the health improved, the population began to grow and more children attended school, which is why the mission school was overburdened. The following combined school enrollment figures tell the story:

Year	Enrollment
1931	208
1932	157
1933	195
1934	n.a.
1935	172
1936	n.a.
1937	238
1938	227
1939	246

In 1932 ten youngsters received tuition support to attend the local county-operated school in Dulce. Every effort was made to have the Jicarillas take advantage of nonreservation schools. The superintendent felt that the educational standards of off-reservation schools were superior to those of Dulce, but the majority continued to attend either the mission school or the sanatorium.[47]

The few students who attended the local public school made little difference to the mission, which by 1935 had exceeded its capacity by twenty students. No provisions were made by the mission board or the government for additional buildings. In that year the superintendent wrote that "the gradual increase in enrollment due to the continued success of the department of health, finds the Mission school rooms too crowded, as well as the dormitories, with a number of children not in school for lack of room. The teaching personnel is too small for the number of scholars, and the rooms inadequate in size and equipment."[48] Several of the school census reports indicated that children were sent home for lack of dormitory space.

In 1936 the school enrollment hit an all-time high. Fortunately, by this time the agency had found vacant buildings to use as classrooms, and had established the Jicarilla Apache Consolidated Day School. The mission still furnished the dormitories. The new arrangements between the agency and the mission caused another kind of problem for the children: that of divided authority. The superintendent acknowledged that the mission workers were very conscientious, but the children were unhappy and ran away because "the child is frequently placed in a difficult position when faced with the problem of choosing between the contradictory points of view of the mission workers and the school authorities."[49] Perhaps the superintendent was referring to the schism between the strict religious control that the mission had over the students and the secular learning that was emphasized at the school.

The mission exercised a strong influence over the Jicarillas not only because it had a monopoly over education for over two decades, but also because the Indian Office did not provide the people with community service facilities. The church filled this void and offered services such as performance of marriages and funerals, vacation Bible studies, recreational programs, and clothing drives for all newborn babies. The church became a fixture in the lives of most Jicarillas; it served as a place to turn when the government was unresponsive. It also had a way of ingratiating itself with the people. Parents were allowed to stay overnight at the mission at no charge when they had traveled long distances by wagons to get to town. Christmas gifts were given to all the people and they were appreciated since most were so poor.

The mission's influence was not curbed by its missionary and community activities. The minister, Denton Simms, became a leading figure in the community. His son married one of Emmitt Wirt's daughters and the two became a powerful duo. They were called upon to testify during investigations, served as advocates for the tribe, accompanied agency officials to important meetings, and in these ways they were able to influence affairs on the reservation.

While the health of the children was gradually getting better, community health was not. The quality of Indian health care, especially with regard to eradicating tuberculosis (which was decreasing) did not meet the expectations of the health authorities. In 1937, two medical directors from the Indian Health Department and the Jicarilla superintendent expressed their dissatisfaction with the persistence of tuberculosis among the adults. For one thing, no effort was being made to hospitalize the adults who had active cases of the disease. One of the medical directors commented: "I come away with the feeling that the medical service at Dulce is of a low grade country practice type with not very much consideration given to modern medicine and very little to public health as such."[50] The other agreed: "I am in entire agreement with you regarding the TB problem at Jicarilla. Your observations coincide with mine when I was there about a year ago. I wanted to arrange for Dr. Cornell's transfer but for various reasons this could not be done at that time."[51]

Awareness of the lack of good medical care might have prompted the relocation of the agency hospital near the sanatorium for better coordination of service. The old hospital became a classroom building for the government day school, which also helped in consolidating the school complex at one location.

The problem of overcrowding at the mission was solved in 1940 when two new dormitories with a capacity of 250 students were built just below the sanatorium. In that year, the administration decided that the pathological enemy had been conquered, and the remaining patients were either transferred to the hospital, or, if their conditions were still critical, they were taken to the Indian sanatorium in Albuquerque. The sanatorium at Dulce was then converted into another dormitory, with space left over for more classrooms and living quarters for some employees. With this change, the schools were no longer congested. In addition, other facilities, a school gymnasium, and a large playground were built.

TABLE 3
Jicarilla Apache Schools
Average Attendance Figures

Year	Boarding	Day	Total
1943–44	...	...	164
1944–45	162	15	177
1945–46	200	16	216
1946–47	202	24	226
1947–48	207	33	240
1948–	207.32	41.43	248.75
(First 9 weeks)			

SOURCE: Jicarilla Apache Agency School Program, November 30, 1948, RG 75, Jic. Agency CCF, No. 806, 1948, FRC, Suitland.

The 1940s presented a complete contrast to previous years in that progress was visible. Student enrollment soared (see table 3) and health was no longer a pressing problem. Finally, the Jicarillas proudly produced a number of high school graduates.

The Jicarillas' journey toward education required patience and perseverance in coping with hardship and suffering. The search for knowledge could have been less agonizing had it been possible to separate it from its interrelationship with the rest of Jicarilla society. The socioeconomic pattern that prevailed after 1887 dictated the course of education. Without proper social and economic environments, the formal learning experience was handicapped. The government, through its slipshod and laggard manner in administering its educational responsibilities, served to prolong its guardianship over the Jicarilla Apaches.

Chapter 8
The Impact of the Indian
Reorganization Act: 1934–49

The Wheeler-Howard Act of June 15, 1934, also known as the Indian Reorganization Act, began a new era for many tribes throughout the United States, among them the Jicarilla Apaches, who accepted the provisions of this act on August 3, 1937. The impact of this new legislation on the reservation economy and political organization was practically immediate. The tribe adopted a constitution, bylaws, and a corporate charter that made it possible to implement other IRA programs: the relinquishing of allotments, the purchase of the Wirt Trading Post, the acquisition of livestock, and the adoption of conservation programs. All of this amounted to a visible increase in individual and tribal income, which, in turn, improved social conditions on the reservation. As a result, the Jicarillas changed from a dying, poverty-stricken race to a prosperous people with a thriving livestock economy.

The Indian Reorganization Act was passed in the hope of reversing the trend started by the Dawes Act of 1887. It was given additional support by the findings of congressional investigations and surveys conducted before 1934. Specifically, it was passed in response to the recommendations of the Meriam Report of 1928, which condemned the Dawes Act and other federal Indian policies that had contributed to the dire economic and social conditions prevalent on Indian reservations.

The basic purposes of the Indian Reorganization Act were (1) to improve the economic condition of the Indians by protecting and preserving their remaining resources, enlarging their land base, and encouraging a more effective use of all land resources; (2) to ensure the political and civic emancipation of the Indians by increasing their participation in their own affairs, including the assumption of increased authority and responsibility; and (3) to foster Indian ethical, spiritual, and cultural values through the improvement of Indian education.

In order to improve Indian economic conditions, the Bureau of Indian Affairs, under the direction of Commissioner John Collier, laid down the following policies relating to land: no more lands were to be allotted or fee patents issued, and there were to be no more sales of allotted and inherited lands. Instead, there was to be an active program of acquiring land through purchase with gratuity and tribal funds. For the more effective use of Indian resources by the Indians themselves there was to be a consolidation of their lands, especially pasture and timber lands, and fractional heirship interests were to be consolidated into usable units. As much individual land as possible was brought into tribal ownership through exchange and purchase. Allotments were to be exchanged for life assignments to the land based on beneficial use.

Provisions for adequate credit funds from gratuity appropriations and tribal funds were to be stimulated. Credit funds were to be used for productive purposes instead of for relief and appeasement. Leasing of Indian agricultural and grazing lands was to be discouraged. Emphasis was laid on the creation of a broader production base instead of concentrating on the existing narrow one. Cooperative and corporate productive enterprises were to have priority over individual ones. All Indian lands were also to be used in accordance with principles of soil conservation and erosion control.

Political emancipation of the Indians was to be accomplished by organizing the Indian tribes and then transferring to them responsibility and authority in areas such as the administration of justice by the establishment of Indian tribal courts and judicial codes. Where Indian communities were widely scattered, efforts were to be made to consolidate them. Tribal members were also given preference for jobs in the Indian Service.

To generate a larger sense of responsibility along with greater authority, spiritual emancipation was to be fostered by a retreat from benevolent paternalism. Liberalized and modernized educational methods were to be used with the objective of stimulating Indian initiative. Racial pride and the preservation of native culture were to be encouraged, and the constitutional rights of free speech, free assembly, and freedom of worship were guaranteed. Indian arts and crafts were to be improved both as a means of self-expression and as a source of revenue.[1]

The Indian Reorganization Act was primarily directed toward Indians who desired land or who had some land holdings that could be consolidated. Its emphasis was undoubtedly economic improvement, social enhancement being only a secondary consideration. Economic advancement hinged to a large degree on the land base, without which the IRA really could not be implemented. On the Jicarilla Apache Reservation, all the necessary prerequisite conditions were present.

At the turn of the century, legislation had provided for the sale of timber on the Jicarilla Reservation. The money realized from the sale had been used to purchase livestock for eventual distribution to individual Jicarillas on a per capita basis. By the 1920s, when more funds became available from the proceeds of timber, several more distributions of sheep were made. To provide for the increasing herds, the southern portion of the reservation was added by Executive Order in 1908. By the 1930s, the Jicarillas already had livestock and thousands of acres of grazing lands at their disposal.

In 1932 a severe winter wiped out a large portion of the herds and the government generously extended a loan for their replenishment. Within a few years the Jicarillas had paid off this loan; but more important, they had established a good credit record with the government. Later when they again applied for a loan through the revolving credit fund, this previous experience was a valuable asset. The government knew that the Jicarillas not only had the ability, but that they were willing to pay their debts. Hence, the Jicarillas had a solid foundation to build on when the IRA was enacted, so their reservation became a special target for the Collier administration.

Collier was aware of the Jicarilla situation, and was keenly interested in getting tribal support for the act. Shortly before the act came up for a vote in Congress, administration representatives came to the reservation to survey conditions and assess the attitudes of the Jicarillas toward the pending legislation. The officials learned that the Jicarillas did not support the bill; neither did they want to come under its provisions.

In addition to sending out representatives, Collier flooded all agencies with circulars designed to explain and clarify the provisions of the bill to agency superintendents and tribal leaders. Superintendent

Charles L. Graves of the Jicarilla Apache Agency received one such circular in February 1934. Graves apparently was not very enthusiastic about the bill, but he did report to Collier that the Jicarillas did not have a tribal council or any other governmental organization. After interviewing the leading members of the tribe, he found that the consensus was that reorganization was not possible or advisable, especially during the early spring season when the men were busy attending to their livestock. More important, the Jicarillas felt that formal organization was possible only if they could first settle their own grievances.[2] Tribal factions and conflicts were strong and the Jicarillas were aware that these schisms would be stumbling blocks to the acceptance of the IRA.

Collier was not impressed by this lame excuse and again urged Graves to bring the Jicarilla leaders together to reconsider the new legislation, and to distribute more literature. This Graves did in March 1934. He traveled with the leaders to a conference in Santa Fe to meet with anthropologist Oliver La Farge and former agency superintendent Chester E. Faris, who served as a persuasive liaison between the Jicarillas and the commissioner. Accompanying the Jicarilla delegation were Emmitt Wirt, the post trader, and the Reverend J. Denton Simms of the Dutch Reformed Church.

Although the bill was thoroughly explained by Mr. La Farge, this did not change the Jicarillas' position. The Jicarillas definitely decided they were not ready for self-government and did not wish to assume any responsibilities. Taking out a charter did not seem to interest them, and they were emphatically against the cancellation of their allotments. This position was maintained by the leaders throughout the next several years.[3]

The main single reason for the Jicarillas' opposition to the reorganization bill was linked to the issue of the cancellation of allotments. The loss of land as a direct consequence of the Dawes Act had not been a problem on the Jicarilla Reservation. Many Jicarillas had been looking forward to getting title to their lands and they did not take well to this reversal in Indian policy. For these reasons, they did not feel compelled to support the bill. As a matter of fact, some believed that this new legislation would inevitably lead to the loss of their lands because a patent meant that one had title to the land, while community land ownership under Executive Order status was too uncertain. Congress could not be trusted and a mere abrogation of an Executive Order, as in 1874 and 1881, which still rankled in the memory of some members of the tribe, would mean the loss of lands.[4]

Collier was aware of the Jicarilla opposition to the cancellation of allotments. Since this was an important feature of the bill, and it was clear that Collier was not getting an overwhelming response from Indians throughout the United States, he needed the support of the Jicarillas. He sent Faris to the reservation in April 1934 to convince them that the cancellation was in their best interest. Faris tried to convince them that "the main purpose of the bill . . . was the prohibition against the alienation of land, individual or tribal."[5] Faris told Collier that the Jicarillas were definitely in support of the bill, which was not true, but with this assurance Collier turned his attention to other tribes.

The issue concerning the cancellation of allotments was dropped in favor of other concerns and remained unresolved for the next several years. Collier's immediate interest in the Jicarillas petered out as support for his bill increased within Congress and its passage was assured. Collier took the position that after the bill was passed it would be only a matter of time until the Jicarillas would accept its provisions. He believed that community ownership was desirable on the Jicarilla Reservation, and that he could convince them of it. He knew that once the bill was passed, it would permit community acquisition of all lands through the process of relinquishment, since it provided for compulsory relinquishment should some Indians refuse to comply voluntarily.[6] Collier must have calculated that if a formal government was established and a charter adopted everything else would fall into place. His hunch proved to be correct.

For the next two years, Collier's administration directed its efforts toward the acquisition of lands within the boundaries of the Jicarilla Apache Reservation, perhaps as an incentive to the Jicarillas. Throughout 1935 and 1936, the Bureau of Indian Affairs was busy looking into the purchase of some 2,959.01 acres of land at an appraised value of $66,381.40.[7] These lands were owned by thirteen different non-Indian individuals. The majority had inherited them from their parents or relatives who had homesteaded before 1887. These owners had held onto their properties even though they had had the chance to sell out to the Jicarillas from time to time. In the past, the presence of these owners had created problems, some of which the purchase of their lands would solve. For example, the acquisition of these tracts would not only increase the amount of arable land, but it would stop the trespassing of livestock on Indian lands and lessen the traffic in liquor. The process of land acquisition was time-consuming, but the effort by the government was now a reality. Under the appropriation act of 1935, most of the holdings were bought, with the exception of about five, including the Wirt holdings and the Gómez estate.[8] The Wirt lands were later sold as part of the trading post purchase.

The goodwill created among the Jicarillas by this action was just what Collier had in mind. It showed them that the government was interested in their well-being and economic progress. Collier's next move was to get an actual acceptance of the act. Again he sent out representatives to make last-minute evaluations of the tenor of opinion on the reservation. This time there were some surprises.

Collier had great faith in the advice and opinions of anthropologists, and used many of these scholars to implement his programs. Among these was Morris E. Opler, whose opinions and observations about the untenable situation on the Jicarilla Reservation received considerable attention in Washington.

Opler's report stemmed from his visit to the reservation during 1934 for a study on Apache culture. The duration of his visit made it possible for him to get fairly well acquainted with the people and their situation. The main point of his report was that the Jicarilla reservation was under the absolute control of Emmitt Wirt, the post trader, and his son-in-law's father, J. Denton Simms. Both of these men had a profound influence on the Jicarillas; and they had become well-entrenched over the past decades. Wirt's control amounted to an economic stranglehold; he had a virtual monopoly on trading with the Indians due to their physical isolation. By extending credit, he bound them to his store through indebtedness. They were penalized severely for any deviation in their trading patterns. Since he charged high prices, most of the government employees did not trade with him. Wirt, according to Opler, was dictatorial and ruthless. He not only had complete economic control over the Indians, but he controlled agency affairs as well.[9] His control was made possible partly because of his political connections with the Republican party of southern Colorado and northern New Mexico, and partly because of his long acquaintance with and residence on the reservation.

United States field representative Louis Balsam was sent out by Collier to inspect this situation Opler had reported. After overcoming some initial skepticism, he virtually confirmed Opler's observations. Balsam was a bit more poignant and blunt about his findings. He wrote that Wirt's power rested upon a rather strong base: his ability to get what he wanted from congressmen and governors; for this reason he encountered no opposition. According to Balsam, it was Wirt himself who told him, "When Graves left I began to worry that they might send me a 'crackpot' down here as superintendent, so I wrote Faris a letter to be sure we got the right kind. Faris did not answer so to make sure I had Jack Dempsey, the Senator, go in to see Mr. Collier. Right away Dempsey wrote me that he had seen the Commissioner and that no one would be appointed Superintendent here who did not meet with my approval"[10] Since A. E. Stover, the next superintendent, met with Wirt's approval, he got the appointment over another man from Montana.[11]

Another story that Wirt told Balsam that illustrated his power had to do with the money advanced to the Jicarillas in the aftermath of the severe winter of 1931. Wirt and Graves, so the story went, had gone to Washington and obtained an outright grant. "Mr. Graves has said that due entirely to my pressure upon Senator Sam Bratton and Commissioner Rhoads a bill was put through Congress giving Mr. Graves the power to spend that $80,000 free and without red tape as he saw fit. Mr. Graves then turned the bulk over to me and I personally went out and bought his sheep for him. Within two years the Indians had paid off my debt."[12]

The reports of Opler and Balsam perhaps had some truth in them, although, interestingly, their opinions are in direct contrast to those popularly held about Wirt. Occasionally, similar views are found in some of the pre-1934 inspection reports. Faris perhaps best reflected what Jicarillas and former associates of Wirt preferred to think. Faris sums it up this way: "The story of the Jicarillas cannot be divorced from Emmitt Wirt. He came to the reservation in 1889. He was gruff and determined to the outside, but there is an interchange of sympathy and understanding with the Indians."[13] Faris also credits Wirt with urging the southern addition to the reservation in 1907–8 against aggravated popular feeling when the president was besieged with demands that this land be restored to the public domain. Without question, according to Faris, Wirt was the deciding factor in the outcome in spite of his party affiliation. Faris went on to credit him with the consistent opposition to the sale of allotments and inherited estates, even when he had money at hand with which he might have acquired a majority of such lands at a minimal figure.[14]

Wirt was of particular interest to the Collier administration. In part, the success and adoption of the act hinged on this man's support; at least, his power had to be circumvented. Wirt's noncommittal and vague attitude toward the IRA kept the administration guessing. Collier wanted to size up his attitude without alienating him in case this elderly man still had the power attributed to him in the reports. Another and more important reason for this keen interest in Wirt was that once the Jicarillas organized a formal government and took out a charter, the purchase of the old trader's store was on their agenda. Without Wirt's cooperation, this might not be possible.[15]

The more immediate concern of Collier was, of course, getting the Jicarillas to accept the IRA so that a program of economic development could begin. In spite of initial opposition, the Jicarillas gradually yielded to the tactful pressure applied by the administration, and by 1936 there was a willingness to accept the IRA. In February 1937, the first draft of the proposed "Jicarilla Apache Constitution and By-Laws," similar to other tribal constitutions, was circulating among concerned personnel for review and comments. After it was approved by officialdom, an election was held on July 3, 1937, in which the constitution was overwhelmingly accepted and ratified by the voters, 247 to 2. It was approved by the secretary of the interior a month later, on August 4, 1937.[16]

The new constitution provided for a tribal government to consist of a representative tribal council of eighteen members from the six districts on the reservation: La Jara area was district one; Boulder and Stinking Lake area was district two; Horse Lake and Burns Canyon were districts three and four, respectively; district five covered the La Juita and Carracus area; and the largest areas, Dulce and Dulce Lake, made up district six. All of these districts were located in the northern part of the reservation because that was where the Jicarillas had their permanent homes. A councilman had to live within the district he represented and he had to be at least twenty-eight years old. Initially, half of the members of the council, those who received the largest number of votes, were to serve for four years and the other half for only two years. Thereafter, elections were to be held every two years for half the council.

Members of the Jicarilla Apache Tribe who were twenty-one or older could cast ballots in their respective districts. Membership in the tribe was defined as follows: it included all persons of Indian blood whose names appeared on the official census roll of 1937 of the Jicarilla Apache Tribe, and all children of one-fourth or more Indian blood not affiliated with another tribe, born after the completion of the 1937 census roll, as well as any member of the tribe resident on the Jicarilla Reservation. Membership by adoption could be acquired by a three-fourths majority vote of the tribal council and the approval of the secretary of the interior. All members were granted equal rights to life, liberty, industrial pursuits, and the economic resources and activities of the tribe. No person could be denied the right to worship as he pleased, to speak or write his opinions, assemble with others, or to petition for the redress of grievances.

Regular voting was to take place within the summer season immediately following the approval of the constitution. The commissioner of Indian affairs was to call and supervise the first election and thereafter the council in office was to prescribe in democratic fashion when and where the elections were to take place.

Once a council was elected, the newly installed officials were to select from among themselves an executive committee consisting of five members. Both the general council and the executive committee were to meet twice a year, on the first Saturday of May and the first Saturday of October, in Dulce. Ten members constituted a quorum for the council and three were required for the executive committee. Vacancies were to be filled at the next election, but if no regular election occurred within six months, the council was to call a special one. Any tribal member could be removed from the council for improper conduct or neglect of duty by a three-fourths vote of the council.

This constitution definitely reflected the spirit of the IRA. The administration saw to it that the specific provisions within the act were also written into the various tribal constitutions so as not to leave any doubts. In Article VI, Section Two, the Jicarilla tribal council was given the power to use and manage the unallotted land of the reservation not reserved for government purposes, in conformity with the regulation of the secretary of the interior for the protection of natural resources. The council was to use the lands for the benefit of the tribal members and in any land transaction, the Jicarillas were to be given preference. Individuals of the tribe could be assigned land for their needs. Any land-use codes and regulations needed the approval of the secretary of the interior.

One of the main ideas of the IRA was to preserve the Indian tribes as cultural entities, and this was reflected in the Jicarilla constitution. The council had the power to expend funds for the good of the entire tribe, for its own expenses, and to extend aid to the needy. In deference to tradition, the council was accorded the duty of preserving peace and order. Still reflecting the spirit of the IRA, it was clearly stated in the constitution that all resolutions and regulations passed by the council were subject to review by the secretary of the interior (after the superintendent had approved or disapproved them within ten days).

In Article VIII another important concept of IRA was stressed. The ownership of land was deemed inalienable except to the tribe or between members. All natural resources were subject to conservation practices and had to be developed for industrial or other purposes consistent with the general welfare of the tribe. Per capita payments were to be made only with the consent of 75 percent of the voters and with the approval of the secretary.

The constitution also ensured that some of the anticipated IRA programs were given proper authority. Article IX granted the tribe the power to maintain a flock of sheep for the care of the needy.

An important feature, that of the amendment process, was not neglected. A majority of voters could get the secretary to call an election for that purpose. For an amendment to be approved, at least 30 percent of the voters had to cast ballots and a majority of this number was needed for approval. The council could also request that an election be called. The constitution as written remained the basis of tribal government for the next two decades.

The members of the first representative Tribal Council according to their districts and clan affiliations were as follows:

District One—La Jara:
Garfield Velarde, Ollero
Lindo Vigil, Ollero
Henry Ladd Vicenti, Ollero
Juan Vigil, Ollero
District Two—Burns Canyon:
John Mills Baltazar, Llanero
Herbert L. Vicenti, Llanero
District Three—Horse Lake:
Sixto Atole, Llanero
Albert Velarde, Ollero
District Four—Stinking Lake and Boulder Lake:
Grover Vigil, Ollero
Norman TeCube, Ollero
District Five—Carracus and La Juita:
Antonio Veneno, Llanero
Dotayo Veneno, Llanero
District Six—Dulce and Dulce Lake:
Laell Vicenti, Ollero
Anastacio Julián, Llanero

Ramón Tafoya, Llanero
Cevero Caramillo, Llanero
DeJesús Campos Serafín, Ollero
Agapito Baltazar, Llanero.

This new government was truly representative of Jicarilla society. The election districts were set up to correlate with the settlements or local groups defined by the peoples themselves. The Jicarillas had a tendency to live with or near their own bandsmen, and they named their people according to the geographic area they inhabited. For example, those who lived in district one were referred to as La Jara people; the Canyon people lived at Burns Canyon; and the Sagebrush people were from district five. Those who lived near the agency were called "Around the House" people, the house being the agency headquarters. They were considered a group apart because they were Ollero and Llanero intermixed and had no special leader. It was well known which districts were Ollero, which were Llanero, and which were mixed.[17]

The Jicarillas were still a conservative people in 1936, the majority of them adhering to traditional customs and religion. The first elected council was quite representative of the majority. About five of the members were traditional leaders whose fathers were chiefs or headmen. For example, Anastacio Julián was the son of a former chief of one Llanero clan, Juan Julián. Albert Velarde was the son of the Ollero chief Huerito Mundo, and the Vicentis and Vigils also represented the descendants of Augustine Vigil and Vicentito. Ramón Tafoya and Dotayo Veneno also came from a family closely related to the family of San Pablo and Santiago Largo, former Llanero chiefs.

The majority of the leaders also represented the religious beliefs of the people. They were men who practiced and appreciated their Apache religion. Out of the eighteen members, ten were either medicine men of one kind or another, or spiritual leaders. These ten were Garfield Verlarde; Lindo, Juan, and Grover Vigil; Sixto Atole; Dotayo Veneno; DeJesús Campos Serafín; Ramón Tafoya; Cevero Caramillo; and Anastacio Julián. Not all of them were active at the time of their election, but their later service as medicine men or participation as spiritual leaders indicated their strong belief in, and commitment to, the religion of their ancestors. The remaining seven were not necessarily nonbelievers; however, they were neither as active nor as visible as the rest. They, too, represented a good number of Jicarillas with similar persuasions on religious matters. This large number of

Jicarilla men who believed in their religion was an indication that the tribe was not only well represented traditionally, but also that in spite of their exposure to missionary activity, the majority had not completely given up their own beliefs.

There are some indications that might lead one to believe the council less representative than it actually was. If representation were based on family groupings, it would seem that there was overrepresentation of four to five families. There were three Vigil brothers, two Baltazar brothers, two Vicenti brothers, two Veneno brothers, and a Velarde uncle and nephew in the council—a total of eleven closely related individuals. It is difficult to draw any valid conclusions from this arrangement, because when one analyzes the entire population, all Jicarillas are related in one way or another. Besides, the Vigils and Vicentis represented a good number of the Jicarilla population. Viewed from the traditional standpoint, brothers were usually the leaders of certain clans, so it was not unusual to have so many brothers on the council. It was also left up to the people to pick their own leaders and they chose brothers knowingly. Also, many of the brothers came from different districts.

When the distribution of wealth is considered, the council must be viewed in an entirely different light. Based on the Jicarilla agency's fiscal report of December 31, 1936, there were 702 Jicarillas, divided into 214 families. The average per-capita income was $580.55, which came from salaries and the sale of cattle, lambs, wool, goats, hay, grain, vegetables, and baskets. In determining the relative wealth of the councilmen, the base used was income from sheep and cattle alone, since that was the primary source of income on the reservation. Sheep raising was the number one industry and ewes were the stabilizing factors in a herd, so only their numbers were used to figure how many were owned by the councilmen. There was a total of 21,422 ewes on the reservation. The seventeen council members owned approximately one-fourth of this number, or 5,586. Records of one member, Herbert L. Vicenti, were not available. Nine members had more than the average income from the sale of lambs and wool alone, and six of those nine also owned cattle, as did other members of the council. Together these nine men owned 345 head of cattle, almost half of the 771 head on the reservation. Also, on the reservation, there were only twenty-two cattlemen.

The five wealthiest men on the reservation in 1936, John Mills Baltazar, DeJesús Campos Serafín, Grover Vigil, Lindo Vigil, and Laell

Vicenti, were on the council. These men were not always the wealthiest on the reservation, but they were never considered poor by Jicarilla standards. Only the Vigils represented inherited wealth. When the Jicarillas returned from the Mescalero Apache Reservation in 1886–87, Augustine Vigil, the patriarch, was the only one who could have been considered well-off. He had a large herd of sheep and horses. He was able to hold on to his wealth and increase his holdings as time went on.[18] Only two men on the council could be considered poor; they had fewer than seventy head of sheep each. The remaining had moderate to medium-high incomes.

One conclusion that may be drawn is that the ability to accumulate wealth was an indication of motivation, incentive, and perhaps leadership, and, as in other societies, it was rewarded. Or one can conclude that this council, like many other governing bodies, was made up of the rich, who had vested interests in the government. The composition of this Jicarilla body might upset the popular belief that among Indians, the poorer ones were usually the traditionalists and the rich ones were the progressives, and that it was the traditional Indians who practiced ancestral religion and customs, whereas progressives did not. This certainly was not the case with the Jicarillas. It was their belief that one's ability to obtain economic wealth was enhanced by retaining one's religion. This conviction, however, became the exception rather than the rule as time went on.

In terms of educational background, five of the older, traditional leaders who were members of the council had had no formal schooling. Their practical experience, however, compensated for their lack of educational training. The remaining thirteen had been to school at least through the sixth grade. The best educated councilor was Norman TeCube, who had finished high school and attended Sherman Institute in California. He was also the youngest member of the council and served as its interpreter. The average age was about fifty years, ranging from TeCube, who was about thirty, to Garfield Velarde, the dean of the council at eighty-two.

This first council chose Agapito Baltazar as its chairman. There was no specific provision for this position in the constitution, but the council did have the power to elect its own officers. Baltazar remained chairman until his death in 1941. He was succeeded by his brother John Mills, who served in that office until 1950.

The council was a good one. It was responsive to the needs of all the people, cautious in its spending, and deliberate in its decisions. Its main problem was the lack of adequate education that was badly needed to run the affairs of an increasingly complex corporation. This made the councilmen rely heavily on the superintendents, who at times were all-knowing benevolent father figures. Toward the end of the 1940s, these councilmen were unjustly being labeled as too traditional and too conservative. They were pushed aside by the superintendents, who wanted more "progressive" and younger men. To them these younger "progressives," regardless of intellect or experience, were synonymous with progress. These "progressives" seemed more willing to go along with the superintendent in all that he wanted or ordered. The older leaders did not go along as easily and this presented a problem for the agency.

One indication of how the first councilmen worked is found in a letter from Stover to Collier in 1938.

I would like to present you a peculiarity of tribal-unit action among the Jicarilla Apaches which I have never known before among any tribe that I have worked with in my twenty years in the service: of the numerous problems I have laid before this tribe and their council for consideration, there has never been a problem presented on which the Indians did not have a difference of opinion . . . discussions were carried on between members at every instance. Yet after complete discussion among the tribe you will note that every decision has been unanimous. This . . . represents good Indian leadership and a willingness to let the majority rule. [19]

These men not only were political but spiritual leaders, charged with maintaining law and order. The job they did was unsurpassed. In the 1944 annual narrative report, the superintendent stated: "Since these Indians organized under the Indian Reorganization Act and have come cooperatively into the program of managing their own affairs, I have known of no other persons in the country where problems of Law and Order have been so reduced in importance."[20] Unfortunately the situation did not remain this way much longer. The 1950s saw the rise of petty crime on the reservation, and this has continued.

Although at first the Jicarillas rejected the IRA, once they accepted its terms, they were ensured a vital economic pattern of growth. The Jicarillas became a model for which Collier often congratulated both himself and Stover. The accomplishments did not go unpublicized and with good reason, for the Jicarillas entered into an unmatched era of economic development. The establishment of the tribal government was only the necessary beginning.

One of the first items of business was taking out a corporate charter.[21] On September 4, 1937, the Jicarillas voted to become a chartered federal corporation under the name of Jicarilla Apache Tribe, composed of all members of the tribe. The tribal council was to act as the governing board with the powers to own, hold, manage, operate, and dispose of real and personal property, subject to certain limitations, such as the prohibition of the sale or mortgage of any lands within the Jicarilla Reservation. All natural resources were to be used cautiously and they were to be protected through the employment of conservation practices. The corporation was not to sign any leases involving a period longer than ten years except mineral leases, or those requiring substantial improvements to land. All contracts were to be approved by the secretary of the interior. This charter surely reflected the spirit of the IRA.

The corporation was also empowered to borrow funds from the revolving credit fund and deposit tribal funds in a bank insured by the Federal Deposit Insurance Corporation. Officers of the tribe were to maintain public accounts of tribal financial affairs and to furnish an annual balance sheet and report to the commissioner of Indian affairs. The charter was not to be revoked or surrendered except by an act of Congress, but amendments could be proposed by resolutions of the tribal council when approved by the members and the secretary. This charter became effective when two-thirds of the adult population ratified it.

With this charter in hand, the administration felt more comfortable in carrying out programs desired by both it and the Jicarilla Apaches. Actually, the programs envisioned by the administration were practically laid out in the constitution and the charter.

One of the first actions of the council was to secure a loan from the revolving credit fund in the amount of $85,000 to purchase the Wirt trading post.[22] It was to be called the Jicarilla Apache Cooperative Store, and it was to be managed by a person hired by the corporation. The manager was not only to run the enterprise, but he was to determine the amount of credit to be extended to the members of the tribe. Credit was a necessary feature of this operation since the tribal members received their monetary incomes twice a year if they were sheepmen and once a year if they were cattlemen. The manager of the store was to be supervised by the superintendent and the Tribal Executive Committee. The supervisors were to review the credit records every three months. In case of a difference of opinion between the council and the manager, the decision of the superintendent prevailed. From the net profits of the store, 50 percent was to be repaid to the government each year; 20 percent was to be placed in a reserve account for operating expenses; and 30 percent was to be distributed in dividends to the members. If per-capita payments were to exceed $10,000, the approval of 75 percent of the voters and that of the secretary of the interior was necessary for distribution. When the 20 percent share of the profits set up in the reserve account equaled $100,000, no further deposits were necessary and this 20 percent was then available for distribution on a per-capita basis.

In the supporting materials that were included with the application for this loan, it was made clear that the manner in which Wirt operated his trading post would continue. For half a century, Wirt had been the manager-operator. In this capacity he had advanced credit to the Indians to buy food and to carry on their livestock business. Expenses incidental to the operation of the business, such as shearing, lambing, and herding, had been funded through the store. Payments were made twice a year and credit was kept under strict control by Wirt. "This has been due to Mr. Wirt's intimacy with the Indians, which gave him a knowledge whereby credit was not extended beyond the borrower's ability to repay and secondly, a gentlemen's agreement existed between Mr. Wirt and every Indian borrowing from the store regarding repayments of the indebtedness and delivery of Indian products. When wool and lamb sales were made, which were marketed through the store, the proceeds were applied to indebtedness to the store. Debit balances of the accounts were carried on the books to be paid from anticipated returns from future operations, and credit balances are paid in cash at the time the transaction is completed."[23]

The operation of the store under new management was to continue along the established traditional lines, though a few variations were made. Several branch stores were proposed throughout the reservation, but only one, at Otero, was approved. With the purchase of the store, the Jicarillas also bought Wirt's residence and all his landholdings. The majority of the funds were for the store, its inventory, and all unliquidated debts of Jicarillas, which amounted to about $20,000. The application was submitted on September 28, 1937, and shortly thereafter, it was approved.

The Jicarilla Apache Cooperative Store became the hub around which the wheel of Jicarilla economy revolved. There was no part of the life of the Jicarilla people that was not influenced by this enterprise directly or indirectly. The entire economy was handled through the store.

By 1940, two years after it came into existence, it was doing very well financially. All obligations to the revolving credit fund had been met and dividends were paid to the tribal members both on a consumers' cooperative basis and on a per capita basis. The volume of business was increasing yearly, going from approximately $125,000 in 1939 to $270,000 in 1949. This cooperative was not only a retail service for the tribe, but a wholesale enterprise for all their collective products, individually produced. It also provided a means of setting up deserving individuals in the livestock business.[24]

Ninety-five percent of the business was conducted on credit sales. In the 1950s, credit was allowed to run rampant and resulted in the death of that enterprise, but during the 1940s credit was cautiously used. In 1942, accounts receivable exceeded $10,000, but after debts were paid, this figure was reduced to slightly more than $7,000.[25] This indicated that the people assumed responsibility and had the ability to pay their debts. They were kept informed about their accounts and the books were open to inspection. The tribal council examined the accounts at least three times a year.

This enterprise was so successful that the tribe decided in 1942 to invest the amount that would have gone for per-capita payments in United States defense bonds. In addition, the Cooperative Store decided to purchase a $100 bond for each month of 1942. The Indian Office approved this investment since the Jicarilla corporation had more than sufficient capital to carry on its operations. This required a slight change in the loan agreement. Since this seemed too cumbersome, it was decided that rather than using per-capita dividends, a certain amount from the cash reserve would be used instead.[26] What plan the administration finally decided on was not determined, but nonetheless, the tribe did buy almost $1,000,000 worth of bonds by the time the war had ended. Since some of the livestock men used these dividends to pay off part of their debts at the store, how the purchase of the bonds affected their credit payments was also not determined. The important thing seemed to be the Jicarilla participation in America's victory.

By 1945, three years ahead of schedule, the tribe had paid off their loan from the government.[27] Part of the success of this enterprise was the general prosperity made possible by the IRA program, the demand for agricultural products during the war, and the good leadership and agency administration. Even more important was the pride engendered among the people in owning their own business and the development of a sense of responsibility toward the use of credit, on which their livelihood depended.

By the end of 1940, the Jicarillas had set up a formal government, a corporation, a wholesale-retail enterprise with complete financing, and had purchased all but a very few tracts of land within the boundaries of the reservation. With these fundamentals out of the way, they were able to turn their attention to other matters—matters directly related to their economic base.

A lingering concern was taken care of in 1943. In that year the council adopted an ordinance by which all allotments were to be surrendered to the tribe by transferring their titles to the United States government; the titles were to be held in trust for the tribe. The increase in the value of the individual's share in the tribal asset was considered sufficient compensation for the surrender of the allotted lands or interests in the lands.

To make an equitable distribution of the tribal lands, now held in tribal ownership, every head of family was given the opportunity to apply for an assignment of sufficient land for a home site and, if available, irrigable land for farming. The assignments were exclusive so long as the assignee made continuous and beneficial use of the land. Improvements on the property were considered the private possessions of each individual. Every adult member of the tribe was also entitled to a proportionate share of the grazing lands until the range was in use to full capacity. There was to be an agreement among all the land users as to how the grazing lands in the summer and winter ranges were to be used. The maximum acreage permitted was a range unit sufficient to run one thousand head of sheep or its equivalent in cattle, provided everyone had been given the opportunity to make an application. Surplus land was granted temporarily to livestock owners who needed it; but if someone who had not received any other land assignment needed it, the surplus land had to be given up. The range capacity was not to be exceeded. All the animals were registered with the council so that land use could be monitored. A land code, which contained all these provisions, was adopted by the council and approved by the secretary.[28] This system of land assignments remained in effect until the late 1950s when all Jicarilla livestock operators were essentially taxed for the use of the range. They had to pay grazing fees according to the number of head of livestock owned.

At the time, the Jicarillas were fairly well satisfied with these arrangements. Most of the people registered their home sites, which in most cases were where they had lived over the years and where they or their parents had been assigned allotments. The system had simply verified the existing pattern of land use. There was little or no problem with the use of the southern portion of the reservation since those ranges had been used on a communal basis since the 1920s.

Besides the land assignments, other matters were also given effective consideration. An Old People's Herd, a flock of sheep belonging to senior citizens and incapacitated members of the tribe, was established.[29] The authority for this was written into the constitution, but it grew out of an existing arrangement, initiated as a result of a sheep issue made on December 4, 1930. The money for this issue was appropriated out of tribal funds derived from the sale of timber. Each member received an equivalent of 14²/7 sheep, representing a $100 investment. A problem arose for seventy Jicarillas who were too old or too incapacitated to care for their sheep and who, in a short time, would not have any visible means of support. So the plan was devised whereby all these Indians brought their sheep together to form a flock of about 1,000; this was designated the Old People's Herd. The expense for running this herd was the responsibility of the Tribal Council.

Each of the shareholders retained a one-seventieth interest in the herd and a similar interest in the proceeds of the sale of its lambs and wool each year. This plan proved to be so successful that it served as a springboard for the creation of another tribal enterprise that improved the quality of livestock on the reservation. Upon the death of any of the original seventy shareholders, the value of the shares did not increase, and the herd's size was maintained at 1,000. The income from the yearly increase was placed in an Old People's Herd Accumulation Fund, which was used for operating expenses. Eventually, after all the original shareholders died, the herd continued as a welfare source for all Apaches in need of help.

In addition to this, the herd was used to raise rams for a new enterprise, the tribal ram herd, begun in 1932. Before that, each sheep owner raised and cared for his own breeding stock. This resulted in a poor breeding program, which produced inferior sheep. But once all the rams were put into one herd and were taken care of by hired help, a controlled breeding program was started and the quality of all the herds improved. Unlike the Old People's Herd, which had originated as a private venture, The Tribal Ram Herd began as a tribal enterprise. It proved to be as successful as its forerunner. Within a few years, both herds had improved the quality of the stock so much that the Jicarillas owned some of the best sheep in northern New Mexico. They also sold their surplus rams to off-reservation sheepmen. The two herds were united in 1948, when the last fifteen shareholders were bought out, and became the Jicarilla Apache Sheep Breeding Enterprise. The following year this enterprise produced a net income of $8,000. Financially it was off to a good start.[30]

By and large, the Indian Reorganization Act was beneficial to the Jicarilla way of life. It had dramatic effects on the economy, especially the livestock sector. This in turn increased tribal and individual incomes and, therefore, improved the standard of living. In the 1940s there was a rapid increase in the number of animals owned by the Jicarillas. For example, sheep alone totaled 32,319 in 1940; a high of 37,312 was reached in 1944, but beginning in 1946 there was a noticeable decrease. In this same decade, the income from livestock and livestock products rose from about $120,000 in 1940 to approximately $320,000 in 1948. The number of families having agricultural income over $1,000 also increased during the 1940s.[31]

The rise in income had obvious implications for the Jicarillas. Clearly it meant previously unknown prosperity. It also meant better living conditions. The new prosperity had beneficial effects socially. The attitude of the people toward education gradually improved. Health care became more readily available. Perhaps the best indication of the new spirit created by these changing circumstances was the increase in the population.

Politically, the IRA had a tremendous impact on the Jicarilla Apaches. The constitution and the corporate charter proved to be important stepping stones toward the establishment of a modern legally recognized tribe. Before 1937, the Jicarillas had held uncertain legal status. The Dawes Act required the allotment of lands, but on the Jicarilla Reservation only the northern portion had been allotted, while the southern addition was communally owned. The Dawes policy was also to sever the trustee relationship: yet administratively, from the 1920s on, the Bureau actually increased its involvement in Jicarilla affairs. The Jicarillas were not being hurt by the Dawes policies because they were benefiting from the continuing guardianship of the federal government. This situation had caused confusion in the minds of the Jicarillas when confronted with the IRA, but once they formally accepted it, their legal status was made clear.

Dollars Received from Livestock and Livestock Products

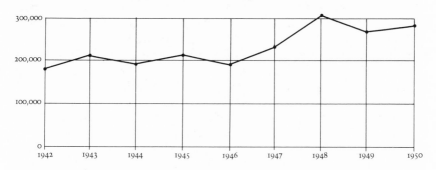

Number of Families Having Agricultural Income of $1,000.00 and Over

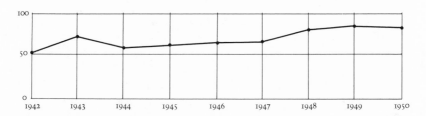

SOURCE: Jicarilla Agency Annual Report, 1951, R675 BIA, National Archives

The constitution and charter clearly embodied the ideas outlined in the Indian Reorganization Act and for this reason they contain both broad and narrow concepts. The tribal constitution recognized tribal self-government, established a common and inalienable land base as well as the communal ownership of all natural resources, and reinforced the federal trustee relationship. It is the recognition of these basic principles that legitimizes tribal existence. It is from these bases that the Tribal Council continues to derive its powers. And it is for these reasons that the tribe continues to exist as a separate cultural identity in spite of all changes that occur.

Over time, the tribal councils broadly construed their powers to protect these principles: these powers have enabled them to assign and distribute land, to sign leases with oil and gas companies, to revise the constitution, to develop a tourist industry, and to bring pressure to bear on the federal government to improve the quality of life on the reservation. It is these principles that distinguish them as an Indian tribe; without them they would be much like any other local government or municipality.

Since the primary documents embody IRA concepts, there are several provisions that were narrowly construed. The IRA was primarily designed for Indian people with an agricultural way of life and it overemphasized economic development; hence the tribal documents. This was reasonable and logical at the time. There were specific provisions in the two documents for programs like the relinquishment of allotments and the maintenance of a tribal herd, which were timely in their application. Within a decade, however, these and other provisions had little meaning for a society undergoing rapid change. The constitution was not relevant in the face of changes brought on by a different set of circumstances and by the 1960s it needed to be revised.

Like all other programs that the government has supported and implemented on the Jicarilla Reservation, the economic emphasis has always outweighed the social and educational. Perhaps for this reason, federal Indian policies have experienced a high rate of failure, because without social development, economic growth will not continue.

Overall, the IRA had a positive impact on the Jicarilla Apaches and their way of life. The Jicarillas had been fighting for an economy that would support them adequately and this was finally realized. Ironically, this accomplishment was short-lived. The 1950s and 1960s brought different values to the reservation, and the agrarian way of life became a thing of the past.

Chapter 9

In Pursuit of the American Dream: The 1950s

After a long and not always successful history, the Jicarilla Apache livestock economy finally became profitable during the 1940s. But in the face of sweeping changes brought on by World War II, the Jicarillas no longer desired that type of economy. The war had radically altered American society, ushering in a life of affluence that affected all segments, including the Jicarillas. In the 1950s they actively pursued a life-style that would guarantee their participation in the American dream, which seemed possible because of the new policies of the Bureau of Indian Affairs and the rise in tribal income from natural resources.

After World War II, federal Indian policies were carefully scrutinized. The principles embodied in the Indian Reorganization Act of 1934 were no longer suitable in light of post–World War II conditions. During the war there was a large exodus from Indian reservations. Approximately 65,000 men and women left the reservations to enter the armed services and to seek employment in war industries. This was the first time in recent American history that thousands of Indians had entered a war on the side of the United States. The atmosphere of war and patriotism deeply affected postwar Indian policies, and led to the reexamination of the policy that treated American Indians as trustees of the federal government.

The IRA came under severe criticism in Congress. This law was accused of clouding its original purpose by "keeping the Indian an Indian," condemning him to perpetual status as ward, instead of making him a full-fledged citizen. The BIA was also charged with building a self-perpetuating institution at the expense of the Indians' self-reliance.

The years following the war constituted a stormy transitional period that led to the development of a policy aimed at the elimination of the Bureau and of all special government services for Indians.[1] On February 8, 1947, the Senate Committee on the Post Office and Civil Service heard testimony on the gradual liquidation of the Bureau. Assistant Commissioner William Zimmerman, Jr., presented a list of ten tribes, which, in the opinion of the Bureau, were ready for the withdrawal of federal services. Twenty more groups were identified as potentially eligible within the next ten years. The remaining tribes, which had not met the government's criteria for a well-developed reservation economy, were considered ineligible for at least the next ten to twenty years.[2]

The impatient Congress requested a report from the Bureau by 1952 outlining a specific plan for terminating its trust responsibilities.[3] So for the next four years the Bureau compiled extensive socioeconomic data on Indian tribes. In the process, the Bureau realized that ending the federal relationship required upgrading the standard of living among the Indians and that the transfer of its functions to the tribes or to the local and state governments would have to be on an incremental basis. It did, however, publish a document in 1953 listing tribes ready for "freedom from wardship."[4] When the 83rd Congress passed House Concurrent Resolution 108, it used the list to name several tribes that were to be terminated at the earliest possible time. This resolution reaffirmed the historical intent of Congress to subject Indians to the same laws, privileges, and responsibilities as all other citizens by severing its special legal ties with them.

The termination policy was piecemeal, and incorporated several different approaches. There were features like relocation, a program that provided assistance and employment training for Indians relocated to cities, as an answer to the high unemployment on reservations. Public Law 280 permitted willing states to assume jurisdiction on Indian reservations, and the Indian Health Service was transferred to Public Health. The provisions of the Johnson-O'Malley Act of 1934 were involved for contracting the education of Indian children to state school districts. The state of New Mexico did not accept responsibility under Public Law 280, but it did take advantage of the provisions of the Johnson-O'Malley Act. Relocation was not stressed as a solution to the unemployment problem on the Jicarilla Reservation.

Within a year after Resolution 108 was passed, pressure mounted against these policies. In 1958, Commissioner of Indian Affairs Glenn L. Emmons implied that the policy of the Republican administration did not call for the hasty termination of federal trust responsibilities in Indian affairs. He emphasized that it called for the need for thorough study, careful planning, and full consultation with the Indians, recognizing and stressing the rights of the Indians to continue to hold their lands, and to maintain their tribal organizations for as long as they wished after the federal trusteeship had been terminated.[5]

Emmons was, on the whole, correct in his pronouncement, because for tribes like the Jicarilla Apaches, which were not considered eligible for termination, the Bureau from 1953 to about 1961 worked with a policy that had four goals. These were: (1) improvement of Indian health programs; (2) encouragement of Indian children to attend federal or public schools; (3) development of economic programs to improve resources in the reservations and to attract industry to or adjacent to reservations to furnish employment for Indians; and (4) continuation of Bureau services to Indians who wished to leave reservations to find employment.[6] All of these objectives were carried out to a certain extent on the Jicarilla Reservation.

Since the Jicarilla Apache Tribe was not one of the target tribes, this made it easier for the people and the Bureau to work together in reaching the common objective of improving the quality of life on the Jicarilla Reservation. The tribe and the Bureau had different motives, however, for wanting to accomplish this mutual goal. The Jicarillas simply wished to share in the American way of life; the Bureau wanted to end federal supervision.

The most influential factor that ensured the Bureau's continuing presence was the tribe's need for assistance in the management of its increasing revenues from oil and gas. During the 1940s some minor mineral exploration had taken place, but it was not until 1950 that energy companies began drilling on a large scale on the southern part of the reservation. In that year, the receipts from the sale of leases alone amounted to about $250,000, and within seven years there was almost a tenfold increase in all revenues from the oil and gas industry. In addition, the tribe had other sources of income from the sale of timber and from interest paid on minor investments.[7]

While tribal revenues rose, individual incomes fell. During the postwar recession, there was a sharp decline in the demand for agricultural products. The Jicarilla economy began to suffer: small livestock producers began experiencing decreasing profits and rising costs of living, and they had unpaid debts from a more prosperous yesterday. These circumstances provided still another reason for the Bureau to prolong its guardianship.

TABLE 4

Annual Income to the Jicarilla Apache Tribe
for Selected Years, 1937–60

Fiscal Year	Timber	Oil and Gas	Other	Total
1937			$3,220	$3,220
1938			2,815	2,815
1939	$163		684	847
1940			15,312	15,312
1942			559	559
1944			685	685
1947	12,640	$ 57,751	20,868	91,259
1950	350	20,112	2,311	22,773
1951		1,125,110	9,728	1,134,838
1952			2,623	2,623
1953		3,357,892	614,627	3,972,219
1954	2,167	1,812,874		1,815,041
1955		1,128,416	548,560	1,676,976
1956	23,787	534,144	11,199	569,130
1957	109,380	496,371	120,325	726,076
1958	44,124	3,020,971	246,281	3,267,252
1959	80,266	1,716,175	261,335	2,057,776
1960		1,330,881	263,534	1,594,415

SOURCE: H. Clyde Wilson, "Jicarilla Apache Political and Economic Structures,"
Publications in American Archaeology and Ethnology, 48 (Berkeley, University of
California Press, 1964).

From 1945 on, there was a steady decrease in the total number of
sheep, reflecting the slump in the reservation economy.[8] In 1950, an
unusually severe year, the average precipitation was 8.78 compared to
the normal 18.5 inches—the lowest since 1906.[9] The scant snowfall,
together with dry, windy days and cold nights, caused an early short-
age of feed and water, which became critical by May. It was this
drought that crippled the livestock economy.

For the Jicarilla stockmen this translated into a smaller crop of
lighter-weight lambs at market time. It also meant facing the winter
with sheep in poor condition. As in 1896, the majority of the owners
never recovered from these devastating losses. The small- to medium-
sized operators gave up and moved to Dulce in the hope of finding
some kind of relief.

TABLE 5
Annual Number of Cattle and Sheep on the Jicarilla Apache Reservation, 1932–59

Year	Number of cattle	Number of sheep
1932	154	22,000
1933	220	24,500
1934	465	23,359
1935	515	25,841
1936	862	22,889
1937	1,094	25,705
1938	1,403	27,512[a]
1939	1,611	28,776[a]
1940	1,471	32,319[a]
1941	1,345	33,501
1942	1,372	36,001
1943	1,431	38,654
1944	1,559	37,312
1945	1,670	36,698
1946	1,729	33,614
1947	1,747	27,830
1948	2,009	25,549
1949	2,112	21,710
1950	2,091	20,617
1951	1,956	18,916
1952	1,845	15,690
1953	1,798	17,152
1954	1,155	17,480
1955	1,401	18,922
1956	1,100	15,988
1957	1,177	15,029
1958	1,226	15,144
1959	1,068	15,768

[a] Includes from 1,000 to 2,000 goats.
NOTE: Figures for a given year vary depending on whether or not tribal and government sheep were counted and the time of the year the count was made. The figures for the number of sheep are accurate, the figures for the number of cattle are less so.
SOURCE: Wilson, "Jicarilla Apache Political and Economic Structures."

There was one bright spot, however, in the livestock business throughout the 1950s. In 1940 there were 1,500 head of cattle on the reservation; by 1950, the number had increased to 2,100. The agency had initiated a program known as "ID" cattle in the early 1940s. Jicarillas had received cattle on a share basis from the tribal herd to start their own herds. Every year the cattlemen were required to return a number of yearlings to the tribal herd as a method of payment, and this allowed others to acquire cattle. The arrangement was a welcome alternative for Jicarillas who were not interested in raising sheep.

Although the cattlemen were doing quite well, a recession had taken hold of the whole industry. A 1954 survey indicated that there were about 18,000 sheep among 60 owners, 1,500 goats among 46 owners, and 1,900 head of cattle for 47 owners.[10] (The actual condition was more bleak than the survey indicated. The figures were not accurate because the ranchers often owned mixed herds and were counted more than once.) The decrease in the number of livestock meant a decrease in total reservation income. Income from livestock during the 1950s was never more than 30 percent of all income earned on the reservation.

The decline of agriculture had a direct relationship with the mass movement into Dulce. In 1954, 80 percent of the Apaches made their homes within seven miles of the agency, 10 percent resided at least fifteen miles away, and the rest lived off the reservation.[11] By the end of the decade, 90 percent lived in the vicinity of Dulce. The Bureau seemed encouraged by the migration pattern and readily accepted this phenomenon. This trend helped to create greater reliance on the Bureau. The self-perpetuation of the Bureau on the Jicarilla Reservation was assured because the old economic system had failed for the most part, and although the Bureau was aware of the failing economy, it chose not to revitalize it. Furthermore, the philosophies of the IRA that had established a successful industry were considered outdated, so that those Jicarillas who wished to return to their old occupations were not encouraged to do so. Instead, the Bureau was trying to create a new community of wage earners. Without encouragement, the majority of the people accepted their predicament and settled into Dulce.

One faction, spearheaded by David and Albert Velarde, Jr., with the tacit support of tribal chairman Frank Vigil, was determined not to give up.[12] They reasoned that since the income of the tribe was on the rise and exceeded the cost of tribal operations, why not pay dividends to all tribal members? The pumping of funds into the livestock economy would put it back on its feet, again providing personal income for the bankrupt livestock owners, who would then be able to raise their standard of living. The rationale for this approach was indicative of a new shift in attitude among the Jicarillas. They had begun seriously to look to the tribe, instead of to the federal government (especially in light of its termination policies), for assistance in cases of economic hardships.

In 1952, after the Bureau decided that the tribe had sufficient funds for a per-capita payment, the secretary of the interior approved $300 for each tribal member.[13] Although the approval was given for the reasons stated in the petition, the Bureau's main concern was to clear up the financial situation of the foundering Jicarilla Apache Cooperative Store.[14] Using the same rationale as the petitioners, the Bureau hoped that if the people were given some funds perhaps they could pay their debts at the store; this, in turn, might put it back on a sound basis.

Instead of revitalizing the livestock economy and helping the store out of its difficulties, the increase in personal incomes triggered more problems. The Cooperative had been established in 1937, and had had a long history of poor management. Although in the early years it had operated fairly satisfactorily, within less than a decade it began to have problems. These developed in part because of the decline in the livestock industry, but also because the management extended unlimited credit to a small group of Jicarillas. The tribe began to pour tribal funds into the business to keep it afloat. Some members interpreted this as an opportunity to transfer the responsibility for their personal debts to the tribe. Instead of paying their debts, they went on spending sprees.

The Bureau knew that the Cooperative had to be a well-managed business before the Jicarillas could be terminated, since it was the hub around which the entire economy revolved. For this reason, the Bureau gave its approval for more per-capita payments in 1953 and 1954,[15] still hoping that the store's operations would be bolstered by another infusion of funds.

Unfortunately, the solution was not more payments, and the Bureau could no longer afford to ignore the situation. In 1954 the Gallup Area Office Branch of Credit conducted a study to put the problem in proper perspective and provide some answers. The conclusion reached was to sell the store to a private businessman. Apparently, the secretary of the interior agreed with the recommendation, for, in his approval of the 1954 per-capita payment, he included a provison whereby the Tribal Council had to agree to sell the store at the earliest practicable date, with the understanding that no more tribal funds would be advanced for its operation and that the new manager would be required to operate on a strictly cash basis.[16]

The council was not in favor of selling the store, but agreed to lease it to a private operator. Even this arrangement did not solve the credit problem and losses continued. The new manager, who was indifferent, did not stop extending credit, nor did he curtail its use. The accounts receivable were so high that the area director requested authority from the commissioner to close the store in August 1955. It remained closed for about a month and then reopened under private management on a cash-only basis.[17]

In the meantime, the losses, which amounted to a little over $200,000, were absorbed by the tribe.[18] As a corporate entity, the tribe had to take the loss for which certain privileged individuals were more culpable than others since they had abused the credit privileges. Indirectly, everyone as a member of the corporation had to pay whether he owed money to the store or not.[19]

In a sample study, 275 store accounts (25 of which belonged to members of the Tribal Council, the Credit Board, and council members who had been reelected in August 1953) were selected by the Bureau as a representative cross-section of the entire population. This was an erroneous assumption. The study showed that as of December 31, 1953, these 25 individuals owed approximately half of all the accounts receivable.[20] There was a definite correlation between having a position of authority or being a close relative of a council member, and the amount of credit one had at the store. A comment was made in the study that "these leaders are in no position to control the credit of others when they have no control over their own spending." For this reason there was certainly gross inequity in the distribution of tribal wealth because of the special privileges granted to only a small group of people.

The store's predicament was due not only to the irresponsibility of a few tribal members or to bad management, but also to ineptitude in the Bureau itself. The Bureau was aware of the problems, but it pretended helplessness, as indicated by one official who wrote that "although, under the Plan of Operation, the Bureau did have some responsibilities, it could not stop the investment of 'local' tribal funds in the store operations which made the excessive extension of credit possible."[21]

This statement was obviously misleading. The Bureau handled all financial matters related to the store's accounts, controlled all expenditures of tribal funds, and exercised the authority to hire a competent manager. Anywhere along the line it could have curbed the rampant credit available. Time and again, several lower-echelon officials of the Bureau out of the Gallup Area Office recommended the use of credit applications. If a customer did not maintain a good credit rating, credit would be cut off until debts were paid. If this simple procedure had been implemented, the abusive few would have been identified and the tribe's losses would have decreased.[22]

There was also some question about the Bureau's adherence to certain procedures as outlined in the Plan of Operation. In August 1955, a Bureau official indicated in a letter to the Washington office that he had not been adequately informed regarding the operations of the store and that the audits had not been received from the previous year.[23] This was the fiscal year in which the store had to be closed for a month because of lack of adequate operating funds. The Bureau did have the power, the duty, and the responsibility to make sure that the operation of the store did not get out of hand: instead it contributed to its failure. As long as the Bureau looked the other way, the privileged few took advantage. It was almost as if the Bureau wanted the store to fail so it could claim that the Indians still needed the Bureau.

Moreover, the per-capita payments were sanctioned by the Bureau, which in a cavalier manner blamed the tribal gratuities for stifling the Apaches' initiative to work and earn a living. One official wrote, "Many had no regard for their debts and again many had no desire to work."[24] Another official stated that "many able-bodied men are not interested in working to support themselves or their families."[25] "Many stockmen are driving around the country in cars and pickups that were paid for with money that should have been used to pay debts due the store and at the same time increasing these debts by purchasing gasoline on credit."[26] Still another wrote, "This free and easy credit has had serious effects on the general daily living of these people"[27] and "this was not conducive to good business training nor is it teaching the people to meet their individual responsibilities and to manage their own affairs."[28]

This entire situation did not reflect well on all the Jicarillas, or on the Bureau's management of Indian affairs, so in 1958 the Bureau finally decided on the future disposition of per-capita payments. An additional consideration was that the income from the oil and gas was not inexhaustible, especially since the growing Jicarilla population would put a strain on the income. A plan was adopted whereby instead of distributing lump sums of money, the payments, which decreased over the next five years, were issued in installments at various intervals over the year.[29] This paternalistic arrangement penalized those Jicarillas who were "prudent" in their spending habits and those who genuinely had no other source of income through no fault of their own.

With regard to the plan to deal with the indebtedness of the Cooperative Store, a portion of the old debts was to be paid out of future per-capita distributions. One-third of the payment to each member who was indebted to the store and one-third of the spouse's share were to be withheld. This applied to debts that were considered reasonable or debts that could be paid within a period of ten years without causing too much hardship.[30] There is no evidence as to whether or not this plan was carried through.

An innocuous request to help revive the livestock industry by providing capital to ranchers who had lost their herds to drought and an unfavorable agricultural market had mushroomed into a maze of dependence and irresponsibility that was neither intended nor anticipated. This rise in tribal income from oil and natural gas, which had made the per capita payments possible, precipitated some undesirable results. It would be unfair to conclude that the rise in revenue created only problems, however. A sizable number of Jicarillas benefited in a positive way. Several long-term benefits were derived from the increased income, especially for the youth. Two large funds for the direct use of minors were set aside—the Chester E. Faris Scholarship Fund and the Minors' Trust Fund.

By the 1950s the tribal population totaled 1,060, of whom 628 were under twenty-one years of age.[31] Both the Bureau and the tribe felt that more tribal funds should be invested for the direct benefit of the children, so that when they became young adults, whether they wanted to pursue a higher education, enter into vocational fields, or just set up a household on the reservation, they would have some financial resources. Consensus was that the per-capita payments were also the property of the minors and that quite a number of adults were incapable of properly managing the moneys for their children. This conviction was mainly the opinion of Bureau officials, who argued that the Jicarilla adults had a long history of dependence on the government, and that this, augmented by their relations with the trader, had not led to responsible financial management.[32] The credit abuse at the store had tarnished the reputations of all Jicarillas.

A conference was held between Bureau personnel and the Tribal Council in May 1954, when it was decided that not more than one-half of the minors' share of future per-capita payments would be turned over to parents and guardians. The other half would be deposited in a commercial bank, which would act as trustee for the Minors' Trust Fund. This was in keeping with Bureau termination policies, which designated commercial banks rather than the government to act as trustees.

The Trust Fund had the wholehearted endorsement of the Tribal Council and its constituency. While the Jicarillas as a whole were not educated in the principles of financial management, accounting, trusts, and so forth, they had a long tradition of and interest in general tribal welfare, whether it was caring for the old people or sharing livestock ranges. So although the Trust was more sophisticated, its intent was within the tribal tradition. It was also a rather odd arrangement: trusts are usually established for the more well-to-do in society. This trust was set up for the benefit of all tribal children, including the very poor. The final plan for the Minors' Trust Fund was approved in 1955.[33] One-fourth of the funds accumulated in the trust were to be distributed to the minors when they reached the age of eighteen and another fourth each year for the following three years.

Another unprecedented and much publicized action was taken by the tribe and Bureau in September 1955. The Chester E. Faris Scholarship Fund in the amount of $1,000,000 (the equivalent of a contribution of $833 from each member of the tribe) was established, with the First National Bank of Albuquerque as the trustee. Funds were thus available to all Jicarilla Apaches who wanted to pursue either a college education or vocational training. Moneys from this fund were not available until 1957, when it had earned a year's interest.[34]

The Bureau and the tribe did not fail to publicize this event. One press release was headlined, "Emmons Hails Jicarilla Apache Action in Establishing $1,000,000 Scholarship Fund."[35] Emmons congratulated the tribe and described that action as "an outstanding example of tribal progress." This event was noted in newspapers and magazines such as the *New York Times* and *Time* magazine.

Although the establishment of these two funds was progressive and socially beneficial for the youth, the accompanying publicity helped to create the false image that the Jicarilla Apache Tribe was rather wealthy. To a certain extent, this reputation made the tribe a target for every merchant, service, and promoter in the area with a scheme, plan, or proposal. The people and the Tribal Council were also quite vulnerable to the suggestion that they were wealthy. This image did not help the spending habits of the Tribal Council.

Adults with families also benefited from the natural resources income. Although the per-capita payments were much criticized, they helped the people who migrated to a town that had no housing facilities, no jobs for the unskilled, and few community services. Without this income, the new arrivals would not have been able to sustain themselves. Per-capita payments were their major source of income.

Employment opportunities in Dulce were inadequate. The majority of the existing jobs that paid decent wages were filled by non-Indians who staffed most of the BIA administrative positions, served as teachers and personnel in the schools, and took the temporary and skilled jobs that were occasionally available on the reservation. The Jicarillas who had jobs were usually found in the blue-collar work force as temporary laborers, janitors, bus drivers, clerks, and night attendants at the BIA boarding school dormitories.

By 1955 the population in Dulce had reached a thousand. It was clear that this trend was not going to reverse itself and the only realistic approach was to deal with the changing needs of the people. As early as 1952, the Bureau began revising its economic policies for the Jicarilla Reservation, in accordance with the administration's four-point plan to aid tribes that were not ready for termination. But it was not until about 1955 that the new policies took shape.[36]

The prevailing thought was that the tribe should invest a large part of its natural resources income in productive enterprises that would provide long-term income from wages for tribal members. Highlighted was the idea of diversifying the economic base by investing the income from natural resources in new industries that would use the reservation's raw materials. These enterprises would provide jobs and give alternatives to dependence upon agricultural pursuits. There were, for example, abundant timber resources. If a logging operation consisting of a sawmill and lumber finishing plant with the capacity to produce millions of feet of lumber per year were purchased, it would help to alleviate unemployment.

Although the new emphasis was on labor and wages, the Bureau was aware that livestock raising was still very important. In its planning, the Bureau continued to place some emphasis on the improvment of the quality of livestock and its production and management by developing the forage resources. The livestock business still yielded the most profitable earned income at this time. The tribal budget in 1954 appropriated a good share of its funds for the livestock industry and related activities.[37] The range management plan was initiated on a limited scale and was to be expanded only if the tribe could realize a profit on its investment. To ensure some degree of return, the payment of grazing fees by livestock owners was implemented. This aspect of the overall policy set a hitherto unknown and unacceptable precedent of essentially taxing members for the use of their own lands. It violated the spirit and intent behind relinquishing private allotments. The original allottees gave up their allotments in favor of tribal ownership of land, to be governed by the concept of beneficial use. It was their understanding that as long as a tribal member put the land to good use, it would belong to him without payment.

Forage development, however, was a minor concern compared to the plans made for community development. One focus was on the establishment of small local retail enterprises such as a service station, an automobile repair shop, a restaurant, a motel, and related service industries. Tribal members were dependent on off-reservation businesses for all that would normally supply services to a community.

Another policy objective was to develop community facilities. The people moved into a town that had inadequate residential housing and public office buildings, poor water and sanitation, and almost no community recreational facilities. The only available services were those provided for the school children and government personnel.

The new income made it possible for the council to allocate more of the tribal budget for community services. In 1954, the tribe was spending approximately $90,000 on services to maintain law and order, a sanitation program, and to provide the salary for a social-economic specialist.[38] The goal of community development became a number-one priority by the end of the decade.

The most urgent need in the town of Dulce was housing, so it became a focus of attention. The Bureau proposed that the tribe loan money to individuals to build homes that would meet national minimum housing standards. These loans would be repaid over a long term, at convenient interest rates, from per-capita payments or other income. The standard of living was disturbingly low among the majority of the Apaches. A 1954 survey pointed out that Jicarilla families were living in substandard housing, with inadequate water and sanitation facilities.[39] According to this study, by necessity the livestock owners had to move from the summer to the winter ranges every year, and therefore they had no desire to acquire good, decent, permanent homes. This may well have been true; but only a small percentage of the people were livestock owners moving from place to place.

The more disturbing fact brought out in the survey was the actual condition of some of the homes.[40] It seemed that little progress had been made in the quality, comfort, and conveniences found in most of the homes. It was reports of this nature that convinced the government that the Jicarillas were in dire need of good housing. A start was made on a limited basis through the loan program, but mass construction of homes did not begin until the 1960s, when federal aid became available.

As part of the overall program to develop the resources to improve the community, the tribal government was reorganized. This change was initiated by the Bureau so that the Jicarillas would be able to control and manage their own affairs upon termination. Changing residential patterns and increased tribal business were other reasons for the reorganization of the council. The tribe's governmental structure had to be modified, and the amendment process was the obvious vehicle for doing so.

The 1937 district system of electing councilmen was quite obviously out-of-date by 1953. The scattered elections no longer attracted large numbers of voters, mainly because they were held out on the reservation and most of the people resided near Dulce; but since this was the only system available, it was used until 1958. The Tribal Council minutes of August 17, 1953, describe how the council selected voting places and set the time and date for casting votes. District One, which was La Jara, was to vote at Alex Vigil's place at 10:00 A.M. on August 24, 1953. The District Three (the Horse Lake and Stone Lake area) polling was to be near Henry Lee Petago's shearing grounds at 3:30 P.M. on the same date. The sparsely populated district of La Juita and Carracus was to hold its election at Wells Lookout, a forest fire station, at 2:00 P.M.

The system lent itself to informality and voter apathy. The only voting requirements were that a tribal member be at least twenty-one years of age and that he or she must have resided on the reservation for six months before the election. There were no separate district requirements, such as length of residence or property ownership. Within the districts, there were no strict voting procedures involving registration or the use of secret ballots; since there was no extensive campaigning, there were no promises to keep or platforms to uphold. The candidate receiving the largest number of votes was elected. Out in the sparsely populated districts, if a few members showed up, they could agree on a representative without actually casting a ballot and return home. Conceivably, a man could get elected by his wife and a few relatives if they were the only ones in attendance at the election site.[41]

The impracticality of this system was yearly becoming more evident. At the October 7, 1955, council meeting, it was reported that there had been no elections in Districts Five and Six. The council decided that the two members who were up for reelection should continue as members of the council.[42] A resolution was passed approving this action and its constitutionality was never questioned (which attests to the lack of general interest in the conduct of tribal government).

It was becoming increasingly clear that what was once a representative government was no longer representative in the wake of changing residential patterns. Thus in 1958 the council amended the constitution to provide for the reduction of its membership from eighteen to ten, elected by popular vote rather than by the old district system. The positions of chairman and vice-chairman were created. The new arrangement, however, did not seem to provide greater representation, ensure more turnover in the composition of the council, or stimulate larger voter participation. Since 1960 there have been councils that have overrepresented several families with the same surnames and the membership has remained fairly stable.[43] In many of the elections, only 30 percent of the voters have cast their ballots.

It is a wonder that the council and the Bureau did not consider redistricting the area around Dulce to ensure a more representative council. The general resettlement pattern in and near Dulce was similar in its family groupings to the former district settlements. Yet the district system was eliminated without much thought being given to its advantages and merits.

Two other amendments were added, which lowered the age from 28 to 25 for eligibility as a council member and changed the tribal membership requirements. The 1937 Constitution had extended membership to all children whose parents' names appeared on the 1937 census roll and who resided on the reservation. The amendment included those Jicarilla children who resided off the reservation if they could prove they were descendants of the 1937 enrollees. These children, however, had to have the proper blood quantum, which remained at one-fourth.[44]

There were several other changes made in tribal government. Since 1954, the responsibilities of the tribe had grown immensely. The business before the council had practically tripled since 1950 and the budget rose from just under $50,000 in 1954 to more than $1,000,000 in 1959.[45] There was also a rise in the cost of tribal administration. For example, between 1956 and 1959, it jumped from $20,000 to $67,000.[46]

This increase in business required the council to meet more often. In the 1937 Constitution, the council was required to meet twice a year, but after 1950 it met at least once a month, with executive committee meetings more often. To provide more attention to the increasing business, an amendment was approved in 1956 which required that the council meet twice a month. Before 1955 all councilmen were paid a per diem rate for their attendance at all meetings, including those of the executive committee. This was modified at the December 12, 1955, session, when an additional increase in the per diem rate was approved for the executive committee and credit board members, and the tribal judge.[47] The increase was effective only during the winter months when it took an extra effort to get to Dulce due to road conditions, but this was later changed to apply to all meetings regardless of season.

With the amount of business, it was no longer efficient for the entire body to consider all matters, so a committee system was adopted. The committees dealt with specific issues and problems like land claims, per-capita payments, loans, and scholarships. There were no standing committees. When a problem arose, a committee was created to handle it, and when it had been resolved, the committee no longer existed.[48]

To take care of the more complex business matters, a business manager was employed by 1955.[49] Most of the council members were not educationally prepared to deal with complex corporate business and the agency was charged with giving only technical assistance. Besides, even the Bureau could not handle all the complicated business alone. By 1954 it was obvious that a tribal office building was necessary, so the council set aside funds for this purpose. In 1955, the superintendent was asked to draw up plans for the building. Within a year, the council had hired an architect and accepted bids for construction. The building was finished, dedicated, and opened for business in 1957.[50] This was symbolic of the attempt to separate the tribe from the agency, despite the Bureau's strong control.

The Bureau retained authority over the more technical matters. Decisions made by the council were of a procedural rather than a substantive or innovative nature. In effect, the council only confirmed Bureau-initiated programs and appropriated tribal funds to carry out or to supplement government-funded programs that were predetermined at the national level. A study conducted by two scholars who were specifically hired by the tribe to study the political changes on the reservation found that the tribe had become increasingly more active as a decision-making body since 1952. A crude index was used to provide quantitative data on the number of council meetings and the number of resolutions passed by the councils from 1946 to 1959. The data indicate that there were only three meetings held in 1946, in which 32 resolutions were adopted. In 1959 there were seventeen meetings and a surprising number of resolutions—337—were approved. The increase was due primarily due to changes in administrative procedures in 1957 and 1958, after which the council was required to pass a resolution on each budget item at the time of expenditure. In 1959 this practice was discontinued and there was a consequent decline in resolutions.

The study showed that the number of resolutions offered no indication as to the relative importance of the decisions. There were two types of decisions. One involved transactions concerned with the orderly operation of tribal affairs and the implementation of previous decisions. Innovative decisions related to the development of new policies that struck out in new directions made up the second type. These were infrequent and were likely to be initiated by agency officials. Although the council was more active in the decision-making process, the superintendent retained the ultimate authority, especially in the area of his trust responsibilities, and any action taken by the council became effective only with his approval.[51]

With a more flexible governmental structure, the Bureau and the council concentrated on their policy priority: the improvement of the community. But rather than relying solely on the Bureau for advice in this matter, the council decided to seek outside assistance from professionals. Since the tribe was financially capable, the agency encouraged this approach. The Bureau's policy was to plan its social and economic programs carefully so that when the tribe was released from federal supervision, its standard of living would be comparable to that of the rest of society.

Several planning strategies were considered, the most feasible of which appeared to be the employment of several consultants and scholars who had experience with and expertise in Indian community development. Announcements were sent out to potential firms and candidates. The Stanford Research Institute of Menlo Park, California, got in touch with the tribal attorney, who introduced a representative from the institute to the council in June 1955.[52] SRI proposed to conduct a study on the economic needs of the Jicarilla Apache Reservation and to make recommendations for long-range economic and community development programs.

It seemed that SRI was actively soliciting business of this nature from Indian tribes. The attorney explained that the institute had worked with both the Navajos and the San Carlos Apaches along these same lines. In March 1957 the council approved a contract with SRI, which allowed the SRI to conduct social and economic research on the reservation.[53] In the meantime, SRI was successful in obtaining another contract with the Jicarillas to do the historical research for the Jicarilla Apache land claims, which were then before the Indian Claims Commission. SRI began its community study in June 1957 and completed it in March 1958. Basically its task was to assemble information on the tribe and its resources; prepare alternative methods of developing resources under various types of tribal organizations; evaluate different economic and social development projects; and present a unified overall plan. A sizable section of the study was devoted to a quantitative measurement of the sources of tribal income.

SRI's economic development program was to increase both tribal and individual income through gainful employment, thus deemphasizing dependence on the sale of depletive resources or on percapita payments from the tribal treasury, which were considered neither self-supporting nor socially healthy. Since the people were the greatest tribal resource, priority would be given to developing their job opportunities through training programs. The creation of jobs would make the families more self-reliant and this would strengthen the tribal organization. Also, if attention were directed toward the development of northwestern New Mexico and a program of road construction were initiated, this would make the area less isolated, would attract tourist trade, and industry could move in. SRI emphasized that economic growth would require better education and job training for all tribal members and elected officials. This was the surest way for the Jicarillas to attain the living standards and economic security of a comparable modern western community.[54]

The council and the Bureau used this study to support their existing programs. The report had useful recommendations and suggestions, but since they were so similar to Bureau policy, plans, and intentions, it is difficult to determine whether it was worth the financial expenditure, especially since a less expensive and less elaborate study was made in 1954 which produced very similar conclusions.[55] SRI did provide analysis and technical information, however, which had not been readily available: information on minerals, a summary of tribal finances, and a forecast of future tribal income. Warnings regarding the distribution of per-capita payments and their drain on the tribal treasury had been heard before the study was made, but perhaps obtaining this independent and objective opinion gave them more weight. This report anticipated the economic and social development programs that were implemented in the 1960s and 1970s.

The decision to employ professionals from various fields to assist with economic and social development started another trend in the conduct of tribal affairs. From 1954 on, the tribe relied heavily on professional advice and became quite liberal in extending contracts to obtain it. A community specialist was hired in 1957 to aid SRI in conducting the survey, and to coordinate existing economic and social programs.[56]

By the end of the 1950s, a foundation for the community had been built with the assistance of the Bureau and it had access to tribal funds to obtain expert advice. The Jicarilla Apache Tribe was ready to continue to build on this foundation in the ensuing decades.

In the 1950s, the Jicarillas sought a share in the prosperity of the country, not as urbanites, but as reservation residents who wanted their own modern community. The technological revolution of the postwar period had whetted their appetite for a modern life-style. The increasing gross tribal income made this life-style possible, at first by providing per-capita payments, which were not always spent very wisely. However, the system provided opportunities for management of finances no matter how inept that management might be. The per-capita allocations were often all the people had to rely on for income. The situation was similar to that in the period from 1900 to 1930, when the Jicarillas continued to rely on the medicine man's services, even if they were inadequate, because modern medical care was lacking. Per-capita payments too were inadequate, but jobs were virtually nonexistent for an unskilled labor force fresh off the old homesteads.

The tribal gratuities created problems, but presented some alternatives for the Jicarillas. For example, other Indian tribes that did not have the same opportunities migrated to the cities under the Relocation Program, thus breaking up tribal groupings and families. Because the Jicarillas had a choice, their tribe remained united. The minors' trust fund provided means for young adults and minimized their migration to cities in search of jobs. The scholarship fund also offered an alternative to seeking a job, although few Jicarillas took advantage of this option. While the tribal income afforded the Indians opportunities, however, it also provided the Bureau with the basis for prolonging federal guardianship. Economic conditions were in a state that necessitated further guidance. In 1952 when the livestock business foundered and the people were migrating to town, there were two directions the economy could have taken. One was to build an even stronger livestock industry based on the existing modern technology. This, however, was never given serious consideration by the Bureau, although the capital was available, the land was plentiful and suited for raising sheep and cattle, and the people had had many years of experience in the profession. Only a small minority continued to benefit from it, however, while the rest were compelled to move to Dulce in search of a livelihood.

The other alternative was to build an entirely new wage and labor economy practically from scratch; an economy that required the Bureau's technical assistance, which it was willing to make available to the tribe. It conveniently had the tribal funds to facilitate its administration by obtaining expert advice for economic and social development. Despite its success in perpetuating itself, the Bureau did establish programs and policies that the tribe seemed to accept and heartily support in the coming years.

Chapter 10

The Era of Growth: 1960–70

While the 1950s had been shaped by the desire to share in the prosperity of the country, the years from 1960 to 1970 were molded by a change in federal Indian policies, from termination to self-determination. Thus, the Jicarilla Apaches gained control of their own affairs, which nurtured progress and growth on the reservation. This change occurred with somewhat more abruptness than was usual because of the amount of federal funding that was made available to Indian tribes.

The publication in 1960 of the *Fund for the Republic Study* by the Commission on Rights and Responsibilities of the American Indian focused attention on the injustices inherent in the termination policy, the paternalistic attitudes and practices of the Bureau of Indian Affairs, and the inadequate services provided for Indians. It argued for reorganization of the Bureau's education program and increased Indian involvement in determining programs affecting Indians. Concurrently, a conference of Indian leaders in Chicago formulated the "Declaration of Indian Purpose," which also repudiated the termination policy of the 1950s and expressed the Indians' desire for greater participation in planning their own programs and in determining the reorganization of the Bureau.[1]

The Kennedy administration responded to these positions with its own study of Indian affairs. A task force headed by Secretary of the Interior Stewart Udall produced a report in 1961, which deprecated termination, and suggested that economic and natural-resource development on Indian reservations, especially through the attraction of industrial firms, be the main basis of a new federal Indian policy. As a result, the Bureau of Indian Affairs shifted its policy direction between 1961 and 1965 and embarked on a program of economic and community development. To implement this, the Indians were included as beneficiaries of all federal programs and assistance, such as, for example, that offered by the Economic Opportunity Act of 1964. For the first time, the Indians were given the opportunity to propose and to work out projects tailored to their specific needs, using resources of the Job Corps, Vista, Headstart, and Community Action Programs. The last demonstrated the scope of the Indians' initiative and self-determination, and their ability to carry out their own programs effectively. Indian tribes were allowed to obtain grants for technical services directly from the Office of Economic Opportunity, bypassing the Bureau, which now had to share its once exclusive domain with a host of other federal agencies.[2]

Federal Indian policies in the 1960s generally favored economic and social progress for all Indian peoples, albeit tempered by their own ideas as to the direction and speed which the progress was to take. This philosophy has not always been followed to the letter, nor has it always had wide acceptance. There have been numerous setbacks in its implementation, especially when viewed from a national perspective; but for the Jicarilla Apache Tribe, the policies did change the quality of life on their reservation, and gave it new dimensions.

It had always been the intention of the Bureau of Indian Affairs to upgrade the standard of living on Indian reservations. It took the War on Poverty programs, however, to focus attention on reservation social and economic conditions throughout the United States. On the Jicarilla Reservation the "war" escalated in 1960 because the tribe had ample ammunition at hand. First, there were the extensive surveys conducted in 1957 by the Stanford Research Institute, supplemented by other, similar studies that had developed planning strategies. Second, the tribe's income continued to increase at about the same rate that federal assistance became more available to all Indian tribes in the 1960s.

The first weapon used to combat poverty was the Family Plan, aimed at giving each Jicarilla family a direct opportunity to improve its standard of living. This was the beginning of a long-range economic and social program. The economic conditions on the reservation and the growing disrepute of the per-capita payments led to the adoption of the Family Plan on January 16, 1959, when the Tribal Council passed a resolution granting $1,600 per person on a family basis. A petition signed by 77 percent of the eligible voters indicating

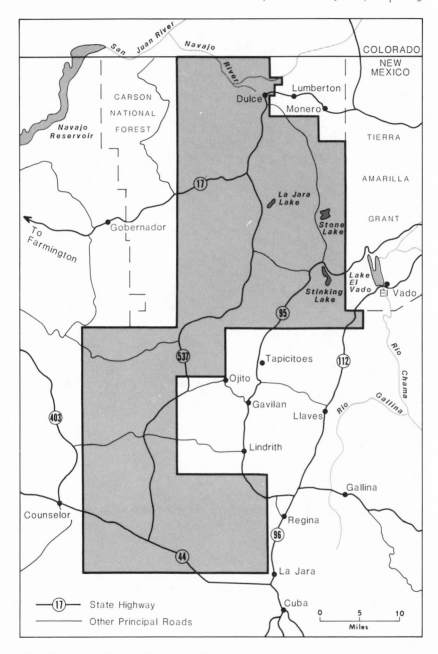

The Modern Jicarilla Apache Reservation

acceptance of the Family Plan was submitted to the council on August 3, and final approval was given by the commissioner on July 15, 1960, although minor alterations were made thereafter.[3] The purpose of this program was to give all the Jicarillas opportunity to lay the foundation for some income-producing activity, or to better their living conditions. The plan was family-based, whether the family lived on or off the reservation. It required each family to submit its plans to one of three subcommittees: livestock, business, or welfare. Separate plans were made for unattached minors, the elderly, the handicapped, welfare recipients, and off-reservation residents. The plans were then forwarded to the larger Family Plan Committee and were previewed by the director-administrator. The plans were funded on a first-come, first-served basis.

The Stanford Research Insitute's *Economic and Social Survey* two years earlier had produced findings that bore a direct relationship to the implementation of the Family Plan. Since 1952 the tribe had followed the practice of allocating a portion of its oil and gas income for per-capita distribution. Consequently, this allotment became the basic means of support for most Jicarillas. The tribe requested the institute to outline a long-range economic program to deal with this problem. SRI's conclusion was that the continuation of the per-capita program would result in a decrease of initiative, self-reliance, and employment. The Tribal Council agreed that this conclusion was valid. By 1958 it had initiated a five-year program to decrease each year the amount of the payments, until no more were distributed. To enforce this, the 1960 Revised Tribal Constitution provided that annual dividends would be payable from the net operating surplus, but that royalties received from oil and gas production would not be included in that net surplus.[4]

Another study conducted by H. Clyde Wilson in 1960, entitled "Analysis of Low-Income Families on the Jicarilla Apache Reservation," provided background information and data to support the Family Plan, but did not share the conclusions of the institute study. It examined concrete issues, going beyond the superficial blanket accusation that the per-capita allotment was the "ruination of the Jicarilla Apaches." In its foreword, Robert Bennett's statement was quoted in support of the Family Plan.

There is still a large proportion of the Jicarilla Apache who do not benefit from any tribal program except per-capita payments and welfare. They do not own livestock, so do not benefit from range and

water development and the services of the State and Federal em-
ployees concerned with livestock; they did not finish high school,
so are not in position to benefit from a scholarship program geared
primarily for college education; they do not have the ten percent
security for tribal loans nor the possibility of repaying these loans;
and they lack the experience and skill to obtain tribal and govern-
ment jobs available on the reservation. These are the individuals
characterized by low economic status. They are also the indi-
viduals on the reservation about whom the least is known.[5]

The data for this study were collected in the spring of 1959 from 223
Jicarilla families living on the reservation. Their income was of two
types: earned income from wages, sale of livestock, and veteran's
disability payments; and total income received, i.e., income plus per-
capita payments. A family was considered to be in the low-income
category if its earned annual income fell below $300 per adult person.
For each additional member, a minimum of $144 was required. If this
additional member was a child in boarding school, which took the
burden of support off the parents for nine months, then only $68
would be needed. A family of five members—two adults and three
children in boarding school—would require an annual earned minimum income of $648. Table 6 shows the income breakdown for the
tribe.

The conclusions drawn from the data were that 95 families, or 42.6
percent of the total reservation families, were in the low-income
bracket. The 411 members of these families, who constituted 36.6
percent of the total Jicarilla membership, received only 4.3 percent of
the total earned income and only 18.3 percent of the total income
received. It was pointed out that these families could not maintain a
subsistence level without outside help. The per-capita payments provided this help, and raised the median and mean total income level to
about $1,500 above the earned income level.

The study found that discontinuing the per-capita allotment without an alternate plan to increase earned income would not only lower
the standard of living for the 95 families (putting them below the
subsistence level), but would also increase their dependence on their
relatives. This would, in turn, lower the relatives' living standards and
would result in an increase in public and tribal welfare. These 95
families could not invest their Family Plan money in capital assets
unless they were provided with an income to take care of their basic
needs. It was recommended that they be provided with an income

TABLE 6
Earned Income, 1958

Income Bracket	Number of Families
$ 0– 99	54
100–199	5
200–299	8
300–399	7
400–499	3
500–599	5
600–699	6
700–799	3
800–899	3
900–999	1
	95

The median earned income to these families was $86.96; the mean earned income was $205.16.

(i.e., per-capita) sufficient to assure adequate support and that they be encouraged to use their Family Plan money to improve their living standards through the purchase of livestock, better housing, and so forth.[6]

Although these 95 low-income families were the main concern, it was recognized that the situation was not much brighter for the remainder of the tribe. Only about 10 pecent enjoyed standards comparable to those of middle-class America—and these were doing only slightly better because they, too, benefited from the per-capita payments.

Educationally the group that escaped the low-income bracket was no better off, and its employment picture was also gloomy. In December 1959 there was an estimated able-bodied work force of 652—312 males and 340 females. Of the total employable group, 281, or 43 percent, received earned income, compared to 64.5 percent for the nation as a whole. Primarily, these were unskilled workers. Out of the 218, 72 had occupational skills, but the majority of this group (46) held jobs such as dormitory attendants, garage workers, trainees as forestry and sanitation aides, clerks, cooks, and general maintenance personnel. The remaining 26 were policemen, plumbers, heavy equipment

TABLE 7
Total Income, 1958

Income Bracket	Number of Families
$ 0– 249	0
250– 499	3
500– 749	6
750– 999	6
1,000–1,249	12
1,250–1,499	15
1,500–1,749	17
1,750–1,999	3
2,000–2,249	13
2,250–2,499	1
2,500–2,749	4
2,750–2,999	3
3,000 and over	12
	95

The median total income of these families was $1583.25; the mean total income $1718.31.

operators, accountants, managers, and teachers. The job opportunities were provided mainly by the tribe (188 positions) the Bureau agency (48), and public health (4); 15 were privately employed. The cattle industry provided self-employment for 72 people.[7] Table 7 shows tribal income figures for 1958.

The Family Plan was proposed as a short-range program with an operational period of approximately three years, but it took five years (1960–65) to complete. The program emphasized the goals of enhancement of family livelihood opportunity and improvement of living standards. In all, 455 plans involving 1,341 persons were completed at a direct cost of $2,145,600, plus $119,715 in administrative costs, all paid from tribal funds. In all, 110 new homes were constructed, of which 98 were on the reservation; 115 were remodeled (again with 98 on the reservation) and 67 house trailers were purchased (56 on the reservation). Also, 157 tents were bought. In July 1959, there were 214 dwelling units on the reservation: as of January 1966, 154 units had been added. New wells supplying potable water were drilled for seven families. New and modern house applicances were bought by 348 families.[8]

Five families expended funds for commercial businesses and other self-employment activities—a garage–service station, a self-help laundry, a barbershop, a poultry enterprise, and a bakery unit. Of 72 chain saws purchased, approximately 50 percent were to be used for cutting fence posts and firewood as a means of earning additional income. Cattle and sheep were acquired by seven families for completely new enterprises, and twenty-one families increased their existing cattle or sheep herds. Many others were helped through the use of funds for the management of livestock—operating expenses, equipment, payment of tribal loans, land improvement, and so forth.[9] More families wanted to enter the livestock business than could be accommodated with land assignments, and some of these applicants had little or no experience in the business.

To ensure the success of these enterprises, the tribal credit fund was increased to $500,000; this fund was used to supplement family plans primarily pertaining to livestock and housing. The Dulce branch of the First National Bank of Río Arriba facilitated the handling of family accounts after 1963.[10]

The Family Plan was an effective program that stimulated economic growth and improved living conditions. It provided equal opportunities for all tribal members, whether they lived on or off the reservation. The amount of benefit derived was determined by a family's initiative and how much it really wanted to get out of the program. Some got a great deal more than others, based on their own planning and cooperation, but all had similar experiences. The family unit appeared to be strengthened.

The majority of all houses constructed or improved and the house trailers bought were located near existing school bus routes; therefore, the children could walk or ride the bus to school rather than being compelled to live in the dormitories.

The Family Plan had the potential for lasting impact, but would be jeopardized if the general overall plan to upgrade the entire reservation economy were not carried out. It was imperative to develop the economy along with the community. From 1960 to 1964, more feasibility studies were contracted to outside firms for town zoning, the building of community and shopping centers, the development of a small commercial industry, a timber survey, and a revision of the tribal investment program. Another study for reorganization of the tribal government was also undertaken.

In March 1958 the Tribal Council adopted a Master Plan, prepared by Stanford Research Institute, for the Dulce community. The tribe hired professional engineers to plan subdivisions of the community areas designed for development. The surveys were completed in July 1960 and base maps were prepared. It was the decision of the council that a modern water and sewage system be installed to service the planned subdivisions.

Construction began in June 1961 and was completed in November 1963, funded by the Public Health Service, the Bureau of Indian Affairs, and the tribe. This project was a major step in implementing the Dulce Community Development Plan and made improved housing possible for tribal members.[11]

A year after the water and sanitation plant was finished, the tribe began negotiating with Southern Union Gas Company to bring natural gas to Dulce, resulting in a gas franchise agreement on August 3, 1964. The agreement set out a schedule of rates for domestic consumers as well as for industrial consumption by the tribe and its enterprises.[12]

When these facilities were completed, the tribe began planning for commercial developments. In 1962, a ground-breaking ceremony was held, but the Master Development Lease between the Jicarilla Tribe and a private firm, Jicarilla Development Inc., was not approved until two years later. The lease provided for the development, with private funds, of a shopping center consisting of a supermarket and general store, a motel and restaurant, service station, garage, bank, post office, and a barber and beauty shop. A new tribal office building was also to be built. The commercial establishments already in operation in 1963 were the self-help laundry and the package liquor store. The latter was possible because on July 19, 1962, Acting Secretary John A. Carver, Jr., had legalized the sale and possession of intoxicating beverages on the Jicarilla Apache Reservation pursuant to state liquor laws.[13]

Employment opportunities were still scarce, but several projects and training programs, albeit temporary in nature, offered some relief. In 1962, through a combined effort of the BIA and the tribe, a 2,000-hour heavy-equipment-operator training program was initiated for tribal members. Under this program, fourteen Indians were trained and received certificates. An agreement between the state and the New Mexico Highway Department for the construction of a 32-mile fence along State Road 44 furnished some jobs. More unskilled work was made available in October 1963 by the Public Works Projects, building roads and small conservation facilities, and in addition, moneys were received for forest projects. Altogether, about sixty-five men were temporarily employed during the summer. The tribal recreation program also provided some summer youth employment as well as a few permanent positions.[14]

Local acceptance of and participation in various federal, state, and local housing programs was very slow at first. Although improvement had been made under the Family Plan, there was still much to be accomplished in this area. In 1963 the Jicarilla Apache Housing Authority was created to seek assistance from the Public Housing and Home Finance Company for low-rent and mutual self-help housing. The first twenty-five units of low-rent housing were constructed in the summer of 1965; fifteen more units were approved in 1967 and forty more in 1969.[15] Since not all tribal members were eligible for these programs, a tribal credit plan was established to finance home construction, and other federal assistance was sought from agencies such as the Farmers Home Administration. Very few, however, could qualify for housing under programs other than those generated by the Housing Authority.

The Jicarilla Apache Tribe, with the assistance of the Bureau of Indian Affairs, was making slow but steady progress in the implementation of its social and economic programs. In 1964 Secretary of the Interior Stewart Udall requested the final studies of Indian reservation economy with recommendations for the ten-year long-range plans. The Jicarilla Tribe had already submitted a provisional Overall Economic Development Program in 1963, but revised it the following year. The planning was designed in full accord with the goals of the Task Force and the philosophy of the president's War on Poverty. The major objectives were the elimination of poverty, and the training of reservation youth not only to take their place in the mainstream of American life, but also to assume responsibility as citizens of the United States and as citizens of their tribes.[16]

The Jicarilla Apache Tribe's Ten Year Plan was basically a continuation of the planning strategy of the 1950s, but it placed more emphasis on employment and on finding a replacement for the diminishing oil and gas income. The tribal focus was on industrial development and a commercial Outdoor Recreation and Tourism Program. By 1964, the Jicarilla Apache Buckskin and Leather Industry was employing approximately 20 full-time craftsmen. The tribe purchased the sawmill two years later and operated it as a tribal enterprise until it was destroyed by fire in 1968. It was not rebuilt despite the fact that it had an annual Indian payroll of over $100,000.[17] Experimental sales of livestock in Dulce proved to be a more successful enterprise—so much so that a group of cattlemen from Río Arriba County organized a marketing association and made a request to the Jicarilla Livestock Association to continue joint sales. Spurred by this, the tribe budgeted funds to construct a modern livestock sales barn in 1965. The council hired a non-Indian manager to operate this facility, which provided several part-time jobs. It has proved to be quite successful, cattle sales having averaged 3,500 head per year.

The largest effort to attract industry to the reservation was made in January 1970 when the tribe signed a contract authorizing the construction and operation of a 16,200-square-foot electronic assembly plant. It was anticipated that sixty individuals would be employed as assemblers, supervisors, and technicians. A job training program was sponsored by the Department of Labor, and funds for training purposes were promised by the North Central Concentrated Employment Program.

In 1968 and 1969 the tribal income was over $1,000,000. The economic projects appeared to be going so well that the tribe felt brave enough to invest in a risky business venture. In 1970 a resolution was passed providing for the investment of $2 million in a movie entitled "A Gunfight," portions of which were to be filmed on the reservation. The tribe was to receive 25 percent of all net profits and share in the music and television rights, and foreign sales.[18] It is not clear whether this was a successful endeavor; however, the Jicarilla tribe was subsequently bombarded with requests from Hollywood to sponsor other films, though all were rejected.

The more reliable investment in recreation and tourism promotion was stepped up. Before 1966, all development efforts had been concentrated on the sale of hunting and fishing licenses, which increased the number of off-reservation people mainly at La Jara and Stone Lakes, despite the lack of visitor facilities. Though advertisement of the hunting and fishing was mainly by word of mouth, there was an influx of sportsmen bringing recognition of the need to build facilities for camping, small retail tourist establishments, a restaurant and motel, a better road network, lake improvements, and the development of more lakes. In 1970, Lower Mundo Lake was improved to accommodate the growing recreation industry. A lodge and restaurant and a branch of the Dulce Liquor Store were built at Stone Lake. Most of the moneys for these projects came from federal and tribal matching funds.

The development of natural resources in four areas—forest, range, realty, and roads—became as important as the improvement of the community and the tourism industry. The Bureau and the tribe undertook a commercial forest program from which the tribe has realized an estimated income of $150,000 per year. This industry provides 35 man-years of employment per year, with fire protection generating an additional 4 man years. The program includes timber sale administration, forest development plans and surveys, logging and wood-using enterprises, and the improvement of fishing, wildlife habitat, and other recreational resources. Forestry also employs students as part of the summer youth program funded by the tribe.

The supervision of 733,950 acres of range has emphasized range and soil conservation through better livestock management in cooperation with federal and state agencies. In 1966 the tribe established its own cattle industry on land vacated by previous stockowners. A large portion of this land was designated as tribal grazing ranges for this enterprise.

The management of real property and the building of roads have also received attention. Approximately 400,000 acres of land were leased to gas and oil companies in 1970, the income from which constituted the bulk of tribal wealth. A 500-mile pipeline gathering system has been constructed on the reservation by El Paso Natural Gas Company and Northwest Pipeline Company. Similar industrial development programs have included the construction of roads, bridges, and small dams.

The tribe has always allocated sizable portions of its financial resources for the care and social well-being of its members. The Chester E. Faris Scholarship Fund, the Minors' Trust Fund, and the Family Plan are all examples of this tribal tradition cloaked in modern attire. The long-established practice of caring and sharing has never been totally supplanted by the American value of individualism. When the War on Poverty committed the nation's resources to help solve the economic and social problems of less fortunate Americans, the tribal government was willing to do its share. The reservation War on Poverty was, therefore, directed not only toward the elimination of economic problems, but of social problems as well. It was fully recognized that the economic battle could not be fought without combatting social ills.

The Jicarillas, like all groups in transition, have a number of social problems. In the 1950s, when the migration to Dulce began, the majority of the people had had virtually no contact with the mechanization and sophistication of modern urban life. The average reservation adult resident was familiar only with an isolated rural life-style in which he devoted himself to livestock raising. Homes were usually two- or three-room frame houses with no electricity or running water and furnished only with the bare necessities. Until the mid-1950s it was not uncommon for people to live in tents on a year-round basis while following the seasonal demands of their occupation. Very few livestock owners had the luxury of even owning an automobile. Nine months out of the year the children were at the Bureau boarding school. Although they learned about the outside world through their studies, they could not afford to emulate it.

This mode of living neither demanded complete adherence to the "American way of life," nor did it completely interfere with the traditional life-style as it existed at the time. Indeed, life was rather simplistic; but all this changed in the post–World War II era when the conflict between the persistence of tribal customs, mores, and attitudes, and the cultural changes brought about by the aftermath of war sharpened. Some Jicarillas were better able to cope with the conflict than others.

With the growth of the Dulce community, a new set of social problems emerged—problems that the tribe and the Bureau had to address, such as alcoholism, child neglect, juvenile delinquency, a growing number of welfare recipients, and so forth.

Child welfare programs have been a major concern for the tribe. A shelter home was established in 1963 on an experimental basis for chidren deprived of parental care, but in 1967 the council determined that it did not meet the needs of the children as adequately as foster homes. The tribe preferred that the children be placed in reservation foster homes, but this was not always possible. For example, in 1969 there were nine children in foster homes; five of these were on the reservation, one was in a non-Indian home, and three lived in licensed foster homes in Santa Fe because they needed health care that was available at the Indian hospital there.

Programs designed to fight alcoholism have been another prime concern of the tribe. A regular alcoholism program, including an Alcoholics Anonymous chapter, has been available since 1960.

In the 1950s the tribe started its own general welfare program with the establishment of a Health and Welfare Committee, which has since increased the number of its social-service activities. The continual need for social-welfare services has led to the Tribal General Assistance program, which furnishes financial help to those in need,

TABLE 8
Family Size

Number in Family	Number of Families
1	11
2	14
3	16
4	17
5	9
6	7
7	10
8	5
9	3
10	1
11	2
	95

The median family size is 3.85 members and the mean family 4.33.

Family Composition: The low-income families have been divided into the following classes:

A. Nuclear Families—husband, wife, children.
B. Incomplete Nuclear Family—widow or widower and children; childless couples.
C. Extended Family—nuclear family plus married and unmarried children.
D. Incomplete Extended Family—widow or widower and married chidren and/or other relatives.
E. Composite Family—nuclear family and one or more relatives or other persons.
F. Joint Families—brother-brother, sister-sister, brother-sister, or unrelated couples, or two or more unrelated persons.
G. Single person

A breakdown according to these classifications is given in Table 9.

counseling services for problems involving child care and family relations, placement for foster care, and general rehabilitative services.

The federal and state governments have cooperated with the tribe in offering social-welfare services to tribal members by providing welfare workers to coordinate liaison services such as the distribution of food stamps, publicizing available health programs, and consulting with the management of tribal welfare programs. When the tribe reduced its per-capita payments in 1950, coincidentally New Mexico extended its welfare services to tribal members.[19] The state also

TABLE 9
Family Composition

Type of Family	Families
A	41
B	19
C	2
D	12
E	6
F	4
G	11
	95

offered assistance, not directly related to welfare, through socially oriented programs (such as the services of an agriculture extension agent and a home demonstration agent who work with the tribe under Bureau contract with the state).

The education of Jicarilla children has remained a top priority. The education of the youth has been viewed as the answer to the historic "Indian problem," but it has not always been the government's number one priority. On the Jicarilla Reservation progress in education began in the late 1940s. The enrollment figures for the Jicarilla boarding and day schools steadily rose during the 1940s as shown by the average daily attendance records of the Jicarilla agency (see tables 12, 13). In the school year 1944–45, the average daily attendance was 177,

TABLE 10
Sex of the Household Head

Type of Family	Male	Female	Total
A	41	0	41
B	10	9	19
C	2	0	2
D	4	8	12
E	6	0	6
F	2	2	4
G	10	1	11
			95

TABLE 11
Age of Household Head

Date of Birth	Male	Female	Total
Before 1880	1	1	2
1880–1884	4	0	4
1885–1889	4	2	6
1890–1894	4	4	8
1895–1899	3	0	3
1900–1904	4	1	5
1905–1909	8	3	11
1910–1914	6	1	7
1915–1919	5	0	5
1920–1924	8	1	9
1925–1929	10	5	15
1930–1934	10	1	11
1935–1939	4	0	4
1940–1944	4	1	5
	75	20	95

and it grew to 232.2 in 1947–48. Although overall enrollment was decidedly increasing, the percentage increase in the number of students going beyond the seventh grade was very small. In 1948 there were 11 students in the eleventh and twelfth grades, but it was anticipated that this number would be between 15 and 20 the following year. Of the 11, 9 were girls, "indicating that the girls were first to show the way"[20] (according to the agency school report of 1948).

Just a decade earlier, it had not been uncommon for the girls to drop out at the age of thirteen or fourteen to get married, but now the girls were staying until sixteen, seventeen, and eighteen. Generally, both boys and girls stayed in school longer. In 1949 the school principal reported that "the present attitude of the majority of students is to continue on in school and to go on to Santa Fe next year if possible, and others who did not go this year, intend to next year. It seems that the girls are a little ahead of the boys in this attitude. Also the majority of our upper-grade students are girls. The attitude of the boys coming up in the grades seems to be to want to continue school."[21] The number staying in school to complete at least the sixth grade was

TABLE 12
Level of Education

Highest Grade Obtained by
Member of Family 18 Years and Older

Grade	Number of Families
0	6
1-4	13
5-8	47
9-12	18
Unknown	11

Highest Grade
Obtained by Household Head

Grade	Number of Families
0	18
1-4	18
5-8	40
9-12	11
Unknown	8

SOURCE: H. Clyde Wilson, "Analysis of Low-Income Families on the Jicarilla Apache Reservation," mimeograph, prepared for the Jicarilla Apache Tribal Council, Records of the Jicarilla Apache Tribe, Dulce, N.M.

encouraging, but for the majority, marriage and starting a business as a stockman precluded higher education.

By the 1951–52 school year, there were 311 Jicarilla students in all schools, the majority (263) in the Jicarilla boarding school.[22] The others were attending day schools and public schools of the various states. The Johnson-O'Malley Act of 1934 had provided the states with federal assistance for the education of Indian youth, thereby relieving them of the tax burden and providing financial incentive for assuming this obligation. In 1956 New Mexico assumed the responsibility of educating the Apaches. A public school existed on the reservation, and all students in the Dulce vicinity attended. The dormitories housed 263 students. The public school offered classes from kindergarten through the twelfth grade. Its facilities consisted of

TABLE 13
Jicarilla Apache Enrollment Information,
1951–52 to 1956–57

Type of School	1951–52	1953–54	1954–55	1955–56	1956–57
Public School	16	14	22	26	331
Federal Schools	295	346	325	326	27
Day Schools	32	80	93	99	0
Boarding Schools	263	266	232	227	2
Mission and Other	0	0	3	7	2
Total	311	360	350	359	360

SOURCE: Abstracted from Gallup Area Enrollment Information, 1952–52 to 1956–57 School Years, U.S. Dept. of the Interior, BIA, Branch of Education, Gallup Area Office, Nov. 12, 1957.

twenty-four classrooms, a dining hall, a small gymnasium, an auditorium, a comparatively well-equipped laboratory for physics and chemistry, playgrounds, ball fields, and a teaching staff of twenty-nine.[23]

The expectation was that Jicarilla children would receive a better education in the public school than their parents had received at the boarding school. In 1958 a study indicated that 76 to 90 percent of the adults who made up the 95-family low-income category had not finished the eighth grade. It was further concluded that "there was no indication that the household heads of these families were any less educated than the other adults on the reservation."[24] (Of the 477 adults, both male and female, whose education was known, about 70 percent did not finish the eighth grade.)

Dulce established an independent school district in 1959 when 207 students were attending school from their own homes, leaving only 204 dormitory students.[25] The trend away from dormitory use continued through the 1960s, and the facilities were closed in 1970. The economic status of the parents had improved to the point where they were able to provide for their own children's housing needs. In 1969–70, the Dulce public school enrollment was 582, of whom 446 were Jicarillas and other Indians, and 136 were non-Indians.[26] Over the past years the non-Indian population had been increasing and the students from the nearby town of Lumberton have been bussed in.

With larger enrollment, as well as a change in curriculum, the number of students who became eligible for higher educational opportunities, both vocational and academic, increased. Beginning in 1952, the tribe offered loans and grants to those desiring training and education beyond the twelfth grade. When the Chester E. Faris Scholarship Fund was established in 1956, all Jicarilla students were eligible for grants. Statistics indicate that they did not fail to take advantage of this opportunity. From 1956 to 1965, there were sixty-one vocational training grants and fifty-one college scholarships awarded. However, the attrition rate was very high: of the sixty-one vocational training candidates, only forty completed their training; and of the fifty-one college students, twenty-seven dropped out, usually in the first two years.[27] After 1965, when federal funds for Indian higher education became more readily available and the number of Jicarilla students desiring college degrees increased, the tribe welcomed Bureau financial assistance to help educate prospective scholars.

Recognizing that a large portion of the adult population had not had an opportunity to obtain a solid, comprehensive education, the tribe and the Bureau also focused attention on the needs of reservation adults by offering opportunities through employment assistance and adult education programs, instituted in the 1960s. Nor were the very young neglected. Many preschool children come from under-privileged homes and need early exposure to an educational environment. For these there are the Headstart programs and day care centers.

Like all other aspects of reservation life, tribal government underwent changes in the 1960s, mainly in response to the rapid economic and social progress made in that decade. With the growing agitation for greater participation by the American Indians in the determination of their own affairs, the Bureau was forced to devote more attention to governmental matters on the local level, and began to transfer more responsibilities to the tribal governing bodies. Under the Johnson administration, the preparation of tribal peoples for the eventual assumption of their responsibilities was stressed. The Bureau took steps to encourage the young people to develop more interest in tribal government, a goal strongly advocated by the Stanford Research Institute, which recommended the establishment of a junior tribal council. This recommendation was not implemented,[28] but major revisions were made in the tribal Constitution and the Tribal Council was again reorganized.

The 1960 Constitution provided for a president, vice-president, and a ten-member Tribal Council, all elected at large. It was organized into an executive committee of five members selected by the full council, and seven other committees: Finance, Land Claims, Family Plan, Credit, Health and Welfare, Resources, and a temporary committee to study the constitution. The council and its committees worked closely with the agency staff, drawing heavily upon its technical advice and assistance. The tribal president and vice-president have acted as program directors for many of the tribal programs and committees.

This new constitution allowed the council greater autonomy: it appointed its own committees; made decisions in regard to tribal loans, scholarships, land assignments, and employment of department heads; determined what projects would be given priority in the expenditure of tribal funds; and set the amount of per-capita payments. The council had greater control in the allocation of tribal resources and participated to a greater extent in the decisions of federal and state agencies that extended economic and social aid to the tribe. As in previous decades, there seemed to be continuing emphasis on the strengthening of control over procedural matters, while the substantive aspects of tribal business, such as the negotiation of gas and oil leases and business and consultant contracts, remained the domain of the Bureau.

The 1960 Constitution was revised on February 11, 1963, and amended several more times before 1968.[29] These amendments dealt with diverse issues: for example, the amendment considered in 1964 concerned the removal from the reservation of any nonmember whose presence was injurious to the tribe.

In 1966 the Bureau began to exert pressure to bring about another constitutional revision, although it is not clear why it considered the 1963 document inadequate. Two years later, another constitution was put before the voters, who accepted it on December 15, 1968.[30] Its provisions completely reorganized the tribal government, modeling it on that of the United States, with executive, legislative, and judicial branches—although in effect the previous tribal governments had operated basically on this very concept. This document, like the United States Constitution, defined procedures for the nominating process, the qualification of candidates, terms of office, how to fill vacancies, and causes for removal. It defined the powers and duties of the president, vice-president, councilmen, secretary, treasurer, tribal court and judges, and other elected officials. Each of the three branches had separate powers and no one branch was to exercise those properly belonging to another branch. No specific mention was made of equal powers—only *separate* powers.

As the 1937 Constitution had made direct reference to the federal Indian policy of the period, so too did the 1968 Constitution, which provided that the Bureau continue to give assistance to tribal members until the tribe should assume full responsibility. Tribal membership was redefined to include all persons of Indian blood whose names appeared on the official per-capita–dividend roll of December 15, 1968, and all children of 3/8 or more Jicarilla Apache blood born on or after December 15, 1968, whose mother or father was a member of the tribe. The rights of the members remained much the same as in the 1937 Constitution, but in response to the 1968 Indian Civil Rights Act, they were spelled out in greater detail.

Under this constitution the jurisdictional powers of the Tribal Court were specifically defined to include those matters relating to divorce, adoption, marriage, inheritance, juvenile guardianship, and misdemeanors committed on the reservation. A code of tribal offenses and a penal code dealing with seventy-three offenses were drawn up. The tribal government was given the power to establish a law enforcement program, although the tribe had had an operative law and order code for fourteen years. On April 15, 1956, the tribe had created such a program in response to an incident involving the slaying of Police Officer Ishkoteen Koteen, who had singlehandedly maintained peace and order on the reservation with only the occasional help of several deputies.[31] As the community grew, however, the law enforcement needs of the tribe changed drastically, resulting in the creation of a police department, and, almost concurrently, a tribal court.

The police department was staffed by a chief of police, ten to twelve officers, a juvenile officer, a patrol sergeant, and a police secretary. Since 1965, officer training has been handled through the Bureau of Indian Affairs and the New Mexico State Police Academy. One graduate has become the chief of police, assuming the duties of a non-Indian, a professional who held this office. Up through 1962 the department was financed solely by the tribe.

The tribal police enforce the code, maintain peace and order on the reservation, perform preliminary investigations of all crimes occurring on the reservation, and serve as officers of the tribal court. The New Mexico State Police have a resident officer who enforces the state laws insofar as non-Indians are concerned and cooperates with tribal officers when assistance is requested. The tribal police do not have jurisdiction over major crimes, but it is their duty immediately to notify the federal officers when major crime is committed within the boundaries of the reservation.

A long-standing legal dispute involving the Jicarilla Apache land claims finally was concluded as the 1960s drew to a close. These claims had been in litigation for a quarter of a century—so their settlement benefited a whole new generation.

The Jicarilla land claims had been permitted by the Indian Claims Commission Act of 1946. At that time, Congress felt that since Indian tribes had legitimate claims against the federal government, the trustee relationship could not be severed in good conscience. This legislation was seen as a step in the preparation of the Indians for withdrawal from federal guardianship. It was an attempt to deal honorably with every Indian tribe that had a claim against the United States, and to give the Indian his "day in court."

The Indian Claims Commission was given the power "to hear and determine claims brought by Indian tribes, bands, or any other identifiable group within the territorial limits of the United States." The claims were to have resulted "if the treaties, contracts, and agreements between the Indian tribes and the United States involved fraud, duress, unconscionable consideration, mutual or unilateral mistake whether of law or fact, or any other ground cognizable by a court of equity."[32]

Under this legislative mandate, the claim of the Jicarillas was filed as part of the *Apache Nation* v. *the United States Docket No. 22* on February 3, 1948, and it involved twelve other southwestern Apache tribes and bands. The Jicarilla claim was separated from this docket on January 5, 1958, when it became Docket No. 22-A, *Jicarilla Apache Tribe of the Jicarilla Apache Reservation, New Mexico* v. *the United States of America.* The land claim was for 14 million acres in northeastern New Mexico, portions of southeastern Colorado, and small portions of the western panhandles of Texas and Oklahoma.

The Jicarilla Apache Tribe had signed a land claims contract with James E. Curry and his associate Roy T. Mobley of Alamogordo on October 15, 1947, which began a twenty-four-year arduous litigation process.[33] In 1951, Curry was found in violation of portions of the legal code of ethics for having solicited more than thirty claims contracts, including the one with the Jicarillas.[34] As a result, the tribal council asked him to remove himself from the contract. The tribe entered into a new contract on March 5, 1951, with Mobley and his new associate, Guy T. Martin, of Washington, D.C.[35]

Between 1951 and 1955 the preliminary work on the claims case barely got off the ground. Only two hearings were held by the commission in 1951 and 1953; no substantive issues were adjudicated.

The tribal claims attorneys must have realized that the amount of legal work confronting them was enough for several full-time lawyers, so in 1957, Mobley arranged for two other law firms to assist him and Martin. Approval was given on April 20, 1957, for the affiliation of Robert J. Nordhaus of Albuquerque, New Mexico, and Richard M. Davis of Denver, Colorado.[36] The tribe agreed to employ experts to conduct research and gather evidence for the use of the attorneys, and to serve as witnesses before the commission. In addition, the Stanford Research Institute was contracted to define the boundaries of the Jicarilla aboriginal territory and to determine the value of the lands at the time of preemption in 1887.

An administrative problem arose with SRI in 1956, which could have ended up in court. It was cleared up by the attorneys, however, and as a result, the tribe hired Frank Hibben, an anthropologist from the University of New Mexico, to continue to determine the boundaries. He recommended Alfred B. Thomas, a noted Borderlands historian from the University of Alabama, to do the historical evaluation and analysis of the land claim.

With more attorneys and expert witnesses at hand, the claims case finally came before the commission in 1959. It was litigated in three stages before the final award was ordered by the commission. In the first stage, the commission determined whether or not the Jicarillas had original Indian title to certain lands in northeastern New Mexico and southeastern Colorado and whether the United States was liable for the expropriation of these lands without compensation in 1887. The first hearing was held on June 22, 1959, when the Jicarilla advocates reestablished claim to 14 million acres. Within this area there were Spanish and Mexican land grants that had been assigned by the respective governments prior to 1846. During the period from 1858 to 1860, Congress had recognized these grants as legitimate, and others were confirmed by the United States Court of Private Land Claims. In all, about 4.8 million acres were involved. The Jicarilla attorneys asserted that their clients had maintained undisturbed use and occupation of these grant lands and that these lands had been illegally awarded to other parties.

On August 26, 1963, the commission accepted the boundaries essentially as defined by the lawyers and the expert witnesses. This signaled the beginning of the second phase. The issue before the commission became the determination of the liability of the United States for the taking of Spanish and Mexican land grants located within the award area, the date of valuation, and the exact acreage of lands for which the United States was liable.

Negotiations between the tribal attorneys and the University of New Mexico to evaluate the lands resulted in a contract for the services of Leroy Gordon of the UNM geography department and Donald Cutter of the history department.[37] Gordon was to provide a complete description of the lands within the award area so that a land appraiser might establish their value. Cutter was to determine the legal rights of the Indians under Hispanic law, especially with regard to the land grants. In addition, John Maktos, an expert on international law concerning rights to land under the Spanish and Mexican governments, was hired.

With the help of these experts, the attorneys were ready to confront the government lawyers at the December 1964 hearings before the commission. The Jicarilla protagonists argued that the federal government was liable for all the lands including the land grants. Despite the evidence they furnished, the commission on November 9, 1966, decided to exclude the land grants because they had never become a part of the public lands of the United States; therefore, they said, the United States was not liable. This left approximately 9.2 million contended acres. The boundaries were redefined as roughly the area from Trinidad, Colorado, on the north, along the Texas and Oklahoma borders on the east, the Sangre de Cristo range on the west, and a line beginning at McIntosh (southeast of Albuquerque) and running below Santa Rosa and Tucumcari, New Mexico, on the south. The commission also decided that the day of extinguishment of Jicarilla title was August 20, 1883, when the United States military authorities had removed the tribe to the Mescalero Apache Reservation in southern New Mexico, and not 1887. The next order of procedure was to determine the fair market value of the lands at the date of taking, the amount of monetary damages for the award lands as of 1883, and the offsets from the final award.

This set in motion the third and final stage of the legal process. It continued to follow the pattern already established. Gordon furnished the Jicarilla land appraiser, Allen McMullen of Idaho, with a detailed study of the physiographic features of the award area and McMullen then evaluated the land on the basis of comparative sales of land in the Southwest. McMullen concluded that the fair market value of the area was approximately $12.6 million, whereas Harley M. McDowell, the government land appraiser, set the figure at $3.6 million.

The commission favored the petitioner's valuation and in a preliminary report decided that the lands were worth $1.08 per acre, for a total of $9,950,000. The commission issued an interlocutory order on December 2, 1970, that the Jicarilla Apache Tribe recover that amount minus the gratuitous offsets.[38]

After much negotiation, the attorneys for both parties compromised on $900,000 as the offset figure. On January 21, 1971, the Tribal Council was advised by its lawyers to accept the settlement offer. It had to be approved by the secretary of the interior or his representatives, and the officials of the tribe were also required to testify before the commission accepting the compromise settlement. All adult members of the tribe were notified to attend a general meeting on March 16, 1971, to vote on the settlement. Two hundred and sixty-four votes were cast in favor of the offer, with none in opposition. This whole meeting was strictly a procedural matter; no negative vote was expected, especially since it had taken twenty-four years to litigate, and the council had already adopted a resolution accepting the award. All this was approved by Commissioner of Indian Affairs Louis Bruce on April 1, 1971,[39] and confirmed by the commission three weeks later on April 20, when a judgment was rendered for the Jicarilla Apache Tribe to recover the amount of the settlement.

The period of litigation had been so long that by 1970, the pendulum of federal Indian policy had swung back toward self-determination. The monetary award then provided additional income for the tribe to continue its development programs and furnished tribal members with additional personal income.

The Tribal Council, with the advice of the local Bureau or agency, submitted a plan for the use of their funds. To improve the community, $1.5 million was earmarked to be invested, or to provide matching funds, for the construction of detention and correctional facilities, expansion of the domestic water system, paving of streets, and the building of a new sewer system. Income from the investment of $3,000,135 was to be used to produce jobs through the development of additional lakes, completion of the planned recreation program, improvement of a tribal livestock operation, creation of additional game parks, and the construction of a tribal sawmill. The largest amount, $4,515,000, was designated for per-capita payments. Each member was to receive a total of $2,000: an initial payment of $800, then $200 each quarter thereafter until a total of $2,000 was reached.[40]

The compensation awarded by the Indian Claims Commission topped off the good faith expressed by the federal government toward its Jicarilla trustees in this period. The progress of the Jicarilla Apache Tribe during the 1960s had been made possible by the close cooperation between the Bureau of Indian Affairs and the tribe, and the availability of federal assistance from numerous agencies. The Bureau and the federal government finally formed a working and workable relationship with the tribe, which theoretically should have been in operation since 1848—a relationship that would have obviated the need for the compensation awarded by the claims commission.

With the claims money, and federal funding and assistance, the Jicarilla Apache Tribe has had the opportunity for growth and progress. By 1970 the town of Dulce resembled any other American rural community. Here are to be found the offices and facilities of the tribe, the Bureau of Indian Affairs agency, and the Public Health Service. A tribally-owned shopping district consisting of a supermarket, motel, restaurant, garage and maintenance shop, cocktail lounge and package liquor store, service station, and laundromat today serves the approximately 2,000 residents. A private firm leases office space to the tribal government, a bank, and the post office. The police department and tribal court system are centered here. Other tribal enterprises located in the town are the Jicarilla Apache arts and crafts center, an electronics assembly plant, and a livestock sales barn. The businesses provide employment for Jicarillas, but a majority are owned by non-Indians.

The community center has a junior-size Olympic swimming pool, bowling alleys, a gymnasium, conference rooms, and general offices. In addition there is also a rodeo arena complex with lights for night activities. These all contribute to the tribe's developing recreation and tourism industry.

The community is served by a water system which has a river-intake reservoir, a filter and treatment plant, and a 250,000-gallon storage tank. Electric service is provided by the Río Arriba Rural Electrification Administration Cooperative, and telephone service is furnished by an independent company. Commercial natural gas is available from Southern Union Gas Company. Television translator stations provide three commercial channels. State Highway 17 is the main east-west access to the reservation, crossing its northern part, with a connecting north-south road that meets U.S. 84, the main highway between Albuquerque and Farmington, New Mexico.

The community's school system includes a local kindergarten and an elementary and junior-senior high school. Facilities include a gymnasium, football and track field, and housing for teachers. The tribe also runs adult education programs in the tribal community center, but the Bureau houses the day care center and Headstart program. There is a genuine concern today on the part of the tribe and the Bureau for the education of the Jicarilla people. Education is seen as the key to their future; without it, they will not be able to run their own affairs, make intelligent decisions, or become truly self-sufficient.

Growing prosperity and improvement in life-style characterize the community, and prove that with understanding, sound management, education, and abundant patience, the Jicarilla Apache Tribe has triumphed in its endeavor to overcome the deprivation and the concomitant problems that all too often spelled tragedy in early reservation life.

It must be remembered that the progress of the tribe is tied directly to its own economic assets. The government, like a commercial bank, is willing to offer financial assistance in direct proportion to its applicant's economic assets. Because the Jicarillas had the assets, the government was willing to pour money into their economy. At the same time, it must be remembered that it was not just tribal citizens who benefited from this federal windfall, but all the non-Indian business firms that built the tribal homes and buildings, the tribal lawyers, the tribal accountants, the business consultants of every imaginable sort, federal project directors, and merchants on and off the reservation.

To a certain extent, credit for this progress rests not only with the BIA-Jicarilla partnership, but with Indians and their friends throughout the United States who fought for greater opportunity for all Indians. While some portions of the Indian population actively agitated for Indian rights and opportunities, tribes like the Jicarilla, in a less active way, proved that what their more vocal brethren were fighting for was indeed possible. In the final analysis, however, continued progress rests ultimately with the Jicarilla Apaches.

Epilogue

The most important act of self-determination accomplished by the Jicarilla leadership was their 1886 decision to regain the northern reservation after the tribe's forced removal to the Mescalero Apache Reservation. Earlier, in the years from 1855 to the 1870s, they had actively participated in the process of choosing a reservation, either by not cooperating with Indian agents in settling a given reservation or by initiating negotiations with the government. These years provided valuable experience for the leaders, who in 1886 stepped outside the bounds of the normal channels to win the support of Governor Ross, whose coalition of influential individuals, including General Miles, formed a countervailing force powerful enough to get the president to sign the 1887 Executive Order. The victory in regaining the reservation has to be credited in part to the coalition of fair-minded men, but the decision to act rests solely with the Jicarilla leaders.

The importance of the 1886 decision cannot be overstated. Not only did the 1887 reservation become the permanent home of the Jicarilla Apache Tribe, but its natural resources provided a beautiful environment in which to live and income for the tribe. The isolated and mountainous reserve has served as a sanctuary where native Apache customs and beliefs have continued to flourish without interference. Though at times the geographical isolation seemed like a disadvantage, and despite early struggles and defeats, it has been the land that has nourished and nurtured the Jicarillas. This the Jicarillas leaders realized in 1886.

Ironically, it has also been the natural resources that have provided the backdrop to the problems created in the 1950s and 1960s. The economic windfall from oil and gas led to a resurgence of the Bureau's interest in the Jicarillas. The increase in tribal income also led to a rise in social problems that up to that time had not been a major concern.

In the future it will be the protection and management of tribal resources that will present problems. As natural resources are depleted, and become scarcer the world over, the value of and demand for the resources will increase. The problem for the Jicarillas will be to protect their valuable assets. Jicarilla history has proven that the government is limited in its ability and willingness to protect Indian properties, especially in times of economic depression. The real guardian and manager of Jicarilla property will have to be the Jicarillas themselves. The land will continue to be a key to the progress of the tribe.

Since the 1970s, more tribal funds have been spent on the determination of legal issues relevant to natural resources. Jicarilla Apache accounting claims against the United States government were settled in 1971. The Indian Claims Commission determined that the government had been negligent in the management of Jicarilla natural resources since 1887 and had failed to pay the proper amount of interest on the Jicarillas' trust account. Litigation to determine the water rights of the tribe has begun, but has not been settled. The tribe has gone to the federal courts to settle the issue of whether the tribe has the power to tax energy companies for the privilege of extracting oil and gas from the reservation. This case is now before the United States Supreme Court.

The severance tax case evolved out of a new economic venture that the tribe has started as a way to obtain more revenue from its mineral resources. The tribe entered into a joint venture with one of the several energy companies doing business on the reservation. As a result, the tribe owns and operates several oil and gas wells. This is an alternative to leasing the mineral properties for development. In this area the Jicarilla Apache Tribe has become a leader and has provided an example of how an Indian tribe can take control of the management of its natural resources.

The spirit of taking on new economic ventures has carried over to other aspects of tribal affairs. Tribal funds have been appropriated for cultural and historic preservation programs, recreational facilities, and educational assistance to Jicarilla candidates for college degrees.

Federal assistance in all these areas continues to play a large role in the upward trend that has occurred since the 1970s. But the Jicarillas, with their income from natural resources, have provided the matching funds often necessary for obtaining federal aid. The assistance given by the government cannot be construed as a gratuity in the literal sense of the word. It is an obligation on the part of the government, in return for the natural resources that the Jicarillas have in the past contributed to the nation's economy. The Jicarillas, like all other Indian tribes, were illegally and forcibly made to contribute, far out of proportion, to the general welfare and economic prosperity of this nation. It is too early to assess accurately the effects of the wholesale infusion of federal assistance on the Jicarilla Apache Reservation, despite apparent economic growth. Whether it will have a lasting effect will have to be determined at a later time.

Self-determination for the Jicarillas will continue to depend on the government, on whether it carries out its trust responsibilities in good faith. The government and the tribe will have to work in partnership. In the final analysis, however, the tribe will have to assume the major burden for its affairs. The Jicarillas will have to view federal aid not as "our due," but as an opportunity to maintain the cherished values of Indian life, to strengthen the concepts of tribal sovereignty through a tribal government run on the principles of equal rights and equal justice for all tribal members, and to ensure its future survival. The history of the Jicarilla Apache Tribe has proven that they have the ability to achieve true self-determination.

Notes

Prologue

1. This theme has been adopted from conclusions made by Dolores Gunnerson, *The Jicarilla Apaches: A Study in Survival* (DeKalb: Northern Illinois University Press, 1974), p. 296, and Morris E. Opler, "A Summary of Jicarilla Apache Culture," *American Anthropologist*, 38 (1936): 205.

2. Opler, "Jicarilla Apache Culture," p. 205; for other versions of the Jicarilla Apache Origin Story, *see* Pliny Earle Goddard, *Jicarilla Apache Texts*, Anthropological Papers of the American Museum of Natural History, 8 (1911); Frank Russell, "Myths of the Jicarilla Apaches," *Journal of American Folklore*, 40 (1898): 253–71; James Mooney, "The Jicarilla Genesis," *American Anthropologist*, 11 (1898): 197–209.

3. Opler, "Jicarilla Apache Culture," p. 205.

4. Ibid., p. 202.

5. *Jicarilla Apache Tribe of the Jicarilla Apache Reservation, New Mexico v. The United States of America*, Docket No. 22-A, 12 Indian Claims Commission (hereinafter ICC) 439 (1963) pp. 448–49.

6. George P. Hammond and Agapito Rey, eds., *Narratives of the Coronado Expedition* (Albuquerque: University of New Mexico Press, 1940), p. 261; George P. Hammond and Agapito Rey, eds., *The Rediscovery of New Mexico*, (Albuquerque: University of New Mexico

Press, 1966), p. 87.

7. Gunnerson, *The Jicarilla Apaches*, p. 64.

8. Ibid., p. 167.

9. For the source of terms, see Gunnerson, *The Jicarilla Apaches*, pp. 154–58.

10. Alfred B. Thomas, ed. and trans., *After Coronado* (Norman: University of Oklahoma Press, 1935), pts. 1 and 2; Gunnerson, *The Jicarilla Apaches*, p. 164; Elizabeth John, *Storms Brewed in Other Men's Worlds* (College Station: Texas A & M University Press, 1975), chaps. 6–7.

11. Thomas, *After Coronado*, p. 242.

12. Ibid., p. 27; Gunnerson, *The Jicarilla Apaches*, p. 233.

13. Thomas, *After Coronado*, p. 147.

14. Ibid., p. 36.

15. Ibid., pp. 201–12.

16. John, *Storms Brewed*, p. 255.

17. Alfred B. Thomas, ed. and trans., *Forgotten Frontiers* (Norman: University of Oklahoma Press, 1969), chap. 8.

18. Gunnerson, *The Jicarilla Apaches*, p. 290.

19. Ralph A. Smith, "Indians in American-Mexican Relations before the War of 1846," *Hispanic American Historical Review*, 43 (1963): 34.

20. Morris E. Opler, *Childhood and Youth in Jicarilla Apache Society*, Publications of the Frederick Webb Hodge Anniversary Publication Fund 5 (Los Angeles: Southwest Museum, 1946), p. 39.

21. Donald C. Cutter, "An Inquiry into Indian Land Rights...with Particular Reference to the Jicarilla Apache Area of Northeastern New Mexico," in *Apache Indians VI,* American Indian Ethnohistory Series (New York: Garland Publishing Co., 1974), pp. 245–80.

22. William A. Keleher, *Maxwell Land Grant: A New Mexico Item* (Santa Fe: Rydal Press, 1942), p. 29. See also Herbert O. Brayer, *William Blackmore* (Denver: Bradford-Robinson, 1949). Lawrence R. Murphy, *Philmont: A History of New Mexico's Cimarron Country* (Albuquerque: University of New Mexico Press, 1972).

Chapter 1

1. Morris E. Opler, "Jicarilla Apache Territory, Economy, and Society in 1850," *Southwestern Journal of Anthropology* 27 (1971).

2. Morris E. Opler, "A Summary of Jicarilla Apache Culture," American Anthropologist 38 (1936): 216–20.

3. Jicarilla Apache campsites were reconstructed from descriptions in Opler, "Jicarilla Apache Territory," p. 317, and from [Frank Hibben?], "Interview Notes with Juan Dedios," mimeographed (Dulce, N.M.: Jicarilla Apache Tribe, 1958?) and from Map on Jicarilla Land Claim Boundaries: Hibben Line, Claimants' Exhibit, *Jicarilla Apache Tribe* v. *the United States,* Record Group (hereinafter RG) 279, Records of the ICC, Docket No. 22-A, Jicarilla Apache Tribe, National Archives (hereinafter NA), Washington, D.C.

4. "Deposition of Members of the Jicarilla Apache Tribe of Indians," *The Apache Nation et al,* v. *The United States of America,* Docket No. 22, before the ICC, July 27–28, 1953.

5. Garfield Velarde, Jr., to Veronica Tiller, May 1, 1973. Letter in possession of author.

6. Jicarilla Apache Llanero campsites were reconstructed from descriptions in Opler, "Jicarilla Apache Territory," p. 317; [Hibben?] "Interview with Dedios," Map on Jicarilla Land Claim Boundaries: Hibben Line.

7. "Deposition of Members of the Jicarilla Apache Tribe," p. 2.

8. For an account of Lobo Blanco's role as a war leader, see Morris F. Taylor, "Campaigns against the Jicarilla Apaches, 1854," *New Mexico Historical Review,* 44 (1969).

9. Oral history interviews with George Phone, Aug. 24, 1974; Elfido Elote, July 14, 1977; Victor Vicenti, Aug. 22, 1974; Jicarilla Apache Reservation, Dulce, N.M., notes in author's possession.

10. Oral history interviews with Maggie Phone (great-granddaughter of San Pablo), Aug. 25, 1974, Jicarilla Apache Reservation, Dulce, N.M., notes in author's possession.

11. Conclusions drawn from oral history interviews with Dan Vigil, Belle Wells, Hans TeCube, Juanita Monarco, Mary V. Becenti and others, 1974–76, Jicarilla Apache Reservation, Dulce, N.M.

12. Jicarilla Apache informants, including Dan Vigil, Jack Inez, Victor Vicenti, Elfido Elote, Juanita Monarco, Belle Welles, and George Phone, have all confirmed this, but it was general knowledge to descendants, relatives, and relatives by marriage, including Mary V. Becenti, Louis Velarde, Rebecca Monarco Martínez, and Garfield Velarde, Jr.

13. Oral history interview with Belle Welles, July 19, 1977, Jicarilla Apache Reservation, Dulce, N.M., notes in author's possession.

14. Morris E. Opler, *Childhood and Youth in Jicarilla Apache Society,* Publications of the Frederick Webb Hodge Anniversary Publication Fund 5 (Los

Angeles: Southwest Museum, 1946),
p. 14.

15. Ibid., p. 47.

16. Ibid., p. 91.

17. Ibid., p. 31.

18. Ibid., p. 33.

19. For a full discussion of adolescence rites, see Morris E. Opler, "Adolescence Rite of the Jicarilla," *El Palacio*, 49 (1942): 25–38.

20. This observation is based on the author's own experience as a participant in the adolescence ceremony.

21. Morris E. Opler, "The Jicarilla Apache Ceremonial Relay Race," *American Anthropologist*, n.s. 46 (1944): 75–97.

22. Ibid., p. 78.

23. Ibid., p. 97.

24. Opler, "Jicarilla Apache Culture," pp. 214–16.

25. For full discussion, see Morris E. Opler, *The Character and Derivation of the Jicarilla Holiness Rite*, University of New Mexico Bulletin, Anthropological Series 4, no. 3 (1943).

26. *Jicarilla Apache Tribe* v. *the United States*, Docket No. 22-A, ICC, Dec. 1958.

27. Ibid.

28. [Hibben?], "Interview with Juan Dedios."

29. Opler, "Jicarilla Apache Territory," p. 318.

30. Opler, *Childhood and Youth*, p. 39.

31. Ibid., p. 39.

32. This observation is based on the author's own experiences and childhood memories.

33. Opler, "Jicarilla Apache Culture," p. 210. For a tale on a raiding expedition, see Morris E. Opler, "A Jicarilla Apache Expedition and Scalp Dance," *Journal of American Folklore*, 54 (1941): 10–23.

34. Opler, "Jicarilla Apache Culture," p. 211.

35. Ibid., p. 212.

36. [Hibben?], "Interview with Juan Dedios."

37. Ibid.

38. Oral history interview with Nagee Vicenti, Aug. 22, 1974, Jicarilla Apache Reservation, Dulce, N.M., notes and tape in author's possession.

39. Opler, "Jicarilla Apache Culture," p. 206.

40. Opler, "Jicarilla Apache Territory," p. 302.

41. Oral history interview with Juanita Monarco, July 1975, Jicarilla Apache Reservation, Dulce, N.M., notes in author's possession.

Chapter 2

1. J. Fred Rippy, "The Indians of the Southwest in the Diplomacy of the United States and Mexico, 1848–1853," *Hispanic American Historical Review*, 2 (1919): 363–96.

2. John T. Hughes, *Doniphan's Expedition* (Cincinnati, Ohio: U. P. James, 1847), p. 68.

3. Paul A. F. Walter, "The First Civil Governor of New Mexico Under the Stars and Stripes," *New Mexico Historical Review*, 8 (1933): 111–12.

4. George Archibald McCall, *New Mexico in 1850: A Military View*, ed. Robert W. Frazer (Norman: University of Oklahoma Press, 1968), pp. 33–34.

5. Walter: "First Civil Governor of New Mexico," p. 112.

6. Annie H. Abel, ed., *The Official Correspondence of James S. Calhoun* (Washington, D.C.: Government Printing Office, 1915), p. 3.

7. Ibid.

8. Judd to Dickerson, Aug. 16, 1849, RG 94, Records of the Adjutant General's Office, 518-W-1849, National Archives, comps., Stanford Research Institute, *Historical and Documentary*

Evidence concerning the Claim of the Jicarilla Apache Tribe before the Indian Claims Commission: Docket No. 22, The Apache Nation ex. rel. Fred Pellman et al., Petitioners v. the United States of America Respondent (Menlo Park, 1957), book 5 (hereinafter cited as SRI, *Historical Evidence*).

9. John Greiner, "Overawing the Indians," RI 541, William G. Ritch Papers, Henry E. Huntington Library, San Marino.

10. For accounts of the White Party massacre, see Abel, *Correspondence of Calhoun*, pp. 63–74; Edwin L. Sabin, *Kit Carson Days: Adventurers in the Path of Empire*, 2 vols. (New York: n.p., 1935) 2: 618–22; Greiner, "Overawing the Indians."

11. Grier to Adams, Nov. 30, 1849, RG 94, 98-N-1850, SRI, *Historical Evidence*, book 5.

12. Greiner, "Overawing the Indians."

13. Ibid.

14. Burnside to Ward, May 30, 1850, RG 94, 313-M-1850, SRI, *Historical Evidence*, book 5.

15. Grier to McLaws, July 31, 1851, RG 94, 158-M-1850, SRI, *Historical Evidence*, book 5.

16. Robert M. Utley, *Frontiersmen in Blue: The United States Army and the Indians, 1848–1865* (1967; rpt. Lincoln: University of Nebraska Press, 1981), p. 85.

17. Holliday to Allen, Mar. 28, 1851, RG 94, 158-M-1851, SRI, *Historical Evidence*, book 5.

18. Chapman to Alexander, May 26, 1851, RG 94, 295-M-1851, SRI, *Historical Evidence*, book 5.

19. McLaws to Alexander, Apr. 25, 1851, RG 94, 250-M-1851/6, SRI, *Historical Evidence*, book 5.

20. McLaws to Chapman, Apr. 18, 1851, in Abel, *Correspondence of Calhoun*, p. 318.

21. Chapman to Ward, Apr. 21, 1851, RG 94, 250-M-1851/9, SRI, *Historical Evidence*, book 5.

22. Munroe to Jones, May 31, 1851, RG 94, 250-M-1851, SRI, *Historical Evidence*, book 5.

23. Ward to Alexander, May 1, 1851, RG 94, 250-M-1851/15, SRI, *Historical Evidence*, book 5.

24. Ewell to Alexander, May 26, 1851, RG 94, 250-M-1851, SRI, *Historical Evidence*, book 5.

25. Ewell to McLaws, June 8, 1851, RG 94, 294-M-1851, SRI, *Historical Evidence*, book 5.

26. Calhoun to Lea, July 30, 1851 in Abel, *Correspondence of Calhoun*, p. 393.

27. Chapman to Alexander, May 26, 1851, RG 94, 259-M-1851, SRI, *Historical Evidence*, book 5.

28. Greiner to Calhoun, Mar. 30, 1852, RG 75, LR, 1852, SRI, *Historical Evidence*, book 5.

29. Steck to Lane, May 20, 1852, RG 75, LR, NM-1853-N128, SRI, *Historical Evidence*, book 6.

30. Manypenny to Lane, Apr. 19, 1853, RG 75, NMFP, SRI, *Historical Evidence*, book 6.

31. Lane to Manypenney, May 30, 1853, RG 75, NM-1853, N127, SRI, *Historical Evidence*, book 6.

32. Manypenney to Meriwether, Aug. 8, 1853, RG 75, SRI, *Historical Evidence*, book 6.

33. Graves to Meriwether, Aug. 31, 1853, RG 75 NM, LR, 1853, N-153; SRI, *Historical Evidence*, book 6.

34. Cooke to Nichols, Feb. 20, 1854, RG, 393, United States Army Continental Commands, 1821–1920, Fort Union, N.M., Letters Received, 1851–1856, NA (hereinafter cited as RG 393, Fort Union).

35. Bell to Cooke, Mar. 7, 1854, RG 94, 177-G-1854, SRI, *Historical Evidence*, book 6.

36. Cooke to Nichols, Mar. 22, 1854, RG 393, Fort Union, vol. 10, p. 34.

37. Messervy to Head, Mar. 25, 1854, RG 75, LR, SRI, *Historical Evidence*, book 6.

38. Blake to Cooke, Mar. 19, 1854, RG 393, Fort Union.

39. Messervy to Carson, Apr. 7, 1854, RG 75, LR, 1854 N-245, SRI, *Historical Evidence*, book 6.

40. Messervy to Manypenny, Mar. 31, 1854, RG 75 LR, 1854, N-245, SRI, *Historical Evidence*, book 6.

41. Cooke to Nichols, May 24, 1854, RI 646, Ritch Papers.

42. Head to Messervy, Apr. 7, 1854, RG 75, NMFP, SRI, *Historical Evidence*, book 6.

43. Taylor, "Campaigns of 1854," p. 274.

44. Messervy to Manypenny, Apr. 29, 1854, RG 75, LR, 1854, SRI, *Historical Evidence*, book 6.

Chapter 3

1. Labadie to Meriwether, Abiquiu Agency Monthly Report for October 1855, RG 75, Records of the Bureau of Indian Affairs (hereinafter RBIA), NMFP, NA, comps., Stanford Research Institute, *Historical and Documentary Evidence concerning the Claim of the Jicarilla Apache Before the Indian Claims Commission: Docket No. 22, The Apache Nation ex. rel. Fred Pellman, et al., Petitioners v. the United States of America, Respondent,* (Menlo Park, 1957), book 6. (hereinafter cited as SRI, *Historical Evidence*).

2. Carson to Meriwether, Sept. 26, 1855, No. 96, U.S. Cong., Senate, *Report of the Secretary of the Interior,* Senate Exec. Doc. No. 1, 34th Cong., 1st sess., 1855.

3. Labadie to Manypenny, Dec. 31, 1856, RG 75, NMFP, SRI, *Historical Evidence*, book 6.

4. David to Manypenny, Mar. 28, 1856, RG 75, NM-1865, N71, SRI, *Historical Evidence*, book 6.

5. Ibid.

6. Garland to Thomas, June 30, 1856, RG 94, AGO, LR, N96, SRI, *Historical Evidence*, book 6.

7. Telegram(?), RG 75 NM-1856, B84, SRI, *Historical Evidence*, book 6.

8. Pelham to Hendricks, July 28, 1856, RG 75, NM-1856, N158, SRI, *Historical Evidence*, book 6.

9. Meriwether to Manypenny, Aug. 9, 1856, RG 75, NM-1856 158, SRI, *Historical Evidence*, book 6.

10. Meriwether to Manypenny, Sept. 19, 1856, RG 75, NM-1856 N172, SRI, *Historical Evidence*, book 6.

11. Arny to Collins, Sept. 1, 1862, No. 5, U.S. Cong., Senate, *Report of the Secretary of the Interior,* Senate Exec. Doc. No. 1, 37th Cong., 3rd sess., 1862, pp. 386–87.

12. Lawrence R. Murphy, *Frontier Crusader: William F. N. Arny* (Tucson: University of Arizona Press, 1972), p. 102.

13. Murphy, *Frontier Crusader,* p. 108. See also Arrell M. Gibson, *The West in the Life of the Nation* (Boston: D. C. Heath, 1976), p. 416.

14. Arny to Collins, Sept. 1, 1862, *Report of the Secretary of the Interior,* House Exec. Doc. No. 1, 37th Cong., 3rd sess., 1862, pp. 387–88.

15. Ibid., pp. 382, 385.

16. Mausinares to Steck, Sept. 23, 1863, No. 43, U.S. Cong. House, *Report of the Secretary of the Interior,* House Exec. Doc. No. 1, 38th Cong., 1st sess., 1863–64, pp. 231–32.

17. Keithly to Steck, Sept. 22, 1863, *Report of the Secretary of the Interior,* House Exec. Doc. No. 44, 38th Cong., 1st sess., 1863–64, p. 232.

18. Arny to Collins, Sept. 1, 1862, *Report of the Secretary of the Interior,* House Exec. Doc. No. 1, 37th Cong., 3rd sess., 1862, p. 390.

19. Steck to Keithly, Jan. 25, 1864, RG 75 NMFP, SRI, *Historical Evidence,* book 7.

20. Abstract of Papers Accompanying Report of J. K. Graves, Special Agent Relative to Indian Affairs in New Mexico, No. 41, U.S. Cong., House, *Report of the Secretary of the Interior,* House Exec. Doc. No. 1, 39th Cong., 2d sess., 1866, pp. 131–37.

21. Keithly to Steck, Sept. 22, 1863, U.S. Cong., House, *Report of the Secretary of the Interior,* House Exec. Doc. No. 1, 38th Cong., 1st sess., 1863–64, p. 233.

22. Salazar to Graves, Jan. 4, 1866, *Report of the Secretary of the Interior,* House Exec. Doc. No. 1, 39th Cong., 2d sess., 1866, p. 141.

23. Denison to Gallegos, June 12, 1869, No. 49, U.S. Cong., House, *Report of the Secretary of the Interior,* House Exec. Doc. No. 1, 41st Cong., 2d sess., 1869.

24. [Frank Hibben?], "Interview with Juan Dedios," mimeographed (Dulce, N.M.: Jicarilla Apache Tribe, 1958?)

25. Lawrence R. Murphy, *Philmont: A History of New Mexico's Cimarron Country* (Albuquerque: University of New Mexico Press, 1972), p. 85.

26. Denison to Pope, Oct. 6, 1860, SRI, *Historical Evidence,* book 7.

27. Norton to Cooley, July 19, 1866; Cooley to Norton, July 19, 1866, RG 75, SMFP, SRI, *Historical Evidence,* book 7.

28. Carleton to Arny, Aug. 1866, RG 75, LR, NM-1866, SRI, *Historical Evidence,* book 7.

29. Carleton to Campbell, Aug. 25, 1866, RG 75, LR, NM-1866, SRI *Historical Evidence,* book 7.

30. Murphy, *Philmont,* p. 80.

31. Gregory C. Thompson, *Southern Ute Lands, 1848–1899,* Occasional Papers of the Center of Southwest Studies, Fort Lewis College, no. 1, (Durango: Fort Lewis College, 1972), p. 5.

32. Murphy, *Frontier Crusader,* p. 140.

33. Arny to Webb, Aug. 31, 1868, U.S. Cong. House, *Report of the Secretary of the Interior,* House Exec. Doc. No. 1, 40th Cong., 3rd sess., 1868.

34. Ibid.

35. Arny to Taylor, Jan. 14, 1868, RG 75, NM-1868, SRI, *Historical Evidence,* book 7.

36. Arny to Taylor, Dec. 12, 1868, RG 75, LR, NM-1868, SRI, *Historical Evidence,* book 7.

37. Murphy, *Philmont,* p. 107.

38. Arny to Parker (?), Sept. 1870, RG 75, NMFP-1870, SRI, *Historical Evidence,* book 7.

39. Wilson to Clinton, Sept. 22, 1870, RG 75, NMFP-1870, SRI, *Historical Evidence,* book 7.

40. Denison to Pope, Dec. 6, 1870, RG 75, NMFP-1870, SRI, *Historical Evidence,* book 7.

41. Roedel to Pope, Dec. 27, 1870, RG 75, NMFP-1870, SRI, *Historical Evidence,* book 7.

42. Murphy, *Philmont,* p. 111.

43. Ibid., p. 112.

Chapter 4

1. Russell to Commissioner of Indian Affairs, Aug. 16, 1876, U.S. Cong., House, *Report of the Secretary of the Interior,* House Exec. Doc. No. 1, pt. 5, 44th Cong., 2d sess., 1876, p. 507.

2. Russell to Commissioner of Indian Affairs (hereinafter CIA), Aug. 7, 1878, U.S. Cong., House, *Report of the Secretary of the Interior,* House Exec. Doc. No. 1, pt. 5, 45th Cong., 3rd sess., 1878, p. 602.

3. U.S. Cong., House, "Negotiations with Ute Indians," House Exec. Doc.

No. 90, 42nd Cong., 3rd sess., 1863; U.S. Congress, House, "Brunot Agreement": Report of the Commission with Ute Tribe of Indians, House Exec. Doc. No. 53, 43rd Cong., 1st sess., 1874.

4. Dudley to Smith, June 3, 1873, RG 75, RBIA, Letters Received, New Mexico-1873, NA, comps., Stanford Research Institute, *Historical and Documentary Evidence concerning the Claim of the Jicarilla Apache Nation ex. rel. Fred Pellman et al., Petitioners v. the United States of America, Respondent* (Menlo Park, 1957), book 8 (hereinafter cited as SRI, *Historical Evidence*).

5. U.S. Cong. House, "The Brunot Agreement," House Exec. Doc.. NO. 1, pt. 5, 43rd Cong., 1st sess., 1874.

6. Smith to Dolan, Nov. 17, 1873, RG 75, NMFP, SRI, *Historical Evidence*, book 8.

7. Thomas A. Dolan, "Report of Council Proceedings with the Jicarilla Apache Indians," *New Mexico Historical Review*, 4 (1925): 59–72. See also *Executive Orders Relating to Indian Reservations from May 14, 1855 to July 1, 1912* (Washington: Government Printing Office, 1912).

8. Russell to CIA, Nov. 13, 1874, RG 75, NM-1874, SRI, *Historical Evidence*, book 8.

9. McNulta to CIA, Sept. 9, 1875, RG 75, LR, NM-1875, SRI, *Historical Evidence*, book 8.

10. Crothers to CIA, Sept. 14, 1875, RG 75, LR, NM-1875, SRI, *Historical Evidence*, book 8.

11. Crosley to Secretary of Interior, Jan. 3, 1876, RG 75, LR, NM-1876, SRI, *Historical Evidence*, book 8.

12. Russell to CIA, Jan. 25, 1876, RG 75, LR, NM-1876, SRI, *Historical Evidence*, book 8.

13. Ibid.

14. *Annual Report of the Commissioner of Indian Affairs to the Secretary of the Interior for the Year 1877* (Washington, D.C.: Government Printing Office, 1878).

15. Charles C. Royce, *Indian Land Cessions in the United States*, Bureau of American Ethnology, Eighteenth Annual Report, 1896–97, pt. 2 (Washington, D.C.: Government Printing Office, 1899), p. 872.

16. Thomas to CIA, Dec. 20, 1877, RG 75, LR, NM-1877, SRI, *Historical Evidence*, book 8.

17. Godfrey to CIA, Aug. 27, 1878, RG 75, LR, NM-1878, SRI, *Historical Evidence*, book 8.

18. Watkins to CIA, Aug. 19, 1878, RG 75, LR NM-1878, SRI, *Historical Evidence*, book 8.

19. Ibid.

20. Roberts to Thomas, July 1, 1878, RG 75, RBIA, Pueblo and Jicarilla Agency Records, Miscellaneous Letters Sent, 1875–1880, Federal Records Center, Denver (hereinafter cited as RG 75, RBIA, PJA, MLS, 1875–1880, FRC, Denver).

21. Roberts to Thomas, May 16, 1879, RG 75, RBIA, PJA, MLS, 1875–1880, FRC, Denver.

22. Acting CIA to Secretary of the Interior, Sept. 11, 1880, RG 48, LR, Indian Division, 1880, SRI, *Historical Evidence*, book 8.

23. Ibid.

24. Interview with Juanita Monarco, Jan. 1973, Jicarilla Apache Reservation, Dulce, N.M., notes in author's possession.

25. Liebert to Thomas, May 5, 1882, RG 75, RBIA, PJA, MLS, 1880–1885, FRC, Denver.

26. Ibid.

27. Reed to Thomas, June 27, 1882, RG 75, RBIA, PJA, MLS, 1880–1885, FRC, Denver.

28. Reed to Thomas, June 17, 1882, RG 75, RBIA, PJA, LS, 1880–1885, FRC, Denver.

29. Thomas to CIA, July 11, 1882, RG 75, RBIA, PJA, LS, 1880–1885, FRC, Denver.

30. Thomas to CIA, July 1881, RG 75, RBIA, PJA, LS, 1880–1885, FRC, Denver.

31. Ibid.

32. Thomas to Reed, Aug. 14, 1882, RG 75, RBIA, PJA, MLS, 1880–1885, FRC, Denver.

33. Ritch to Secretary of Interior, July 29, 1881, RG 48, LR, Indian Division, 1881, SRI, *Historical Evidence,* book 8.

34. Thomas to CIA, Aug. 1, 1881, RG 75, LR-1881, SRI, *Historical Evidence,* book 8.

35. Ibid.

36. Ibid.

37. Ibid.

38. Thomas to Reed, July 26, 1882, RG 75, RBIA, PJA, MLS, 1880–1885, FRC, Denver.

39. Llewellyn to Reed, Oct. 5, 1882, RG 75, RBIA, Mescalero and Jicarilla Agency, Miscellaneous Letters sent, 1880–1885, Federal Records Center, Denver (hereinafter cited as RG 75, RBIA, MJA, MLS, 1880–1885, FRC, Denver).

40. Ibid.

41. Llewellyn to Reed, Oct. 5, 1882, RG 75, LR, 1882, SRI, *Historical Evidence,* book 8.

42. Howard to CIA, Feb. 13, 1883, RG 75, LR, 1883, SRI, *Historical Evidence,* book 8.

43. Secretary of Interior to CIA, July 13, 1883, Authority 6050, RG 75, SRI, *Historical Evidence.*

44. Howard to Secretary of the Interior, June 11, 1883, RG 75, NM-1883, SRI, *Historical Evidence,* book 8.

45. Interview with Juanita Monarco, Jan. 1973, Jicarilla Apache Reservation, Dulce, N.M., notes in author's possession.

46. Llewellyn to CIA, Aug. 14 and 16, 1883, certificate attached by Stanley, RG 75, LR, NM-1883, SRI, *Historical Evidence,* book 8.

47. Grierson to Assistant Adjutant General, Dec. 1, 1886, RG 94, AGO, LR, 1886, SRI, *Historical Evidence,* book 8.

48. Report on Mescalero-Jicarilla Agency, Nov. 1, 1883, RG 48, Records of the Secretary of the Interior, Indian Division, Inspector's Files—1883, Letters Received, Garner-Mescalero-Jicarilla, National Archives (hereinafter cited as RG 48, Inspector's Files, LR, NA.)

49. Report on Mescalero-Jicarilla Agency, Oct. 13, 1883, RG 48, Inspector's Files—1883, LR, NA.

50. Llewellyn to Gardner, Oct. 23, 1883, RG 48, Inspector's Files—1883, LR, NA.

51. Llewellyn to CIA, Apr. 25, 1884, RG 75, LR, Indian Office, 1884, SRI, *Historical Evidence,* book 8.

52. Stevens to Secretary of the Interior, Nov. 10, 1884, RG 75, LR, 1885, SRI, *Historical Evidence,* book 8.

53. Cowart to Ambrose, Feb. 1, 1886, RG 75, RBIA, Mescalero Agency, MLS, Oct. 1886, FRC, Denver.

54. Cowart to CIA, Apr. 21, 1886, RG 75, Mescalero Agency, MLS, April 1886, FRC, Denver.

55. Cowart to CIA, July 1, 1886, RG 75, Mescalero Agency, MLS, July 1886, FRC, Denver.

56. Ibid.

57. Cowart to CIA, July 16, 1886, RG 75, Mescalero Agency, MLS, July 1886, FRC, Denver.

58. Ibid.

59. Ibid.

60. Williams to CIA, Dec. 18, 1886, RG 75, RBIA, Pueblo Agency, MLS, 1880–1885, RFS, Denver; Grierson to Asst. Adj. General, Feb. 1, 1887, RG 94, Attorney General's Office (hereinafter AGO), LR, 1886, NA, SRI, *Historical Evidence,* book 8.

61. Ibid.

62. Ibid.

63. Ibid.

64. Telegram, Asst. Adj. General, Division of the Pacific to General of the U.S. Army, Nov. 13, 1886, RG 94, AGO, LR, 1886, NA, SRI, *Historical Evidence*, book 8.

65. Cowart to CIA, Nov. 18, 1886, Mescalero Agency, MLS, Nov. 1886, FRC, Denver.

66. Welton to CIA, Apr. 12, 1887, RG 75, LR, 1887, SRI, *Historical Evidence*, book 8.

67. Welton to Perry, Feb. 24, 1887, RG 94, LR, AGO, SRI, *Historical Evidence*, book 8.

68. Welton to Springer, Jan. 28, 1887, RG 94, LR, AGO, SRI, *Historical Evidence*, book 8.

69. CIA to Welton, Mar. 22, 1887, RG 75, LS, 1887, SRI, *Historical Evidence*, book 8.

70. CIA to Secretary of the Interior, Mar. 29, 1887, P͡ 5, LS, 1887, SRI, *Historical Evidence*, book 8.

71. Welton to CIA, May 2, 1887, RG 75, LR, 1887, SRI, *Historical Evidence*, book 8.

72. CIA to Secretary of the Interior, June 23, 1887, RG 94, AGO, LR, 1887, SRI, *Historical Evidence*, book 8.

Chapter 5

1. D. S. Otis, *The Dawes Act and the Allotment of Indian Lands*, ed. Francis Paul Prucha, (Norman: University of Oklahoma Press, 1973), pp. 6–7.

2. Fred A. Nicklason, "Report on the Jicarilla Apache Accounting," Docket No. 22-K, for the years 1887–1892, mimeographed (Dulce, N.M.: Jicarilla Apache Tribe), p. 36 (hereinafter cited as Nicklason, "Jicarilla Accounting").

3. CIA, Nov. 4, 1889, RG 75, RBIA, Letters Received, Indian Office, 1881–

1907, NA (hereinafter cited as RG 75, LR, 1881–1907, NA).

4. CIA to Rankin, June 7, 1890, RG 75, LS 1881–1907, NA.

5. CIA to Special Agent, Mar. 24, 1891, RG 75, LS, Letter Book 213–14L, NA.

6. *Annual Report of the Commissioner of Indian Affairs to the Secretary of the Interior, 1889–1890*, p. 228 (hereinafter cited as CIA, *Annual Report*).

7. Ibid., p. 222.

8. Acting CIA of GLO to CIA, May 6, 1895, RG 75, LR, 1881–97, NA.

9. Taggart to CIA, Feb. 16, 1898, RG 75, LR, 1881–1907, Special Case 147, NA.

10. Walpole to CIA, Apr. 14, 1890, RG 75, LR, 1881–1907, Special Case, 68, NA.

11. Special Agent to CIA, Aug. 13, 1880, RG 75, LR, 1881–1907, Special Case 68, NA.

12. Nicklason, "Jicarilla Accounting," p. 6.

13. Ibid.

14. Welton to CIA, Jan. 26, 1887, RG 75, LR, 1907 Special Case 28, NA.

15. Welton to CIA, July 1, 1887, RG 75, LR, 1881–1907, NA.

16. Welton to Grierson, Sept. 20, 1887, RG 393, Records of the Army Continental Commands, Fort Union, 1821–1920.

17. Acting CIA to Secretary of Interior, Aug. 1, 1887, RG 75, LS, Letter Book 163–164L, NA.

18. Executive Order of Feb. 11, 1887, in *Executive Orders Relating to Indian Reservations from May 14, 1885 to July 1, 1912* (Washington, D.C.: Government Printing Office, 1912), p. 293; Nicklason, "Jicarilla Accounting," p. 12.

19. CIA to Secretary, June 23, 1887, RG 75, LR, 1881–1907, NA.

20. CIA to Secretary, Oct. 6, 1899, RG 75, LS, 1881–1907, NA.

21. Nicklason, "Jicarilla Accounting," pp. 30–32.

22. Ibid., p. 37.

23. Acting CIA to Welton, May 18, 1887, RG 75, LS, LB 159–60L, NA.

24. Ibid.

25. CIA to Welton, Dec. 18, 1886, RG 75, LS, LB 153–54L, NA.

26. Nicklason, "Jicarilla Accounting," p. 13.

27. Duncan to CIA, Dec. 6, 1898, RG 75, LR, 1881–1907, NA.

28. CIA to Welton, Mar. 22, 1887, RG 75, LS, 1881–1907, NA.

29. CIA, *Annual Report*, 1891.

30. CIA, *Annual Report*, 1889.

31. Affidavit, Tarsey against Stollsteimer, Feb. 7, 1887, RG 48, Records of the Secretary of the Interior, Indian Division, Appointments File, Southern Ute-Stollsteimer, National Archives (hereinafter cited as RG 48, ID, AF, S. Ute-Stollsteimer, NA).

32. Welton to CIA, July 5, 1887, RG 48, ID, AF, S. Ute-Stollsteimer, NA.

33. Grierson to Asst. Adj. General, Oct. 13, 1887, RG 48, ID, AF, S. Ute-Stollsteimer, NA.

34. CIA to Welton, Oct. 1, 1887; Welton to CIA, Oct. 6, 1887, RG 48, ID, AF, S. Ute-Stollsteimer, NA.

35. Teller to CIA, Oct. 9, 1889; Stollsteimer to Teller, Oct. 1, 1889, RG 48, AF, S. Ute-Stollsteimer, NA.

36. Taggart to CIA, May 20, 1889, RG 75, LR, 1881–1907, NA.

37. CIA to Secretary, Oct. 6, 1889, LS, 1881–1907, NA.

38. CIA, *Annual Report*, 1895.

39. Bullis to CIA, Apr. 7, 1896, RG 75, RBIA, Jicarilla Agency, LS, 1895–1900, Federal Records Center, Denver.

40. Nicklason, "Jicarilla Accounting," p. 28.

41. Ibid., p. 29.

42. U.S. Cong., House, Allotments on the *Jicarilla Reservation*, New Mexico, House Exec. Doc. No. 134, 59th Cong., 2d sess., 1906, p. 1.

43. U.S. Cong., House, *Jicarilla Reservation*, House Report 6382, 59th Cong., 2d sess., 1907.

44. Executive Order of Jan. 28, 1908, *Executive Orders Relating to Indian Reservations*, p. 293.

45. *Jicarilla Apache Agency Report*, 1919, RG 75, Jicarilla Agency, Narrative Annual Reports, 1919, FRC, Denver.

46. Special Agent to CIA, Nov. 2, 1918, Nicklason, "Jicarilla Accounting," p. 39.

47. U.S. Cong., House, Congressional Record, 56th Cong., 1st sess., 1919, 58, pt. 1, p. 187.

48. Ibid.

49. Ibid.

50. *Jicarilla Agency Annual Report*, RG 75, Jicarilla Agency, Annual Narrative Reports, 1922, NA.

51. *Jicarilla Agency Annual Report*, RG 75, Jicarilla Agency, Annual Narrative Reports, 1930, FRC, Denver.

52. U.S. Cong., Senate, Subcommittee of Committee on Indian Affairs, *Survey of Conditions of Indians of the United States*, Hearing on S. R. 79, 308, 70th Cong., 2d sess., pt. 19, May 11, 1931.

53. U.S. Cong., Senate, Condition of Indians in the United States, Speech of Hon. William H. King, Senate Document No. 214, 72nd Cong., 2d sess., Feb. 8, 1933, p. 11.

54. Ibid., p. 73.

55. U.S. Cong., House, Subcommittee of House Committee on Appropriations, *Hearings on Interior Department Appropriation Bill for 1934*, 72nd Cong., 2d sess., 1934.

Chapter 6

1. Interview with Seguro Lucero, July 1974, Jicarilla Apache Reservation, Dulce, N.M., notes in author's possession.

2. *Report of the Commissioner of Indian Affairs to Secretary of the Interior, 1887* (Washington: Government Printing Office, 1888).

3. Interview with Mary Becenti and Rebecca Monarco Martinez, July 1974, Jicarilla Apache Reservation, Dulce, N.M., notes in author's possession.

4. Interview with Seguro Lucero, 1974.

5. U.S. Cong., House, *Report of the Secretary of the Interior, House Doc.* No. 5, 54th Cong., 1st sess., 1895–96, p. 221 (hereinafter cited as *Report of Secretary of Interior*).

6. First Asst. Sec. to Secretary of the Interior, Oct. 22, 1892, RG 48, Records of the Secretary of the Interior, Indian Division, Appointments File, Jicarilla-Robertson, NA (hereinafter cited as RG 48, ID, AF, Jic.-Robertson, NA).

7. Ibid.

8. Keck to CIA, May 31, 1892, RG 48, ID, AF, Jic.-Robertson, NA.

9. Report on Jicarilla Subagency by Cisney, Aug. 19, 1892, RG 48, ID, AF, Jic.-Robertson, NA.

10. Ibid.

11. Ibid.

12. Robertson to Hogan, July 13, 1893, RG 75, PJA, MLS, 1890–95, FRC, Denver.

13. D. S. Otis, *The Dawes Act and the Allotment of Indian Lands,* ed. Francis Paul Prucha, (Norman: University of Oklahoma Press, 1973), p. 95.

14. *Report of the Secretary of the Interior, 1892,* House Exec. Doc. No. 1, pt. 5, 52nd Cong., 2d sess., 1892–93, p. 337.

15. Jic. Agency, *Narr. Annual Report,* 1914.

16. William T. Hagan, *Indian Police and Judges* (New Haven: Yale University Press, 1966).

17. Rules and Regulations Governing the Police Force at the Jicarilla Agency, Miscellaneous Letters, FRC, Denver.

18. Jicarilla Agent to Wirt, Oct. 14, 1899, RG 75, PJA, MLS, FRC, Denver.

19. Rules and Regulations, 1896, RG 75, Jicarilla Agency, MLS, 1896, FRC, Denver.

20. *Report of the Secretary of the Interior,* House Exec. Doc. No. 1, pt. 5, 54th Cong., 1st sess., 1895–96, p. 221.

21. Lonnie E. Underhill and Daniel F. Littlefield, Jr., eds., *Hamlin Garland's Observations on the American Indian, 1895–1905* (Tuscon: University of Arizona Press, 1976), p. 133.

22. Ibid., p. 136.

23. Ibid., p. 27.

24. Diane Putney, "Fighting the Scourge: American Indian Morbidity and Federal Policy, 1897–1928," (Ph.D. diss., Marquette University, 1980), p. 41. Information on population: CIA, *Annual Report,* 1887–1909; U.S. Census Office, *Survey of Conditions of Indians of the United States;* Jicarilla Agency, *Annual Reports,* 1931–34.

25. Ibid., p. 78.

26. G. L. Williams to CIA, Jan. 25, 1909, RG 75, Jicarilla Agency, Central Files 1907–39, 723, NA.

27. Putney, "Fighting the Scourge," p. 120.

28. Inspection Report by F. Shoemaker, Mar. 20, 1912, RG 75, Jicarilla Agency, Central Files 1907–39, 723, NA.

29. Ibid.

30. Ibid.

31. Jic. Agency, *Narr. Annual Report,* 1910.

32. "Report on Conditions on Jicarilla Reservation," 1912, RG 75, Jic. Agency, Central Files, 1912, NA.

33. Home and Social Conditions on Jicarilla Reservation, 1915, RG 75, Jicarilla Agency, CCF-1915, NA.

34. Jic. Agency, *Narr. Annual Report,* 1910.

35. C. A. Churchill to CIA, Jan. 25, 1911, RG 75, Jicarilla Agency, Central Files 1907–39, 723, NA.

36. O. M. McPherson to CIA, Nov. 24, 1915, RG 75, Jicarilla Agency, Central Files 1907–39, 150, NA.

37. C. A. Churchill to CIA, Jan. 25, 1911, RG 75, Jicarilla Agency, Central Files 1907–39, 723, NA.

38. Ibid.

39. Green to Scott, Dec. 10, 1912; Acting CIA to Adams, Jan. 7, 1913; MacColl to Lane, Nov. 22, 1913; RG 75, Jicarilla Agency CCF-910, NA.

40. Ibid.

41. Inspection Report of Jicarilla Agency, 1912, RG 75, Jicarilla Agency, Central Files 1907–39, NA.

42. Jic. Agency, *Narr. Annual Report,* 1910.

43. Ibid.

44. Inspection Report by W. M. Peterson, Jicarilla, Apr. 13, 1913, RG 75, Jicarilla Agency, Central Files 1907–39, 700, NA.

45. Jicarilla Indian Reservation, Sept. 17–22, 1914, RG 75, Jicarilla Agency, Central Files, 1907–39, 126135–14–150, NA.

46. Jic. Agency, *Narr. Annual Report,* 1914.

47. Special Report on Jicarilla Agency, Mar. 22–26, 1916, RG 75, Jicarilla Agency, Central Files, 1907–39, NA; School enrollment figures from Jicarilla Agency School Census, Jic. Agency, *Narr. Annual Report,* 1931–39.

48. Investigation Report by C. M. Knight, July 26, 1917, RG 75, Jicarilla Agency, Inspection Reports, 1908–40, NA.

49. Report by F. Shoemaker, Sept. 7, 1917, RG 75, Jicarilla Agency, Central Files 1907–39, 150, NA.

50. Jic. Agency, *Narr. Annual Report,* 1919.

51. Ibid.

52. "A Study of the Need for Public Health Nursing on Indian Reservations," Archives of the American Red Cross, 500.003 Indian Demonstration, NA (hereinafter Patterson Report).

53. Ibid.

54. Jic. Agency, *Narr. Annual Report,* 1922.

Chapter 7

1. Bullis to CIA, Sept. 19, 1895, RG 75, RBIA, Pueblo and Jicarilla Agency, Letters Sent, 1890–95, Federal Records Center, Denver (hereinafter cited as RG 75, PJA, LS, date, FRC, Denver).

2. *Report of the Commissioner of Indian Affairs to Secretary of the Interior,* 1903, Jicarilla Agency (hereinafter cited as CIA, *Annual Report*).

3. CIA, *Annual Report,* 1899, p. 254.

4. U.S. Cong., House, Report of the Secretary of the Interior on Indian Affairs, House Exec. Doc. No. 1, pt. 5, 51st Cong., 2d sess., 1890–91, p. cxlvi (hereinafter cited as *Report of the Secretary of the Interior*).

5. Pueblo Agent to Gaylord, Dec. 19, 1897, RG 75, PJA, LS, 1895–1900, FRC, Denver.

6. Robertson to CIA, Sept. 19, 1892, RG 75, PJA, LS, 1890–95, FRC, Denver.

7. Chase to CIA, Sept. 9, 1890, RG 48, Records of the Secretary of the Interior, Indian Division, Inspector's Files— Ramona Indian School, NA (hereinafter cited as RG 75, ID, IF–Ramona, NA).

8. Ibid., Inspection Report, Apr. 11, 1894, RG 78, ID, IF–Ramona, NA.

9. Vigil to Cooper, Apr. 5, 1898, RG 75, PJA, MLR, 1895–1900, FRC, Denver.

10. Jicarilla Agency Narrative Annual Report, 1910, RG 75, Jicarilla Agency, Narrative Annual Reports, 1910–35, NA (hereinafter cited as Jic. Agency, *Narr. Annual Report*).

11. Report on Jicarilla Agency, Nov. 9–13, 1919, RG 75, RBIA, Jicarilla Agency, Central Files 1907–39, NA, (hereinafter cited as RG 75, Jic. Agency, CF 1907–39, NA).

12. Jic. Agency, *Narr. Annual Report,* 1911.

13. Inspection Report on Jicarilla Agency and School, 1913, RG 75, Jic. Agency, CF 1907–39, NA.

14. Inspection Report, Jicarilla Agency, 1915, RG 75, Jic. Agency, CF 1907–39, NA.

15. Jic. Agency, *Narr. Annual Report,* 1910.

16. Ibid.

17. Diane Putney, "Fighting the Scourge: American Indian Morbidity and Federal Policy, 1897–1928," (Ph.D. diss., Marquette University, 1980), chap. 1.

18. Ibid., p. 14.

19. Ibid., p. 23.

20. Ibid., p. 44.

21. Ibid., p. 46.

22. Average is based on figures from the Jicarilla Apache Agency Annual Reports, Narrative Section on Education, 1903–1906.

23. Special Report on Jicarilla Agency, 1916, RG 75, Jic. Agency, CF 1907–39, NA.

24. Jic. Agency, *Narr. Annual Report,* 1910.

25. RG 75, RBIA, Jicarilla Apache Agency, Central Classified Files-723, 1912, NA.

26. Inspection Report by F. Shoemaker, Mar. 20, 1912, RG 75, RBIA, Jicarilla Agency, Central Classified Files-723, 1912, NA.

27. "A Study of the Need for Public Health Nursing on Indian Reservations," Patterson Report.

28. Jic. Agency, *Nar. Annual Report,* 1911, Health Section.

29. Jic. Agency, *Narr. Annual Report,* 1912.

30. Ibid.

31. Ibid.

32. Boarding School Principal to McConihe, Mar. 3, 1915, RG 75, Jicarilla Agency, CF 1907–39, NA.

33. Inspection Report by Radcliffe, May 14, 1919, RG 75, Jic. Agency, CFC 1907-39, NA.

34. Jic. Agency, *Narr. Annual Report,* 1912.

35. Jic. Agency, *Narr. Annual Report,* 1920, 1921.

36. Jic. Agency, *Narr. Annual Report,* 1932.

37. Gossett to CIA, Nov. 23, 1926, RG 75, Jic. Agency, Decimal Files, Inspection-150, FRC, Denver.

38. Gossett to CIA, Nov. 23, 1926; Report of Inspection Trip to Jicarilla Agency, Oct. 1929, RG 75, Jic. Agency, CF 1907–39, NA.

39. Supervisor of Education to CIA, June 21, 1922, RG 75, Jicarilla Agency, CF 1907–39, NA.

40. White to CIA, Dec. 5, 1934, RG 75, Jic. Agency, CF 1907–39, NA.

41. White to CIA, Dec. 5, 1934, RG 75, Jic. Agency, CF 1907–39, NA.

42. Jic. Agency, *Narr. Annual Report,* 1931.

43. Shepard to Collier, May 19, 1933, RG 75, Jicarilla Agency, CF 1907–39, NA.

44. Rhoades to Vice-President, Dec. 20, 1932; Shepard to Secretary of the Interior, July 11, 1932, RG 75, Jic. Agency, CF 1907–39, NA.

45. Health Survey of Jicarilla Apache Tribe 1934, White to CIA, Dec. 5, 1934, RG 75, Jic. Agency, CF 1907–39, NA.

46. Ibid.

47. Graves to CIA, July 15, 1932; Graves to CIA, Feb. 11, 1935, RG 75, Jic. Agency CF 1907–39, NA.

48. Graves to CIA, Feb. 11, 1935, RG 75, Jic. Agency, CF 1907–39, NA.

49. Jic. Agency, *Narr. Annual Report,* 1938.

50. Warner to Towsend, Nov. 29, 1937, RG 75, Jic. Agency, CF 1907–39, NA.

51. Warner to Towsend, Dec. 17, 1937, RG 75, Jic. Agency, CF 1907–39, NA.

Chapter 8

1. "A Bird's Eye View of Indian Policy Historical and Contemporary," 1935;

"Statements Concerning Indian Service Policies by Members of the Washington Staff," June–July 1938, RG 75, RBIA, Jicarilla Apache Agency, Decimal File-120-Policy, Federal Records Center, Denver (hereinafter cited as RG 75, Jic. Agency, DF, FRC, Denver).

2. Graves to Commissioner of Indian Affairs (CIA), Aug. 6, 1934; Graves to CIA, Mar. 26, 1934, RG 75, Jic. Agency, DF, Letters to the Commissioner (LC) 004, FRC, Denver; Graves to CIA, May 1, 1934, RG 75, Records Concerning the Wheeler-Howard Act 1933–37, Jicarilla Files, NA (hereinafter cited as RG 75, RW-H, 1933–37, Jic. Files, NA).

3. Graves to CIA, Mar. 26, 1934, Faris to CIA, May 1, 1934; RG 75, RW-H, 1933–37, Jic. Files, NA; Faris to Collier, Jan. 5, 1937; Stover to CIA, Aug. 22, 1938, RG 75, Jic. Agency, DF, LC 004, FRC, Denver.

4. This position was maintained by Albert Velarde, Sr., one of the main opponents to cancellation of allotments. He was one of the last Jicarillas to turn in his patent. Interview with Rebecca Monaco Martínez, Dec. 1978, Jicarilla Apache Reservation, Dulce, N.M., notes in author's possession.

5. Faris to CIA, May 1, 1934, RG 75, RW-H, 1933–37, Jic. Files, NA.

6. CIA to Graves, Feb. 23, 1934; RG 75, Jic. Agency, DF, LC, 004, FRC, Denver.

7. "Indian Reorganization Act Land Acquisition Jicarilla Project" Dec. 11, 1935, RG 75, Jicarilla Agency–Central Files, 1910–39, 066-pt. 1, NA (hereinafter cited as RG 75, Jic. Agency, CF 1910–39, NA).

8. Ibid; Radcliffe to Stewart, July 23, 1936, RG 75, Jic. Agency, CF 1910–39, 066–9809, NA.

9. Opler to CIA, 1936; Memo Crosthwait to CIA, Dec. 5, 1936, RG 75, Jic. Agency, CF 1907–39, NA.

10. Balsam to CIA, Oct. 26, 1936, RG 75, Jic. Agency, CF 1907–39, NA.

11. Ibid.

12. Ibid.

13. Memorandum Faris to Collier, Oct. 13, 1936, RG 75, Jic. Agency, CF 1907–39, NA.

14. Ibid.

15. Opler to Collier, 1936; Balsam to Collier, Oct. 26, 1936, Faris to Collier, Oct. 13, 1936, RG 75, Jic. Agency, CF 1907–39, NA.

16. Stover to Collier, June 22, 1937; RG 75, Jic. Agency, DF, LC-004, FRC, Denver; U.S. Department of the Interior, *Constitution and By-Laws of the Jicarilla Apache Tribe Indian Reservation New Mexico August 4, 1937* (Washington, D.C.: Government Printing Office, 1937).

17. Interview with Juana Monarco, Seguro Lucerco, Elfido Elote, Lee Martinez, Sr., and Bell V. Wells helped to confirm the residence of the 1937 Council, Summer 1976, Jicarilla Apache Reservation, Dulce, N.M. Notes in possession of author. Stover to Collier, Aug. 11, 1937, RG 75, RW-H, 1933–37, Jic. Files, NA.

18. Tabulations made from Jicarilla Agency's Fiscal Report of Dec. 31, 1936, RG 75, Jic. Agency, CF 1907–39, NA.

19. Stover to CIA, Feb. 25, 1938, RG 75, Jic. Agency, CF 1907–39, NA.

20. "Program of the Jicarilla Indian Reservation, New Mexico," RG 75 Jic. Agency, DF-103 Programs, Post War Resettlement, FRC, Denver.

21. U.S. Dept. of the Interior, *Corporate Charter of the Jicarilla Apache Tribe of the Jicarilla Reservation September 4, 1937* (Washington, D.C.: Government Printing Office, 1938).

22. Walker to Critchfield, July 19, 1937, Jicarilla Fiscal Report of 1937; RG 75, Jic. Agency, CF 1907–39, NA.

23. "Exhibit G," Jicarilla Fiscal Report of 1936, RG 75, Jic. Agency, CF 1907–39, NA.

24. Ibid.

25. Stover to Dietrich, Jan. 21, 1943, RG 75, Jic. Agency, CF 1907–39, NA.

26. Critchfield to Stover, Jan. 30, 1942; Cooley to Pohland, Feb. 25, 1942, RG 75, Jic. Agency, CF, 1907–39, Extension, NA.

27. Area Credit, Gallup Area Office, to CIA, Oct. 24, 1957, RG 75, Jic. Agency–Central Classified Files–1957, Credit, National Records Center, Suitland, Md.

28. Collier to Baltzar and Vicenti, Apr. 26, 1943; RG 75, Jic. Agency, CF, 1907–39, 056, NA; Jicarilla Apache Tribal Council Meeting Minutes, May 1, 1943, RG 75, Jic. Agency, DF-056, FRC, Denver.

Chapter 9

1. S. Lyman Tyler, *A History of Indian Policy,* (Washington, D.C.: Government Printing Office, 1973), Chap. 7.

2. Ibid., p. 163.

3. Ibid., p. 172.

4. Ibid., pp. 162–64.

5. Ibid., p. 179.

6. Ibid.

7. Tribal Council Budget, 1950, from Tribal Council Meetings, June 1950, mimeographed (Dulce, N.M.: Jicarilla Apache Tribe); Stanford Research Institute, *The Needs and Resources of the Jicarilla Apache Tribe* (Menlo Park: Stanford Research Institute, 1957), p. 7.

8. 1950 Annual Extension Report, Jicarilla Indian Reservation, Record Group 75, Records of the Bureau of Indian Affairs, Jicarilla Agency, Central Classified Files 1935–60, Extension, National Record Center, Suitland, Md. (hereinafter cited as RG 75, Jic. Agency, CCF 1935–60, NRC, Suitland).

9. Ibid.

10. Jicarilla Field Trip Report, 1954, RG 75, Jic. Agency, CCF 1935–60, 211, NRC, Suitland.

11. Ibid.

12. Interview with Rebecca Monarco Martinez, Dec. 1978, Jicarilla Apache Reservation, Dulce, N.M. Notes in possession of author.

13. Huber to Deputy Commissioner, Feb. 23, 1958, RG 75, Jic. Agency, CCF 1958, Credit, NRC, Suitland.

14. Galbraith to Area Director, Feb. 23, 1954; Huber to Deputy Commissioner, Oct. 15, 1958; RG 75, Jic. Agency, CCF 1958, Credit, NRC, Suitland.

15. Huber to Deputy Commissioner, Oct. 15, 1958, RG 75, Jic. Agency, CCF 1958, Credit, NRC, Suitland.

16. Ibid.

17. Ibid.

18. Ibid.

19. Ibid.; also memorandum from Inspection Officer to Deputy Commissioner, Sept. 5, 1958, RG 75, Jic. Agency, CCF 1958, Credit, NRC, Suitland.

20. Galbraith to Area Director, Feb. 23, 1954; CIA to Dempsey, 1955(?); Huber to BIA Section 500, July 16, 1954; Bennett to Jenkins, May 12, 1954, RG 75, Jic. Agency, CCF 1954–58, Credit, NRC, Suitland.

21. Huber to Deputy Commissioner, Oct. 15, 1958, RG 75, Jic. Agency, CCF 1958, Credit, NRC, Suitland.

22. Huber to Deputy Commissioner, Oct. 15, 1958, RG 75, Jic. Agency, CCF 1958, NRC, Suitland.

23. Greenwood to Head, Aug. 23, 1955; Inspection Officer to Deputy Commissioner, Sept. 5, 1958, RG 75, Jic. Agency, CCF 1955–58, Credit and Inspections, NRC, Suitland.

24. CIA to Dempsey, 1955(?), RG 75, Jic. Agency, CCF 1955(?), Credit, NRC, Suitland.

25. Galbraith to Area Director, Feb. 23, 1954, RG 75, Jic. Agency, CCF 1954–58, Credit, NRC, Suitland.

26. Ibid.

27. Ibid.

28. Ibid.

29. Acting Supt. to CIA, Feb. 13, 1958, RG 75, Jic. Agency, CCF 1958, Credit, NRC, Suitland.

30. Ibid.

31. Lewis to CIA, May 29, 1954, RG 75, Jic. Agency, CCF 1954, Trust 211, NRC, Suitland.

32. Ibid.

33. Minors' Trust Fund, 1956, Records of the Jicarilla Apache Tribe, Dulce, N.M.

34. Ibid.

35. Press Release, July 12, 1956, Department of the Interior Information Service, RG 75, Jic. Agency, CCF 1956, 220, NRC, Suitland.

36. Summary and Recommendations, 1955, Jicarilla Apache Agency, RG 75, Jic. Agency, CCF 1956, NRC, Suitland; Tribal Council Budget and Justification, 1954, RG 75, Jic. Agency, CCF, NRC, Suitland.

37. Ibid.

38. Ibid.

39. Study on Overall Economic Conditions on Jicarilla Reservation, 1554, RG 75, Jic. Agency, CCF, NRC, Suitland.

40. Ibid.

41. H. Clyde Wilson, "Jicarilla Apache Political and Economic Structures," *Publications in American Archaeology and Ethnology*, 48, no. 4 (Berkeley: University of California Press, 1964), pp. 297–360.

42. Tribal Council Minutes, Oct. 7, 1955, Records of the Jicarilla Apache Tribe, Dulce, N.M.

43. Tribal Council Records 1960–68, Records of the Jicarilla Apache Tribe, Dulce, N.M.

44. The one-fourth blood quantum remained until it was changed to three-eights in the 1968 Jicarilla Apache constitution and bylaws.

45. See Jicarilla Apache Fiscal Budgets, 1950–59, Records of the Jicarilla Apache Tribe, Dulce, N.M.

46. Ibid., 1956–59.

47. Minutes of the Jicarilla Tribal Executive Committee, Dec. 12, 1955,

Records of the Jicarilla Apache Tribe, Dulce, N.M.

48. Harry W. Basehart and Tom T. Sasaki, "Changing Political Organizations in the Jicarilla Apache Reservation Community," *Human Organization*, 23 (1964): 287.

49. Jicarilla Apache Fiscal Budget, 1956, Records of the Jicarilla Apache Tribe, Dulce, N.M.

50. Minutes of Tribal Executive Committee, Nov. 13, 1957, Records of Jicarilla Apache Tribe, Dulce, N.M.

51. Basehart and Sasaki, "Changing Political Organizations," pp. 286–87.

52. Minutes of the Jicarilla Tribal Council, June 28, 1955, Records of the Jicarilla Apache Tribe, Dulce, N.M.

53. Minutes of the Jicarilla Tribal Council, Sept. 21, 1955, Records of the Jicarilla Apache Tribe, Dulce, N.M.

54. Stanford Research Institute, *Needs and Resources of the Jicarilla Apache Indian Tribe*, 5 vols. (Menlo Park: SRI, 1958), "Introduction."

55. See Clarence Forsling, "A Report with Recommendations on the Economic Development of the Jicarilla Apache Tribe," mimeographed, Oct. 18, 1854, Jicarilla Apache Tribe, Dulce, N.M.

56. Minutes of the Jicarilla Tribal Council, Oct. 7, 1957, Records of the Jicarilla Apache Tribe, Dulce, N.M.

57. See Wilson, *Jicarilla Apache Political and Economic Structures*, p. iii.

58. Minutes of the Jicarilla Tribal Council, Mar. 15, 1957, Records of the Jicarilla Apache Tribe, Dulce, N.M.

Chapter 10

1. For a full discussion, see Alvin M. Josephy, Jr., *Red Power: The American Indians Fight for Freedom* (New York: McGraw-Hill, 1972.)

2. For a summary of federal Indian policies in the 1960s, see Donald Parman's "American Indians and the Bicentennial," *New Mexico Historical Review*, 51 (1976): 233–51.

3. Samuel L. Hilliard, "The Family Plan Program," Jan. 31, 1966, RG 75, RBIA, Jicarilla Agency, Central Classified Files 1935–1970, 079, 1804, National Records Center, Suitland, Md. (hereinafter cited as RG 75, Jic. Agency, CCF 1935–70, NRC, Suitland.)

4. Olsen to Commissioner of Indian Affairs, Sept. 26, 1968, RG 75, Jic. Agency, CCF 1935–70, 229, Pt. I, NRC, Suitland.

5. H. Clyde Wilson, "Analysis of Low-Income Families on the Jicarilla Apache Reservation," mimeographed, prepared for the Jicarilla Apache Tribal Council, Records of the Jicarilla Apache Tribe, Dulce, N.M.

6. Ibid.

7. Quinn to Asst. Commissioner, July 5, 1960, RG 75, Jic. Agency, CCF 1935–70, 077–6731, Pt. II, NRC, Suitland.

8. Hilliard, "The Family Plan Program," p. 52.

9. Ibid., p. 59.

10. Ibid., p. 61.

11. Jicarilla Agency, "The Reservation and Status of Its Development," 1967, Jicarilla Agency Records, Dulce, N.M.

12. Superintendent to Area Program Officer, Mar. 18, 1969, RG 75, Jic. Agency, CCF 1935–70, 058, NRC, Suitland.

13. Area Director to Anderson, Oct. 19, 1961, RG 75, Jic. Agency, CCF 1935–70, 170, NRC, Suitland; *Federal Register* 27, 143 (1962): 7046.

14. Ibid., p. 7.

15. Ibid. See also Tribal Ordinance Resolution 63–184, 1963, RG 75, Jic. Agency, CCF 1935–70, 054, Pt. III, NRC, Suitland.

16. Ten-Year Planning Report Requested by Secretary Stewart L. Udall, Jicarilla Reservation, Nov. 18, 1964, RG 75, Jic. Agency, CCF 1935–70, 380, 7363, Pt. 1-A, 1964.

17. Task Description–Sawmill and Timber, 1968, RG 75, Jic. Agency, CCF 1935–70, 339.1, NRC, Suitland.

18. Jicarilla Apache Tribe and Jicarilla Agency Staff, *Together We Strive: An Analysis of Community Development Teamwork and Coordination on the Jicarilla Apache Indian Reservation* (Pagosa Springs, Col.: SUNPrint, 1970.)

19. Quinn to Asst. CIA, July 5, 1960, RG 75, Jic. Agency, CCF 1935–70, 077–6731, Pt. II, NRC, Suitland.

20. Jicarilla Boarding School Report 1948, RG 75, CCF Jic. Agency, School Statistics, 1948, NA.

21. Ibid.

22. Asst. Area Director to Area Director, Oct. 28, 1957, RG 75, Gallup Area Office, Education, 1957, CCF-NRC, Suitland.

23. Carol Kerr, "Education on the Jicarilla Apache Reservation" M.A. thesis, Staten Island College, 1958.)

24. Wilson, "Low-Income Families," p. 9.

25. Supt. to Quinn, June 24, 1960, RG 75, Jic. Agency, CCF 1935–70, 077, 6731, Pt. II, NRC, Suitland.

26. U.S. Cong., Senate, *Providing for Disposition of Funds Appropriated to Pay: Judgment in Favor of the Jicarilla Apache Tribe…Senate Report No.* 92-768, 92d Cong., 2d sess., 1972.

27. "Study of Scholarship Program," Jicarilla Agency, Branch of Education, Dulce, N.M.

28. SRI, *Needs and Resources of the Jicarilla Apache Indian Tribe.*

29. Cummings to CIA, June 18, 1964, RG 75, Jic. Agency, CCF 1935–70, Tribal Programs, NRC, Suitland.

30. U.S. Dept. of the Interior, *Jicarilla Apache Tribal Constitution and By-*

laws, Dec. 15, 1968 (Washington: Government Printing Office, 1969).

31. Interview with Gerald Vicenti, Summer 1978, Jicarilla Apache Reservation, Dulce, N.M., notes in author's possession.

32. ICC Act of Aug. 13, 1946 (60 Stat. 1049; 25 U.S.C. 70-70v.)

33. CIA to Solicitor, Feb. 2, 1972, RG 75, Jic. Agency, CCF 1935–70, 174.1 Attorney Expenses, NRC, Suitland.

34. U.S. Cong., Senate, *Attorney Contracts with Indian Tribes,* Senate Report No. 8, 83d Cong., 1st sess., 1953, p. 5.

35. CIA to Solicitor, Feb. 2, 1972, RG 75, Jic. Agency, CCF 1935–70, 174.1 Attorney Expenses, NRS, Suitland.

36. Ibid.

37. Research Contract Between Jicarilla Apache Tribe and University of New Mexico Regents, Oct. 9, 1958, Albuquerque Area Office, BIA, Tribal Operations, Jicarilla Apache Land Claims Files.

38. 24 ICC 123 (1970).

39. Ibid.

40. U.S. Cong., House, Disposition of Funds of Jicarilla Apache Tribe, Docket 22-A, Senate Report 93-697 to Accompany H.R. 9019, 92d Cong., 2d sess., Dec. 1, 1971.

Bibliography

MANUSCRIPTS

Unpublished Government Documents
Record Group 75, Records of the Bureau of Indian Affairs, National Archives, Washington, D.C.
> Records of the Office of Indian Affairs, Letters Received, New Mexico Superintendency, 1848–80, Microcopy T-21, National Archives Microfilm Publications.
> Bureau of Indian Affairs, Letters Received, Indian Office, 1881–1907.
> Bureau of Indian Affairs, Letters Sent, Indian Office, 1881–1907.
> Bureau of Indian Affairs, Central Classified Files, Jicarilla Agency, 1907–39.
> Narrative Reports, 1910–35, Jicarilla Agency.
> Records Concerning the Wheeler-Howard Act, 1933–37, Jicarilla Agency.
Record Group 48, Records of the Office of the Secretary of the Interior, National Archives, Washington, D.C.
> Indian Division, Letters Received, 1881–1907.
> Indian Division, Letters Sent, 1881–1907.
> Indian Division, Inspectors File, 1873–1907.
> Indian Division, Appointments File:
>> Southern Ute Agency, 1886–87
>> Pueblo and Jicarilla Agency, 1890–92
>> Jicarilla Agency, 1892–1907
Record Group 393, Records of the United States Army Continental Commands, 1821–1910, Fort Union, N.M., Letters Received, 1851–1956.
Office of Adjutant General, Main Series, 1881–1889, Letters Received, 1882, Microfilm Copy 689, National Archives Publication, Papers Concerning the Threatened Starvation of Indians on the Mescalero Apache Reservation, May 1882–August 1884.
Record Group 279, Records of the Indian Claims Commission, Jicarilla Apache Land Claims, Docket Nos. 22 and 22-A.

Record Group 75, Records of the Bureau of Indian Affairs, National Archives
  Branch, Federal Records Center, Denver, Colorado.
Cimmaron and Abiquiu Agencies, Letters Sent to Commissioner of Indian
  Affairs, 1870–80.
Mescalero Apache Agency, Miscellaneous Letters Sent, 1886–87.
Jicarilla Apache Agency, Decimal File, 1900–1935.
Jicarilla Apache Agency, Letters Sent to Commissioner of Indian Affairs.
Record Group 75, Records of the Bureau of Indian Affairs, National Record Center,
  Suitland, Md., Central Classified Files, 1935–70, Jicarilla Agency.
Bureau of Indian Affairs, Jicarilla Apache Agency, Dulce, N.M.:
  Decimal Files, 1968–70.

OTHER MANUSCRIPT MATERIALS

Chicago, Newberry Library. Benjamin H. Grierson Papers.
San Marino, Calif. Huntington Library. "The Indians of New Mexico and Arizona"
  [by Andrew Ferdinand], 1868.
San Marino, Calif. Huntington Library. William Ritch Papers.

UNPUBLISHED MATERIAL

Forsling, Clarence L. "A Report with Recommendations on the Economic
  Development of the Jicarilla Apache Tribe." Prepared for the Jicarilla Apache
  Tribe. Mimeographed. Jicarilla Apache Tribe. Dulce, N.M., 1954.
Gelvin, Ralph A. "A General Survey of the Jicarilla Apache Tribe." Mimeographed.
  Jicarilla Apache Agency. Dulce, N.M., 1939.
[Hibben, Frank?]. "Interview with Juan Dedios." Mimeographed. Jicarilla Apache
  Tribe. Dulce, N.M., 1934, 1958.
The Jicarilla Apache Tribe of the Jicarilla Apache Reservation, New Mexico v. *the
  United States of America*, Docket No. 22-A. Before the Indian Claims
  Commission. Mimeographed. Washington, D.C., Mar. 29, 1965, July 8, 1969,
  Nov. 6, 1969 and Dec. 9, 1969.
Nicklason, Fred A. "Report on the Jicarilla Apache Accounting Claim before the
  Indian Claims Commission, for the Years 1887–1940." Docket 22-K, 2 vols.
  Mimeographed. Jicarilla Apache Tribe. Dulce, N.M., 1970.
Schroeder, Albert H. "A Study of the Apaches, Part II: The Jicarilla Apaches."
  Mimeographed. A report prepared for the Indian Claims Commission on
  behalf of the United States, Docket No. 22-A. Zimmerman Library, University
  of New Mexico, Albuquerque, N.M., 1959.
Stanford Research Institute, comp., "Historical and Documentary Evidence
  Concerning the Claim of the Jicarilla Apache Tribe before the Indian Claims
  Commission," Docket No. 22, *The Apache Nation ex rel. Fred Pellman, et al.,
  Petitioners* v. *the United States of America Respondent.* Mimeographed.
  Menlo Park, Calif.: Stanford Research Institute, 1957.

Thomas, Alfred B. "The Jicarilla Apache Indians: A History, 1598–1888." Mimeographed. Prepared for the Indian Claims Commission in Behalf of the Jicarilla Apache Tribe, Washington, D.C., 1958.

Wilson, H. Clyde. "Analysis of Low-Income Families on Jicarilla Apache Reservation." Mimeographed. Jicarilla Apache Tribe, Dulce, N.M., 1960.

GOVERNMENT DOCUMENTS

U.S. Congress. House. *Report of the Secretary of War, 1854. House Executive Document no. 1,* 34th Cong., 1st sess., 1855.

U.S. Congress. House. *Report of the Secretary of the Interior.* House Executive Document no. 1, 37th Cong., 3d sess., 1862.

U.S. Congress. House. *Report of the Secretary of the Interior.* House Executive Document no. 1, 38th Cong., 1st sess., 1863–64.

U.S. Congress. House. *Report of the Secretary of the Interior.* House Executive Document no. 1, 39th Cong., 2d sess., 1866.

U.S. Congress. House. *Report of the Secretary of the Interior.* House Executive Document no. 1, 40th Cong., 3d sess., 1868.

U.S. Congress. House. *Report of the Secretary of the Interior.* House Executive Document no. 1, 41st Cong., 2d sess., 1869.

U.S. Congress. House. *Negotiations with Ute Indians.* House Executive Document no. 90, 42nd Cong., 3d sess., 1873.

U.S. Congress. House. *The Brunot Agreement: A Report of the Commission with the Ute Tribe of Indians.* House Executive Document no. 53, 43rd Cong., 1st sess., 1874.

U.S. Congress. House. *Report of the Secretary of the Interior.* House Executive Document no. 1, pt. 5, 44th Cong., 2d sess., 1876.

U.S. Congress. House. *Report of the Secretary of the Interior.* House Executive Document no. 1, pt. 5, 45th Cong., 3d sess., 1878.

U.S. Congress. House. *Report of the Secretary of the Interior.* House Executive Document no. 1, pt. 5, 51st Cong., 2d sess., 1890–91.

U.S. Congress. House. House Executive Document no. 1, pt. 5, 52d Cong., 2d sess., 1892–93.

U.S. Congress. House. *Report of the Secretary of the Interior.* House Executive Document no. 5, 54th Cong., 1st sess., 1895–96.

U.S. Congress. House. *A Bill for Sale of Timber on Jicarilla Apache Reservation.* H.R. 15848, 59th Cong., 1st sess., 1905.

U.S. Congress. House. Representative Hogg speaking for a Bill of the Committee of the Whole House. H.R. 15848, 59th Cong., 1st sess., *Congressional Record,* 40, pt. 4, 3967.

U.S. Congress. House. *A Bill to Quiet Titles to Land on Jicarilla Apache Reservation.* H.R. 23650, 59th Cong., 2d sess., 1907.

U.S. Congress. House. *Allotments on the Jicarilla Reservation, New Mexico.* House Document 134, 59th Cong., 2d sess., 1906.

U.S. Congress. House. "Jicarilla Reservation." *House Report 6382 to Accompany H.R. 23650,* 59th Cong., 2d sess., 1907.

U.S. Congress. House. Committee on Indian Affairs. *The Condition of Various Tribes of Indians.* Hearing on the Condition of Various Tribes of Indians, 66th Cong., 1st sess., Vol. I, 1919.

U.S. Congress. House. *A Bill to Exclude Certain Lands from Jicarilla Reservation. H.R. 7113.* 66th Cong., 1st sess., 1919.

U.S. Congress. House. Representative Hernández speaking for the Indian Appropriation Bill of the Committee of the Whole House. H.R. 2480, 66th Cong., 1st sess., May 23, 1919. *Congressional Record,* 58, pt. 1, 187.

U.S. Congress. House. *A Bill to Exclude Certain Lands from Jicarilla Apache Reservation.* H.R. 2909, 67th Cong., 1st sess., 1921.

U.S. Congress. House. *Purchase of Certain Privately Owned Land in Jicarilla Indian Reservation, New Mexico. House Report 1875 to Accompany S. 4942.* 69th Cong., 2d sess., 1927.

U.S. Congress. House. *Communication from the President of the United States.* House Document 745, 69th Cong., 2d sess., 1927.

U.S. Congress. House. Representative Morrow speaking for Interior Department Appropriation Bill of the Committee of the Whole House. H.R. 9136, 70th Cong., 1st sess., Jan. 17, 1928, *Congressional Record,* 69: 1639.

U.S. Congress. House. Subcommittee of House Committee on Appropriations. *Hearing on Interior Department Appropriation Bill for 1934,* 72nd Cong., 2d sess., 1934.

U.S. Congress. House. A Bill to Reserve Certain Lands in New Mexico as an Addition to the School Reserve of Jicarilla Apache Reservation, *H.R. 12073,* 74th Cong., 2d sess., 1936.

U.S. Congress. House. To Reserve Certain Public Domain Lands in New Mexico as an Addition to the School Reserve of the Jicarilla Indian Reservation. *H.R. 2442 To Accompany H.R. 12073,* 74th Cong., 2d sess., 1936.

U.S. Congress. Senate. *Report of the Secretary of the Interior,* Senate Executive Document no. 1, 37th Cong., 3d sess., 1862.

U.S. Congress. Senate. Letter from the Secretary of the Interior Transmitting Senate Resolution of December 11, 1877 in Relation to the Bands of Apaches and Ute Indians of Cimarron, *Senate Executive Document no. 8,* New Mexico, 43rd Cong., 2d sess., 1878.

U.S. Congress. Senate. *Indian Affairs: Law and Treaties,* vol. 3. Sen. Doc. no. 719, 63rd Cong., 2d sess. (edited by Charles J. Kappler [1911–13]).

U.S. Congress. Senate. Purchase of Certain Privately owned Land within the Jicarilla Indian Reservation, New Mexico. *S. Rept. 1298 to Accompany S. 4942,* 69th Cong., 2d sess., 1927.

U.S. Congress. Senate. Subcommittee of Committee on Indian Affairs, *Survey of Conditions of Indians of the United States,* Hearing on S.R. 79, 308, 71st Cong., 2d sess., 1931.

U.S. Congress. Senate. *Conditions of Indians in the United States,* Speech of Hon. William H. King, Senate Document No. 214, 72nd Cong., 2d sess., 1933.

U.S. Congress. Senate. *Condition of Indians in the United States,* Senate Document no. 214, 72nd Cong., 2d sess., 1933.

U.S. Congress. Senate. *Survey of Conditions among the Indians of the United States,* Senate Report no. 310, 78th Cong., 1st sess., 1943.

U.S. Congress. Senate. Repealing the So-called Wheeler-Howard Act, Senate Report No. 1031, 78th Cong., 2d sess., 1944.
U.S. Congress. Senate. Subcommittee on Interior and Insular Affairs, "Partial Report on Attorney Contracts with Indians." Senate Misc. Report no. 8, 83rd Cong., 1st sess., 1951.
U.S. Congress. Senate. Juvenile Delinquency among the Indians. Senate Report no. 1483, 84th Cong., 2d sess., 1956.
U.S. Congress. *Joint Economic Committee of Congress, Toward Economic Development for Native American Communities.* Vol. 2, 91st Cong., 1st sess., 1969.
U.S. Congress. Senate. Committee on Labor and Public Welfare, Special Subcommittee on Indian Education, *Indian Education: A National Tragedy—A National Challenge,* 91st Cong., 1st sess., 1969.
U.S. Congress. Senate. Providing for Disposition of Funds Appropriated to Pay a Judgment in Favor of the Jicarilla Apache Tribe in Indian Claims Commission Docket No. 22-A and for Other Purposes, Senate Report no. 92–768, 92nd Cong., 2d sess., 1972.

GOVERNMENT PUBLICATIONS

Annual Reports of the Commissioner of Indian Affairs, 1870–1934.
Annual Reports of the Secretary of the Interior, 1870–1934.
Executive Orders Relating to Indian Reservations, Washington, D.C.: Government Printing Office, 1972.
Hodge, Frederick Webb, *Handbook of Indians North of Mexico,* Bureau of American Ethnology. Bulletin 30, 2 vols. Washington, D.C.: Government Printing Office, 1907, 1910.
Report of Secretary of War, 1888. Washington, D.C.: Government Printing Office, 1889.
Royce, Charles C. *Indian Land Cessions in the United States.* Bureau of American Ethnology, Eighteenth Annual Report, 1896–97, pt. 2. Washington, D.C.: Government Printing Office, 1899.

THESES AND DISSERTATIONS

Cornell, Lois Adelaide. "The Jicarilla Apaches: Their History, Customs, and Present Status." M.A. thesis, University of Colorado, 1929.
Kerr, Carol. "Education on the Jicarilla Apache Reservation." M.A. thesis, Staten Island College, 1958.
Putney, Diane T. "Fighting the Scourge: American Indian Morbidity and Federal Policy, 1897–1928." Ph.D. diss., Marquette University, 1980.
Tiller, Veronica E. "A History of the Jicarilla Apache Tribe." Ph.D. diss., University of New Mexico, 1976.

ORAL HISTORY INTERVIEWS

Jicarilla Apache Reservation, Dulce, N.M., Jan. 1973–Dec. 1978.

Mary V. Becenti

Cevero Caramillo

Elfido Elote

Jack Inez

Seguro Lucero

Lee Martinez, Sr.

Rebecca Monarco Martinez

Juanita T. Monarco

Japan Pesata

George Phone

Maggie Phone

Juan Quintana

Norman TeCube

Hanse TeCube

Garfield Velarde, Jr.

Lena S. Velarde

Louis Velarde

Nagee Vicenti

Gerald Vicenti

Victor Vicenti

Dan Vigil

Frank Vigil

Bell V. Wells

BOOKS

Abel, Annie H., ed. *The Official Correspondence of James S. Calhoun While Indian Agent at Santa Fe and Superintendent of Indian Affairs in New Mexico.* Washington, D.C.: Government Printing Office, 1915.

Bancroft, Hubert H. *History of Arizona and New Mexico: 1530–1888.* 1889. Reprinted Albuquerque: Horn and Wallace Publishing Co., 1962.

Bender, Averam Burton. *March of Empire: Frontier Defense in the Southwest, 1848–1860.* Lawrence: University of Kansas Press, 1952.

Brayer, Herbert O. *William Blackmore: The Spanish-American Land Grants of New Mexico and Colorado, 1868, 1878.* Denver: Bradford-Robinson, 1949.

Brophy, William A., and Aberle, Sophie D., comps. *The Indian: America's Unfinished Business.* Norman: University of Oklahoma Press, 1969.

Cohen, Felix S. *Handbook of Federal Indian Law.* 1942. Reprinted Albuquerque: University of New Mexico Press, 1971, 1976.

Collier, John. *On the Gleaming Way: Navajos, Eastern Pueblos, Zunis, Hopis, and Apaches, and Their Land and Their Meaning to the World.* Chicago: Swallow Press, 1962.

Cooke, Philip St. George. *The Conquest of New Mexico and California: An Historical and Personal Narrative.* Oakland, Calif.: Biobooks, 1952.

Dale, Edward Everett. *The Indians of the Southwest: A Century of Development under the United States.* Norman: University of Oklahoma Press, 1971.

Deloria, Vine, Jr. *Behind the Trail of Broken Treaties: An Indian Declaration of Independence.* New York: Dell, 1974.

Ellis, Richard N., ed. *The Western American Indian: Case Studies in Tribal History.* Lincoln: University of Nebraska Press, 1972.

Fay, George E., Comp. *Charters, Constitutions and By-Laws of the Indian Tribes of North America.* Part 3, *The Southwest.* Occasional Publications in Anthropology, no. 4, Ethnology Series. Greeley: Colorado State College, Museum of Anthropology, n.d.

Forbes, Jack D. *Apache, Navajo and Spaniard.* Norman: University of Oklahoma Press, 1960.

Gibson, Arrell M. *The West in the Life of the Nation.* Lexington, Mass., D. C. Heath, 1976.

———. *The American Indian.* Lexington, Mass.: D.C. Heath, 1980.

Goddard, Pliny Earle. *Indians of the Southwest.* American Museum of Natural History Handbook Series, no. 2, 4th ed. New York: American Musuem of Natural History, 1931.

———. *Jicarilla Apache Texts.* Anthropological Papers of the American Museum of Natural History, 7 (1911).

Gregg, Josiah. *Commerce of the Prairies.* Edited by Max Moorehead. Norman: University of Oklahoma Press, 1954.

Gunnerson, Dolores A. *The Jicarilla Apaches: A Study in Survival.* Dekalb: Northern Illinois University Press, 1974.

Hagan, William T. *Indian Police and Judges: A Study in Acculturation.* New Haven: Yale University Press, 1966.

Hoopes, William T. *Indian Affairs and Their Administration, with Special Reference to the Far West, 1849–1860.* Philadelphia: University of Pennsylvania Press, 1932.

Hughes, John T. *Doniphan's Expedition, Containing an Account of the Conquest of New Mexico; General Kearny's Overland Expedition to California; Doniphan's Campaign against the Navajos, His Unparalleled March upon Chihuahua and Durango; and the Operations of General Price, with a Sketch of the Life of Col. Doniphan.* Cincinnati: U. P. James, 1847.

John, Elizabeth. *Storms Brewed in Other Men's Worlds: The Confrontation of Indians, Spanish, and French in the Southwest 1540–1795.* College Station: Texas A & M University Press, 1975.

Josephy, Alvin M., Jr. *Red Power: The American Indian's Fight for Freedom.* New York: McGraw-Hill, 1972.

Keleher, William A. *Maxwell Land Grant: A New Mexico Item.* New York: Argosy-Antiquarian Ltd., 1964.

Kenner, Charles L. *A History of New Mexico–Plains Indian Relations.* Norman: University of Oklahoma Press, 1969.

Lamar, Howard, *The Far Southwest, 1847–1912: A Territorial History.* New Haven: Yale University Press, 1966.

Lavender, David. *Bent's Fort.* New York: Doubleday, 1954.

Leupp, Francis E. *Notes of a Summer Tour among the Indians of the Southwest.* Philadelphia: Indian Rights Association, 1897.

McCall, George Archibald. *New Mexico in 1850: A Military View.* Edited by Robert W. Frazer. Norman: University of Oklahoma Press, 1968.

McKittrick, Margaret. *Indian Boarding Schools: Findings of the Meriam Report.* Eastern Association of Indian Affairs, 1928.

Mails, Thomas E. *The People Called Apache.* Englewood Cliffs, N.J.: Prentice Hall, 1974.

Marriott, Alice. *These are the People: Some Notes on Southwestern Indians.* Santa Fe: Laboratory of Anthropology, 1949.

Meserve, Charles F. *A Tour of Observation among Indians and Indian Schools in Arizona, New Mexico, Oklahoma, and Kansas.* Philadelphia: Indian Rights Association, 1894.

Moorehead, Max. *The Apache Frontier: Jacobo Ugarte and Spanish Indian Relations, 1769–1791.* Norman: University of Oklahoma Press, 1968.

Murphy, Lawrence R. *Philmont: A History of New Mexico's Cimarron Country.* Albuquerque: University of New Mexico, 1972.

Murphy, Lawrence R. *Frontier Crusader: William F. N. Arny.* Tucson: University of Arizona Press, 1972.

Opler, Morris E. *The Character and Derivation of the Jicarilla Holiness Rite.* University of New Mexico Bulletin, Anthropological Series 4, no. 3. 1943.

———. *Childhood and Youth in Jicarilla Apache Society.* Publications of the Frederick Webb Hodge Anniversary Publication Fund, 5. Los Angeles: Southwest Museum, 1946.

———. *Dirty Boy: A Jicarilla Tale of Raid and War.* Memoirs of the American Anthropological Association, 52. 1938.

———. *Myths and Tales of Jicarilla Apache Indians.* Memoirs of the American Folklore Society, 31. 1938.

Otis, D. S. *The Dawes Act and the Allotment of Indian Lands.* Edited by Francis Paul Prucha. Norman: University of Oklahoma Press, 1973.

Pearson, Jim Berry. *The Maxwell Land Grant.* Norman: University of Oklahoma Press, 1961.

Philp, Kenneth R. *John Collier's Crusade for Indian Reform, 1920–1954.* Tucson: University of Arizona Press, 1977.

Sabin, Edwin L. *Kit Carson Days: Adventures in the Path of Empire.* 2 vols. New York: n.p., 1935.

Schmeckebier, Laurence F. *The Office of Indian Affairs: Its History, Activities and Organization.* Baltimore: Johns Hopkins Press, 1927.

Sorkin, Alan L. *American Indians and Federal Aid.* Washington, D.C.: Brookings Institution, 1971.

Spicer, Edward H. *Cycles of Conquest: The Impact of Spain, Mexico, and the United States on the Indians of the Southwest, 1533–1960.* Tucson: University of Arizona Press, 1962.

Stanford Research Institute. *Needs and Resources of the Jicarilla Apache Indian Tribe.* 5 vols. Menlo Park: Stanford Research Institute, 1958.

Stanley, F. *The Jicarilla Apaches of New Mexico, 1598–1967.* Pampa, Tex.: Pampa Print Shop,1967.

Stuart, Levine, and Nancy O. Lurie, eds. *The American Indians Today.* Baltimore: Penguin Books, 1965.

Thompson, Gregory C. *Southern Ute Lands, 1848–1899.* Occasional Papers of the Center of Southwest Studies, no. 1. Durango: Fort Lewis College, 1972.

Thrapp, Dan L. *The Conquest of Apacheria.* Norman: University of Oklahoma Press, 1967.

Trennert, Robert A., Jr. *Alternative to Extinction: Federal Indian Policy and the Beginnings of the Reservation System, 1846–51.* Philadelphia: Temple University Press, 1975.

Twitchell, Ralph Emerson. *Leading Facts of New Mexico History.* Vols. 2, 3, 4. Cedar Rapids: Torch Press, 1917.

Tyler, S. Lyman. *Indian Affairs: A Study of the Changes in Policy of the United States.* Provo, Utah: Brigham Young University, Institute of American Indian Studies, 1964.

Underhill, Lonnie E., and Littlefield, Daniel F., Jr., eds. *Hamlin Garland's Observations on the American Indians, 1895–1905.* Tucson: University of Arizona Press, 1976.

Utley, Robert M. *Frontiersmen in Blue: The United States Army and the Indian, 1848–1865.* 1967. Reprinted Lincoln: University of Nebraska Press, 1981.
Van Roekel, Gertrude B. *Jicarilla Apaches.* San Antonio: Naylor, 1971.
Worcester, Donald E. *The Apaches: Eagles of the Southwest.* Norman: University of Oklahoma Press, 1979.

ARTICLES

Abel, Annie Heloise, ed. "Indian Affairs in New Mexico under the Administration of William Carr Lane from the Journal of John Ward." *New Mexico Historical Review,* 16 (1941): 206–32.
———. "The Journal of John Greiner." *Old Santa Fe,* 3 (1916): 189–243.
Basehart, Harry W., and Sasaki, Tom T. "Changing Political Organization in the Jicarilla Apache Reservation Community." *Human Organization,* 23 (1964): 283–89.
———. "Sources of Income among Many Farms—Rough Rock Navajo and Jicarilla Apache: Some Comparisons and Comments. *Human Organization,* 2 (1961–62): 187–90.
Bieber, Ralph P., ed. "Letters of William Carr Lane 1852–1854." *Historical Society of New Mexico Publications in History,* 6 (1928): 178–203.
Blount, Bertha. "The Apache in the Southwest, 1846–1886." *Southwestern Historical Quarterly,* 23 (1919): 20–38.
Carson, William G. B., ed. "William Carr Lane Diary." *New Mexico Historical Review,* 39 (1964): 181–234, 274–332.
Cutter, Donald C. "An Inquiry into Indian Land Rights . . . with Particular Reference to the Jicarilla Apache Area of Northeastern New Mexico." In *Apache Indians VI,* American Indian Ethnohistory Series. New York: Garland Publishing Co., 1974.
Dolan, Thomas A. "Report of Council Proceedings with the Jicarilla Apache Indians." *New Mexico Historical Review,* 4 (1929): 59–72.
Fergusson, Erna. "Modern Apaches of New Mexico." *American Indian,* 6, (1951): 3–13.
Galloway, Tod., trans., "Private Letters of a Government Official [John Greiner] in the Southwest." *Journal of American History,* 3 (1905): 541–54.
Gold, Herbert. "How Rich Is a Rich Apache?" *New York Times Magazine,* February 13, 1972.
Gordon, B. L., et al. "Environment, Settlement, and Land Use in the Jicarilla Apache Claim Area." In *Apache Indians VI,* American Indian Ethnohistory Series. New York: Garland Publishing Co., 1974.
Hodge, Frederick W. "Jicarilla." *U.S. Bureau of American Ethnology,* Bulletin 30 (1907): 631–32.
Mooney, James. "The Jicarilla Genesis." *American Anthropologist,* o.s. 2, (1898): 197–209.
Nicklason, Fred. "The American Indians' 'White Problem': The Case of the Jicarilla Apache." *Prologue* (1980): 41–55.
Opler, Morris. "Adolescence Rite of the Jicarilla." *El Palacio,* 49 (1942): 25–38.
———. "The Jicarilla Apache Ceremonial Relay Race." *American Anthropologist,* n.s. 46 (1944): 75–79.

——. "A Jicarilla Apache Expedition and Scalp Dance." *Journal of American Folklore,* 54 (1941): 10–23.

——. "Jicarilla Apache Territory, Economy, and Society in 1850." *Southwestern Journal of Anthropology,* 27 (1901): 309–29.

——. "A Summary of Jicarilla Apache Culture." *American Anthropologist,* n.s. 38 (1936): 202–23.

Parman, Donald. "American Indians and the Bicentennial." *New Mexico Historical Review,* 51 (1976): 233–49.

Taylor, Morris. "Campaigns against the Jicarillas, 1854." *New Mexico Historical Review,* 44 (1969): 269–91.

——. "Campaigns against the Jicarillas, 1855." *New Mexico Historical Review,* 45 (1970): 119–36.

Walter, Paul A. F. "The First Civil Governor of New Mexico under the Stars and Stripes." *New Mexico Historical Review,* 8 (1933).

Watson, Edithe L. "Jicarillas, the Happy People." *New Mexico Magazine.* December 1945, p. 14.

Wilson, H. Clyde, "Jicarilla Apache Political and Economic Structures." *Publications in American Archaeology and Ethnology,* 48, no. 4, pp. 297–360. Berkeley: University of California Press, 1964.

Woods, Betty, "Jicarilla Fiesta." *New Mexico Magazine,* September 1941, p. 6.

Index

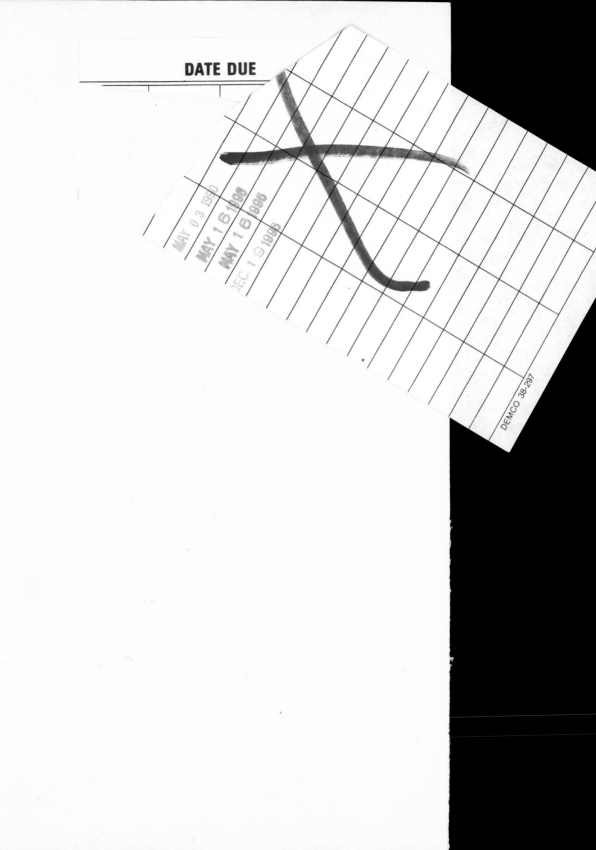